Sparing the Rod
Schools, Discipline and Children's Rights

Sparing the Rod
Schools, Discipline and Children's Rights

Marie Parker-Jenkins

Trentham Books

First published in 1999 by Trentham Books Limited

Trentham Books Limited
Westview House
734 London Road
Oakhill
Stoke on Trent
Staffordshire
England ST4 5NP

British Cataloguing in Publication Data
A catalogue record for this book is available from the British Library
ISBN: 1 85856 159 0 (pb)
ISBN: 1 85856 160 4 (hb)

Designed and typeset by Trentham Print Design Ltd., Chester
and printed in Great Britain by The Cromwell Press Ltd., Wiltshire

Contents

Foreword

During the last thirty years the education service and schools in the United Kingdom have increasingly become the scene of litigation. Parents, pupils, teachers and educationalists generally have recognised that schooling involves a high degree of compulsion and at times of coercion, which nowadays are seen by many as unacceptable. Such complainants argue cogently that schools are, or should be, a microcosm of society, and the values which are upheld by schools will inevitably become the values of society as pupils reach maturity.

Created in the aftermath of World War Two, the European Convention on Human Rights seeks to inhibit the establishment of totalitarian regimes by describing inalienable human rights. But while such rights are well on the way to wide acceptance in countries like the United Kingdom which were early signatories, the extent to which they do or should apply equally to children is seen as debatable. No one argues that the children heading for Auschwitz in the 'Kindertransport' should not have been protected against such evil and violence, but hackles can rise when the argument is translated into violence against pupils in school. Violence by pupils against teachers is seen – paradoxically – as a sign of the imminent breakdown of the social order.

Marie Parker-Jenkins' book takes the reader carefully through these developments and arguments. It covers the field comprehensively, stressing that at no point does the Convention make any distinction between the child and the adult in defining human rights. Nor could such a policy statement reasonably make any distinction, since it would then be in the position of having to define the point at which children became adults. Every parent and teacher knows that to attempt this would be inconsistent and absurd and would inflame the arguments in this area which already exist.

The issue nowadays is one of interpretation of the Convention by the European Court of Human Rights at Strasbourg. The UK has made some appearances before the Court which have been at best unfortunate, resulting in adverse judgements. These are the issues with which this book is concerned.

John Partington
South Wingfield, Derbyshire
February 1998

Acknowledgements

This study began over a decade ago when I monitored from Canada the impact that the European Court of Human Rights was having on education policy in the United Kingdom. That initial interest led me to Strasbourg, where I researched for myself the corporal punishment cases being lodged by British parents. Marc-Andre Eissen, Registrar; Fredrik Sundberg, Administrative Officer; and Siefrid Bein, Law Librarian, assisted me during my time spent in Strasbourg, and through subsequent correspondence. Not only did the Court guide me, but individual litigants such as Miss X, in the case of *Mrs and Miss X v UK* corresponded with me over her experience of petitioning in Strasbourg.

Further afield different countries have been struggling with the controversial decision to remove physical chastisement from their schools. My studies in Australia revealed wide-ranging debates going on over the purpose of education and the appropriateness of sanctions. Particularly helpful to me with this aspect of my work were Ken Cruickshank and Neville Hatton of the Faculty of Education, University of Sydney, and Michael McIntyre, research student at McQuarrie University, New South Wales. Likewise, the South African context has been affected by the recent abolition of corporal punishment, and my research there was supported by Joan Squelch of the Faculty of Education, University of South Africa. Finally, drawing on international perspectives, Albert Miles of the Faculty of Higher Education, University of Alabama, was most helpful in confirming my understanding of the American situation where just over half the states have moved to abolish the practice.

Closer to home, work with a number of organisations have helped inform my knowledge of current practice. Once abolition became inevitable, local authorities began to develop alternative sanctions. In gathering information about the way in which policy has since developed the following government authorities have been particularly helpful: Derbyshire County Council, Nottinghamshire County Council, Leicestershire County Council, and Leeds City Council. Individual educationalists were also supportive of my work. Ann Convery, of the School of Education,

University of Nottingham has been particularly informative about European developments. Likewise, Margaret Eley, of the Noel Baker Community School, Derby, and Patrick McDonough of Lakeview Sixth Form Centre, Nottingham, were most helpful in sharing their knowledge as practitioners at the 'chalk-face'.

Locating the discussion in the contemporary context also required consideration of the issue of discipline affecting teachers in general. In this regard, the National Union of Teachers, the Professional Association of Teachers, the National Association of Secondary Teachers/Union of Women Teachers, and the Commission of Health and Safety all responded to my requests for information regarding policy. Within the context of issues concerning pupils, a variety of groups have assisted me, but particularly helpful have been: the Society of Teachers Opposed to Physical Punishment before it dis-banded, and End Physical Punishment of Children World Wide.

Within the university sector, Peter Hayward, Education Librarian, and Pat Wilkinson, Law Librarian, of the University of Nottingham, were always most helpful. Secretarial support was provided by Caroline Laborde, of the School of Education, University of Nottingham, and when I changed institutions half-way through writing this book, Debbie Hawkesworth, Sima Parmar, Louise Richards and Georgina Baxter of the School of Education and Social Science, University of Derby, generously took over the final stages and completion of the study.

Thanks also to Mary Fitzgerald and Lesley Huckerby who acted as readers.

Finally, I am indebted to Barrie Irving of the College of Guidance Studies, Kent who inspired and encouraged me to write this book, and John Partington, formerly of the School of Education, University of Nottingham whom I have known as both a student and colleague and who graciously agreed to write the foreword.

While a number of educationalists have thus been consulted over issues contained in this study, the opinions expressed are my own; likewise any errors or omissions.

Marie Parker-Jenkins
University of Derby
1998

List of figures

To Will

Introduction

'Our youth today love luxury. They have bad manners, contempt for authority, disregard for older people. Children are tyrants who contradict their parents and tyrannise their teachers' (Socrates, 500 BC.)

How should we treat unruly children in our schools? What punishments are appropriate, and which will help to instill order and discipline in the classroom? These are the perennial questions raised by adults but rarely asked of children themselves. Instead, teachers seek to maintain control by use of a number of strategies developed within well-intentioned statements. Ironically these documents are often entitled 'whole school' policy but seldom do they incorporate the views of pupils!

Schools bear the responsibility for creating an ordered community and in the light of legal and social norms teachers have been forced to abandon physical chastisement as part of their repertoire of sanctions. So alternative sanctions are required which are not only effective but which do not contravene children's rights either morally or legally.

This book explores these issues of schools and discipline within an overall framework of human rights. It does not seek to promote the concept of children's rights in isolation, but instead to locate them within the context of the school as a community in which rights are owed to all members. Furthermore, we increasingly hear talk of 'rights', espoused by a number of groups on behalf of a variety of causes, but rather less is said about corresponding responsibilities. I take the position that rights and responsibilities are owned *by* and owed *to* children, teachers and other people involved in education, and that by promoting this view we make schools a better place for everyone. As such, 'sparing the rod' does not mean 'spoiling the child', but instead encourages young people to have a healthy respect for their rights and those of others in society.

The discussion begins with an overview in chapter 1 of the traditional use of corporal punishment in the home and school. Drawing on biblical and literary sources we see how physical chastisement has been justified with widespread usage in private, independent and maintained schools. Litigation upholding teacher authority is explored with a focus on delegating parental rights to educators to use this form of sanction and which continues to have relevance for schools. Beyond the historical and legal aspects of school discipline, we examine in chapter 2 Britain's involvement in Europe with particular reference to the role of the European Court of Human Rights at Strasbourg in dealing with complaints from individuals who failed to obtain satisfaction through our domestic courts. This serves as a useful backdrop in which to consider the major Strasbourg decisions concerning corporal punishment in chapter 3, and the use of the European Convention on Human Rights by British parents. These disputes centre on the allegation that physical chastisement is a violation of human rights since it constitutes 'degrading punishment', and that by excluding pupils who refuse to accept this sanction, 'the right to education' is also breached. In exploring this challenge to the traditional authority of the teacher, the chapter includes the legislation which finally abolished corporal punishment for the majority of pupils in Britain.

Chapter 4 examines the development of alternative methods with discipline in the classroom and the implications raised for schools. Concepts of 'punishment', 'discipline' and 'social control' provide philosophical consideration of what schools should be about, of how we justify punishment in the pedagogical process, and how we might allow the child's voice to be heard on the matter. Chapter 5 provides a broader perspective regarding our position in Europe vis-a-vis our continental neighbours. Particularly significant is the work in Scandinavian countries which challenges parental rights to punish their children corporally. The US, Australia and South Africa have shared similar Common Law traditions of administering physical chastisement to children and their struggles over the issue of abolishing the practice are noted. For Britain, the impetus for change came as a result of our implementation of the European Convention on Human Rights which directly influences our educational policy. Elsewhere, countries which are not signatories to the European Convention, can rely on the treaty only for moral rather than legal authority. Strasbourg has also been significant for the importance it has placed on children's rights, with a perception of minors as people in their own right who, along with everyone else, deserve to be legally protected from physical assault. The use of corporal punishment in schools has been seen as a denial of children's human rights and the penultimate chapter explores the concept of rights and entitlements when applied to children. Furthermore, rather than seen as simply challenging or undermining teacher authority, consideration is given to how schools can be the place where human rights are given recognition and support. Finally, chapter 8 concludes the discussion about the move towards abandoning physical chastisement and the development of alternative strategies. The majority of schools in Britain have had a decade to adjust so we can explore some of the ideological and political issues which have accompanied this shift.

Debates continue about school discipline and the nature of punishment. There has been a call for the re-introduction of corporal punishment as a response to public concern over youth crime and levels of indiscipline. Britain was the last country in Europe to end the use of physical chastisement, and some would have us be the first to re-introduce the practice! A return to corporal punishment would be at odds with efforts to reduce violence in our society and the rejection of force as a method of resolving conflict. As well as contradicting the developing ethos of non-violence in schools, a return to the cane would again remove the rights of children to the same legal protection as that afforded adults and we would again be answerable to Strasbourg.

Finally, as we address problems of indiscipline in the young, there are demands for protection for children and protection *from* children. This is evidenced by a public outcry over rising crime figures, echoed in Labour Government proposals for youth curfews and fast-track sentencing of juvenile offenders, all of which are clearly not intended to 'spare the child'. Yet crime among the young is nothing new – throughout history children have been seen as unruly delinquents 'with contempt for authority'. Given that the future is so obviously tied up with our young we should not overestimate the seriousness of these problems, nor must we underestimate the complexity of the solutions.

Chapter 1

Physical Punishment in the Home and School

'I grew up beside you, you smote my back, and so your teaching entered my ear' (pupil to teacher, Ancient Egypt, 2000 B.C.)[1]

Physical chastisement has been used universally in both the home and school for instilling discipline into the young. Discipline for children in ancient Greece or Rome, for example, was characterised by harshness and brutality,[2] and the history of childhood chronicles the regular abuse and terrorising of children by their caretakers.[3] Concepts of morality have placed legitimacy on the practice with not only an acceptance, but an expectation, that child-rearing and corporal punishment should go hand in hand, and this has been carried over into school life.

This historical perspective begins with exploration of the Victorian attitude to corporal punishment and the beginnings of state education in 19th Century Britain. Consideration is then given to the development of school regulations governing physical chastisement and litigation which has helped shape our understanding of the authority of the teacher. Discussion moves next to the doctrine of *in loco parentis*, whereby parents have been perceived as having automatically delegated their right to chastise, and this is examined within the context of legal cases which have taken place in our domestic courts when parents have challenged the use of corporal punishment and detention.

The Victorian Attitude Towards Corporal Punishment

Corporal punishment has a long-standing tradition which was sanctioned by the norms and values of Victorian society. Rooted in the concept of 'original sin', this sanction was condoned by parents who expected, and indeed in many instances demanded, that it be inflicted on their offspring. 'Original sin', or a state of being alienated from God, was believed to be manifested in acts of sloth or insubordination and teachers were considered to be ideally placed to lead children out of ignorance and sin.[4] (This attitude still remains part of the ethos of some religious schools when administering corporal punishment).[5] Elsewhere the same reasoning was also prevalent. For example, in New England the use of corporal punishment was 'rooted in the community's understanding of the nature of childhood' states Ryan (1994) and 'adults largely viewed children as 'creatures of sin', who were born evil as well as ignorant' (p72).[6] Indeed 'pre-emptive whipping' of new boys took place in some of the country's boarding schools in anticipation of misdemeanours and to endorse the importance placed on 'flogging' (ibid., p73) Straus (1994) describes it as 'beating the devil out of them'. (The use of corporal punishment in American schools today is explored in Chaper 5).

Justification for using physical chastisement has centred boldly on behaviour-modification in this traditional Japanese perspective on the issue of child rearing:

> In training dogs and horses, they receive a treat whenever they behave, and they are whipped when they don't. The same stance should be taken with children. Children are animals being taught to be human (Kinji Kato).[7]

Similarly, Scott notes in his 'History of Corporal Punishment', that physical chastisement was considered an excellent 'instrument for the correction of children' and was used as a panacea for all breaches of discipline (1938, p.94). In Scotland, for example, use was made of the 'tawse' or strap, whilst in the Isle of Man the 'birch' was favoured. (This was given in evidence in the Tyrer case (1978),[8] detailed later in chapter 3.)

Dr. Samuel Johnson's views on corporal punishment are revealing for what they suggest about early attitudes. He contended that there were three important reasons for using this form of disciplinary measure: 'the need of society to produce people who would conform to accepted norms; a moral need to beat out obstinacy, a symptom of 'original sin'; and as a necessary tool to ensure learning takes place'[9].

Johnson advocated the use of corporal punishment and actually attributed his expertise in Latin to the severe beatings he received:

> my master whipt me very well. Without that Sir, I should have done nothing.[10]

Gibson (1978) notes the obsession of parents with the need to beat their children:

> upper and middle-class Victorians ... never tired of reminding themselves that the beating of naughty children had been strictly enjoined upon them by God (p.48).

It was from the Bible that authority was sought to justify the practice and was amply provided in Proverbs with such precepts as:

> '*For whom the Lord loveth he correcteth; even as a father the son in whom he delighteth*' (III, 12)

> '*He that spareth the rod hateth his son: but he that loveth him chasteneth him*' (XIII, 24)

> '*Chasten thy son while there is hope, and let not thy soul spare for his crying*' (XIX, 18)

> '*Thou shalt beat him with the rod, and deliver his soul from hell*' (XXIII, 14)

Such entreaties are embodied in Samuel Butler's oft-repeated maxim of 'spare the rod and spoil the child', which provided sufficient philosophical and religious justification to carry out what was morally necessary to ensure the salvation of the child. Schoolmasters and mistresses in both boys' schools and girls' dispensed liberal doses of corporal punishment in reflecting the general wishes and expectations of parents. This situation is well captured in William Shenstone's poem, 'The Schoolmistress':

> *In ev'ry village mark'd with little spire*
> *Embow'r'd in trees and hardly known to fame,*
> *There dwells, in lowly shed, and mean attire,*
> *A matron old, whome we Schoolmistress name;*
> *Who boasts unruly brats with birch to tame;*
> *Aw'd by the pow'r of this relentless dame;*
> *And oft-times, on vagies idly bent,*
> *for unkempt hair, or task unconn'd, are*
> *sorely shent.'*

Barnard (1971) states that although this poem describing a 'dame school' was written in 1742, there were schools in existence for more than another century of which the description would still be true (p.2).

Such was the widespread application of corporal punishment in public schools that it earned for the country the ignominious reputation of 'the English vice', which Gibson took for the title of his book on the subject. Apart from the contention that corporal punishment derived its legitimacy from God, Gibson notes that 'obedience and duty' were 'two imperatives which dominate all nineteenth-century discussions on the education of children, and which forbade all insubordination to parental authority ' (p.51). Gathorne-Hardy reiterates these themes in his works on 19th century values and attitudes, claiming that middle and upper-class parents had little hesitation in using corporal punishment and justifying its application in the country's public schools.[11]

Parents of children attending (non-maintained) schools often specifically wished corporal punishment to be used whenever required on their children, and inevitably teachers were delegated to mete out the sanction. (This theme of parental delegation or acting *in loco parentis* is examined in greater detail later in the chapter). That parents were prepared to allow their children to be treated in this manner seems to be entrenched in the fact that they were able to demonstrate emotional detachment in order to ensure their children's steadfastness and ultimate salvation. By sending their offspring away from home for their education, they expected that their moral as well as academic welfare would be attended to. With this assumption in mind, 19th century headmasters like Arnold of Rugby and Thring of Uppingham dispensed swift and regular physical justice. Dr Arnold was a case in point for, whilst widely regarded as a humane and enlightened educationalist, he was also a firm advocate of discipline. In an essay published in 1835, entitled 'On the Discipline of Public Schools', he contended that children's disobedience stemmed from the concepts of 'pride' and 'sin' and that corporal punishment was useful in assisting them in seeing the 'truth' and 'light'.[12] Writing a decade later, he maintained that children were by their very age and nature, subordinate to adults:

> impatience of inferiority felt by a child towards his parents, or by
> a pupil towards his instructors, is merely wrong because it is at

variance with the truth: there exists a real inferiority in the relation, and it is an error, a fault, a corruption of nature not to acknowledge it.[13]

The right to inflict some form of corporal punishment was also in many instances extended to prefects as well as teachers, the extreme example of which is well-captured by the activities of Flashman in Hughes' 'Tom Brown's Schooldays' (1890), who used this right or privilege to 'roast' Tom.

Permeating the whole public school system, corporal punishment was, notes Gibson, 'given prestige... and initiated elsewhere: the assumption being that what was good enough for public school boys was good enough for everyone else' (p.66). Parents could, therefore, expect that it was highly likely that their children would receive physical chastisement, and teachers operating within the maintained system could in turn expect to be charged with carrying out the sanction.

> If ever there was a schoolmaster who felt himself to stand *in loco parentis* to the pupils it is the preparatory school headmaster... the more so given the tender years of those committed to his care (*ibid.*, p.67).

Public school teachers traditionally had a greater responsibility and authority for the welfare of their charges, firstly by virtue of the fact that the children were frequently boarding pupils and secondly, because the use of corporal punishment was an integral part of the educational process. This point is highlighted in the renowned case of *Regina v. Hopley* (1860),[14] reviewed in detail later in this chapter. A pupil ultimately died as a result of receiving a beating from a schoolmaster who had specifically sought permission from the boy's father to inflict the punishment. Upon finding himself indicted for manslaughter, the defending teacher wrote:

> ... while anguish shook the frame, the conscience suffered not one pang. I searched and searched among the deepest secrets of my soul, and could not blame myself... I could look up tranquilly into the face of heaven who knew me to be Not Guilty.[15]

Clearly, he considered that his actions had been justified and that 'he acted for the good, in an age which accepted his actions as not abnormal'.[16]

This initial section has revealed some of the Victorian tenets regarding child-rearing, the use of corporal punishment, and its traditional use in public schools. We look next at the expansion of schooling for 'the masses' and the perpetuation of this form of juvenile chastisement within the state education system.

The Origins of State Education

A brief discussion of the origins of the educational system provides a useful background against which to consider the issue of teacher authority and the use of corporal punishment in schools. A hallmark of 'education for the masses' was low cost and large class sizes.[17] Within such a situation, and given the Victorian predilection for physical chastisement, it is perhaps not surprising that the disciplinary sanction was used widely.

Before 1850 what provision there was for educating the 'poorer classes'[18] was by virtue of the charity schools which were founded by such organisations as the British and Foreign School Society of 1810 and the National Schools established in 1811.[19] The origins of the teaching profession are enshrined in these charity schools which were formed as a direct consequence of the 18th and 19th centuries, 'Age of Philanthropy'. Throughout Britain the churches initiated schooling for the poorer classes as a means of carrying out their evangelical crusade. These schools tried with crude and limited resources, to impart the basics of literacy and numeracy, and teachers functioned under extreme difficulties without the support of government assistance, constantly attempting to accommodate an ever-increasing number of pupils. Census returns for 1851 revealed that over half-a-million pupils attended these private day schools, and whilst government had been subsidising education to a limited degree in the form of treasury grants since 1833, it did not assume the role of instigator for educational provision. Universal free schooling was not implemented until the following century.

During the mid-19th Century, elementary school teachers comprised people who had worked at other trades such as shop-keepers, clerks and semi-skilled craftsmen. Upon entering teaching they were given little, if any training, and normally possessed only a very basic level of competence. Gould (1954) summarises the requisites as: 'the ability to read fluently; spell correctly; be familiar with 'the first four rules of arithmetic', and have some understanding of history and geography' (pp.648-9). The use of the monitorial system, whereby elder children were taught and they in turn instructed younger ones, was also a feature of schooling at that time. Monitorial schools, inspired by the ideas of Andrew Bell and Joseph Lancaster, were established in an attempt to alleviate the difficulties experienced by the charity schools,[20] by providing inexpensive and efficient education for a large number of pupils. Through the monitorial system, the use of corporal punishment was transmitted and the right to use the sanction was on occasions delegated to older children. Likewise, in 19th century American schools, the monitorial system was used because it was in-expensive and there was an acceptance of harsh and frequent physical chastisement of pupils (Ryan, 1994).

The latter part of the 19th century and early 20th century saw teach-ing associations playing an increasingly important role in the struggle for improving the status of teachers and promoting wider acceptance of the need for education.[21] *The Forster Act* (1870) in Britain was con-sidered by these associations to be a victory for their cause. School Boards were established and given the authority to charge their annual losses to Poor Law Relief, in order to provide schools in areas where they were lacking in number and quality and they replaced school managers as the teachers' employers.[22] These organisations decided on the denominational or secular philosophy of each school under their jurisdiction. The legislation also gave them the power to insist that parents ensured that their children attend school. Most impor-tantly, once some form of compulsory attendance was established, parents were now obliged to recognise the parallel roles of education and concurrently, educator.

Whilst the status of teachers at this time improved with the imple-mentation of the new legislation, the exchange of School Board for School Manager as employer did not eradicate all of the problems. More specifically, School Board policy on corporal punishment caused much contention amongst teachers. In 1871, for example, the London School Board forbade pupil-teachers from using this form of punishment and instead determined that the head teacher alone should administer it and maintain a record of such activity. This restricted use of corporal punishment in schools was further extended to include certificated assistant teachers in 1874.[23] It is noteworthy that the controversy surrounding this issue included parents in addition to school boards and teachers. For the latter, it can be stated that the jurisdiction of teachers appeared to be encroached upon by school regulations which were considered unnecessary and constituted an erosion of professional freedom and competence:

> They also maintained that in the elementary schools of the time, corporal punishment judiciously used, was a legitimate, valuable and necessary means of maintaining good discipline (Tropp, 1957 p.134).

Parents from the poorer classes were often exposing their children to some form of regular schooling for the first time. The accepted tradition of corporal punishment in public schools now affected far more pupils by virtue of extended educational provision. Working-class parents were forced to recognise the status of teachers not only in their right to insist on attendance, but also to use disciplinary measures:

> The teachers did, however, lose a great deal of progressive and working class sympathy by their insistence on full freedom to inflict corporal punishment (*ibid.*, p.134).

School regulations governing corporal punishment

The Disciplinary sanctions were subject to regulation, and School Boards, and later Local Education Authorities developed guidelines governing the use of corporal punishment in schools. In conducting a survey of the practice, the British Psychological Society (1980)(BPS) recorded that 'approved' or 'unapproved' forms of corporal punishment were administered in schools, and that 'most definitions of corporal punishment to be found in regulations for schools [were] made not in the context of banning, but in attempts to describe permitted use and to proscribe irregular practice' (p.15).

There was little uniformity in school regulations, noted the BPS, and little general agreement as to what types of corporal punishment were permitted and what types forbidden. Furthermore, there were variations as to the 'type and amount of official corporal punishment' between Local Education Authorities (*ibid.*). This organisation thus concluded that outside of Scotland, where the 'tawse' was the standard form of corporal punishment, 'the most common permitted form of corporal punishment [was] the use of the cane on the open hands or buttocks' (p.16).

In addition to approved or unapproved forms of corporal punishment, school regulations specified certain conditions relating to the person who was empowered to administer the punishment, the number of strokes, the presence of a witness, and the recording of the action in a punishment book. The Inner London Education Authority (1970), for example, stated that all acts of physical chastisement should be reported in a punishment book, and warned that unapproved or irregular forms of corporal punishment 'are in themselves contrary to the Rules of the Education Committee and, if reported, can be the subject of disciplinary action' (p.8). Presumably the head and/or assistant teachers who administered unapproved forms of punishment could have been reported by other members of staff, parents or pupils. since it is unlikely that they would have incriminated themselves. It would be interesting to consider whether illegal acts of corporal punishment are logged by headteachers in the post-1987 era, irrespective of complaint by pupils or their parents. Finally, with the increasing membership of the National Union of Elementary Teachers, forerunner of the National Union of Teachers, more teachers sought legal advice from their union on such matters as defence against assault charges.[24] As evidenced in the next section, the judiciary normally upheld the teacher's right to administer corporal punishment which thereby helped to confirm its traditional use and acceptance in schools.

Litigation concerning corporal punishment

It is through litigation in the 19th and 20th centuries that our understanding of teacher authority has further evolved. The notions of *in loco parentis* and teachers' rights and duties have been expressed through significant judicial decisions of this time and have been given legal definition. It is important for the purpose of this book that an appreciation of the historical development of these aspects of the profession is gained, since they are fundamental to the protracted litigation which came before the European Court analysed in chapter

3. Further, an historical perspective of teachers' legal rights and duties serves as an instructive prologue to consideration of the position of teachers today in 'sparing the rod' and using alternative punishments, as explored in chapter 4.

In loco parentis

When teachers assume some of the legal rights and duties of parents, such as the right to use corporal punishment and the duty to provide care and protection, they are considered to be acting *in loco parentis*. Adams (1984), defines this concept as 'parent substitutes, standing in place of the natural parents' (p.102), Barrell (1978) elaborates further that the teacher 'assumes some of the rights and duties of the natural parent' (p.325). As such, parents are assumed to have temporarily transferred their responsibility to the teacher. According to *Fitzgerald v. Northcote and another* (1865):[25] 'a parent, when he places his child with a schoolmaster, delegates to him all his own authority'.

Analysis of key litigation of the last 150 years demonstrates how this notion of *in loco parentis* has been interpreted and accepted by the courts and how it has given teachers a distinct and well-defined status in society.

In *Williams v. Eady (1893),*[26] a definition of *in loco parentis* was first proffered by the judiciary, which indicated that a teacher's duty is that of a 'careful parent'. The case involved the careless storage of the chemical phosphorus in a Surrey private school, which precipitated an accident whereby a pupil, Kenneth Williams, received burns. Finding for the plaintiff, Lord Esher stated:

> the schoolmaster was bound to take such care of his boys as a careful father would of his boys, and there could not be a better definition of the duty of the schoolmaster.

This now standard definition of teachers' obligation to their pupils has been continually employed by the courts, as recently as in *Myton v. Wood and others 1980,*[27] in which it was stated that 'the standard to be adopted was that of a reasonable parent.' The 'reasonable parent' principle was also cited in *Hudson v. The Governors of Rotherham Grammar School and Selby Johnson (1937);*[28] in which the teacher had been temporarily supervising activities on the school playing field and during his absence, a pupil sustained an injury. In discussing the case against the teacher, the Court stated that one should not place on the teacher 'any higher standard of care than that of a reasonably careful parent.' More recent cases such as *Lyes v Middlesex County Council (1962)*,[29] *Van Oppen v Bedford Charity Trust (1989)*[30] and *Becky Walker v Derbyshire County Council (1994)*[31] have all addressed teacher responsibility and the extent of the duty of care.

A further point must be made about the concept of *in loco parentis* relating to its foundation in Common Law. It is a frequently-voiced opinion of teachers and the general public that a teacher acts *in loco parentis* under the auspices of Common Law, in that the teacher possesses the legal duty to assume what Adams calls the 'mantle of the parent' and act as a wise and sensible guardian. Common Law is the unwritten law of England which derived from ancient usage, as opposed to Statute Law which is law specifically enacted to provide for a particular requirement of society, for example in the 20th century, to regulate the teaching profession.[32] Common Law has served as the source of teachers' legal right to act *in loco parentis* and to assume many of the rights and obligations of a parent. Barrell (1985) develops this theme further:

> Turning to Common Law, it must be noted that much of the education of children is entrusted to the schoolmaster and, if he is to carry out his obligations, some of the rights and some of the duties of the natural parent must be transferred to him so far and so long as may be necessary for him to carry out his duty. In other words the schoolmaster is said to be *in loco parentis*. He may chastise the child, if he does so unreasonably he is accountable to the law. He must take care of the child, and if he fails to do so reasonably he is accountable to the law' (p.5).

Such has been the role of teachers to 'take care' of their pupils, and to use 'reasonable chastisement' when deemed necessary. Notice also the issue of being 'accountable to the law'. This still applies today as teachers are answerable to society for their conduct; a point we return to in chapters 4 and 6.

Corporal Punishment and Detention

The largest number of legal problems, notes Barrell (1985) have been generated by corporal punishment and detention:

> Both of them lie within that field of the law in which they would, were it not for the special status of the teacher, constitute trespass against the person (p.332).

Teachers have not normally risked charges of 'assault and battery' or wrongful imprisonment when they have either of these sanctions, precisely because they were acting *in loco parentis* and assuming the 'mantle' of parents. Corporal punishment is discussed in the context of human rights in chapter 6, but it is useful here to examine cases which demonstrate the legal tradition of a teacher's authority in this area.

Probably the most quoted case of the 19th century involving the issue of corporal punishment is *Hopley*, alluded to earlier. Schoolmaster Thomas Hopley was charged at Lewes Assizes with the manslaughter of one of his pupils, 15 year-old Reginald Chancellor. In order to purge the obstinacy from within the boy, Hopley sought and obtained permission from Chancellor's father to inflict severe corporal punishment – so severe that Chancellor subsequently died of the beating. Lord Cockburn's summing-up of the case is illuminating in what it reveals about the authority teachers enjoyed at the time and is worth quoting at length:

> By the law of England, a parent or a schoolmaster (who for this purpose represents the parent and has the parental authority delegated to him), may for the purpose of correcting what is evil in the child, inflict moderate and reasonable corporal punishment, always, however, with the condition, that it is moderate and reasonable. If it be administered for the gratification of passion or of rage, or if it be immoderate and excessive in its nature or degree, or if it be protracted beyond the child's powers of endurance, or with an instrument unfitted for the purpose and calculated to produce danger to life or limb: in all such cases the punishment is excessive, the violence unlawful, and if evil consequences to life or limb ensue, then the person inflicting it is answerable to the law, and if death ensues it will be manslaughter.'

Manslaughter was the verdict handed down, despite the fact that Hopley had obtained the father's permission to inflict severe corporal punishment, because 'excessive chastisement' could not be authorised.

The reasoning behind this decision indicates that the teacher was a delegate, representing the parent and endowed with parental authority. This delegation of authority consequently formed the basis of the traditional view that teachers had the right to chastise a pupil when they considered it was warranted. It is interesting that such chastisement was 'for the purpose of correcting what is evil in the child'. As discussed earlier, the concept of 'original sin' and the assumed inherent wickedness of minors was a constituent element of the Victorian perception of morality. The punishment, however, had always to be 'moderate and reasonable'. This maxim reoccurs in other court cases and is followed as a guiding principle throughout subsequent litigation. The teacher in the case of *Hopley* received a sentence of four years imprisonment for the manslaughter of the pupil rather than a harsher sentence for 'wilful murder' precisely because, as Barrell (1985) notes, 'he stood in the position of schoolmaster' and was therefore afforded a status different from any other member of society (p.222).

Even when there has been a contravention of school regulations regarding the use of corporal punishment, the courts have looked favourably upon the teacher's position. In *Mansell v. Griffin (1908)*,[33] an assistant teacher at a Gloucester elementary school struck a child with a 'boxwood ruler' (sic), in violation of school regulations which authorised the use of only a 'birch rod or cane'. Further, the teacher had not received the authority of the headmistress to administer corporal punishment, and pleaded ignorance of regulations governing the act. Despite these circumstances, the Court still decided in the teacher's favour because according to Mr Justice Phillimore:

> ... it is enough for the teacher to be able to say: 'The punishment which I administered was moderate; it was not dictated by any bad motive, and it was such as it is usual in the school and such as the parent of the child might expect it would receive if it did wrong.

The Court was satisfied that these criteria were met: and despite the violation of school regulations, the authority of the teacher was recognised in this case.

The authority of the teacher was also acknowledged in *Hutt and another v. The Governors of Haileybury College and others (1888)*,[34] in which public school pupil Henry Robert Mackenzie Hutt claimed that he was libelled, slandered, wrongly imprisoned and assaulted because of a theft which, he claimed he did not commit. In his summing-up, Mr Justice Field examined the issue of teacher authority:

> What is the authority of a master of a public school?... It seems... clear that the master is the delegate of the parent... The law... does justify a parent in a case where he honestly considers correction necessary in administering blows in a reasonable and proper manner. But then this power is not limited to corporal punishment, but extends to detention and restraint. I think... that the father parts with all these powers and delegates them to the master under whose charge he places the child... Therefore, unless limited by special contract, I think that the master has the power of judging when a punishment is required and also to what extent.

Again the notion of *in loco parentis* was alluded to, this time as a delegation of authority to include not only corporal punishment but extending to 'detention and restraint', thus widening the type of disciplinary measures a teacher could impose upon a pupil. It also credits the teacher with the professional discretion necessary to judge 'when a punishment is required and also to what extent.' Thus both this case and the former one of *Mansell v. Griffin* serve to demonstrate that teachers in both the private and state school sectors were afforded the right in law, to administer physical punishment. Parliament also endorsed this right in the *Prevention of Cruelty to Children Act (1904)*[35] (later changed to the *Children and Young Persons Act (1933)*), which contained a clause specifying that:

> nothing in this section shall be construed as affecting the right of any parent, teacher or other person having the lawful charge of a child or young person to administer reasonable punishment to him.

In addition to being allowed to legally administer corporal punishment within the school environment, the courts have recognised the authority of the teacher beyond the school boundaries. The case of *Cleary v. Booth (1893)*[36] highlights this point as two pupils, Callaway and Booth were caned after the former had assaulted a third pupil, Godding, on their way to an elementary school. Action was brought by Booth's parents because whilst their own son had been present at the event, he had not actually struck the victim. At issue here was whether a teacher's authority was enforceable beyond the school premises. In the appeal heard by the Divisional Court of the Queen's Bench, similar reasoning was used in support of the headmaster as had been echoed in earlier cases, namely that the parent delegates his authority to the teacher. Further, Mr Justice Lawrance referred to the broad responsibility of a teacher, to instil 'moral training and conduct':

> Can it be reasonably argued that the only right of a schoolmaster to inflict punishment is in respect of acts done in the school, and that it is only while the boys are there that he is to see that they are well-mannered, but that he has exceeded all the authority delegated to him by the parent if he punishes a boy who within a yard of the school is guilty of gross misbehaviour? It is difficult to express in words the extent of the schoolmaster's authority in respect to the punishment of his pupils; but in my opinion his authority extends, not only to acts done in school, but also to cases where a complaint of acts done out of school, at any rate while going to and from school is made to the schoolmaster.

Barrell clarifies understanding of this important case and others with a similar theme, by stating that:

> it is probable that it would be held not only that it was within his power but that it was his duty to deal, for example, with any of his scholars engaged in street feuds with pupils from a neighbouring school (p.332).

Teachers' authority beyond the school confines was also a feature in *R. V. Newport (Salop) Justices, ex parte Wright (1929)*.[37] In this instance, a boy was caned for smoking in the street even though he had his father's permission to do so. A protracted dispute ensued, but the final decision concluded that the action was in term-time and violated an established and reasonable school rule which came within a teacher's authority by virtue of being *in loco parentis*. A more recent case, *Cook v. Attock (1955)*[38] involved a pupil being caned for running across the road in front of a teacher's car. Once again the Court decided in favour of the school and acknowledged the teacher's authority outside the school premises. Adams is insightful on these two cases:

> The judges in these cases all recognised the obvious fact that if schools could not deal with matters occurring outside the school gates then it would be impossible to maintain order and discipline (p.168).

It is evident from the cases reviewed thus far that the judiciary was prepared to support a teacher's authority to inflict punishment arising from incidents taking place both within and beyond the school boundaries, and whilst the nature of sanction has changed, the same principle would hold true today.

Two major themes emerge from this examination of litigation involving a teacher's authority: firstly, that by acting *in loco parentis* a teacher had a right, and clearly at times was expected to administer corporal punishment; and secondly that teachers also had the obligation to act as a wise and reasonable parent to ensure correct moral upbringing as well as pupil safety. The judiciary has tended to be very supportive to the teaching profession and with regard to pupil chastisement specifically, Barrell (1985) notes that '... the courts have consistently upheld the teacher's right to administer physical punishment' (p.336).

Within the distinction of teacher's rights and duties, Barrell argues that the 'former can be restricted by mutual consent but the latter cannot be abrogated' (p.345). The judiciary has tended over the years, to increase the level of the 'duty of care', and legislation has been passed giving a clear definition of teachers' responsibility and duty within their 'scope of employment'. The teacher's traditional right to administer punishment is of particular concern to our discussion, and, as reviewed later, the curtailment of this right is fundamental to many of the cases which were examined by the European Court. Further, the duties which teachers are required to perform are allegedly becoming more difficult to implement as their authority is subjected to challenge.

Summary

Physical chastisement has been a common feature in child-rearing, carried over into schooling as teachers in both private and state schools were expected to administer the sanction. The courts have accepted the principle of reasonable punishment by a teacher acting *in loco parentis* as a defence in cases of physical punishment. This assumption has now been challenged vigorously in Strasbourg, as discussed in chapter 3. Clearly, a tradition has evolved in which the teacher has sought approval under the umbrella of *in loco parentis* in order to administer corporal punishment and to use detention as a disciplinary measure with impunity. This is not to infer, however, that there have been no limits placed on teachers. The courts have adjudicated on many cases involving discipline and from litigation accumulated over the past one hundred years a number of precepts have emerged. These are that the punishment be reasonable and given 'in good faith'; that factors affecting the child should be taken into account; and that the sanction be consistent with school policy and such as the parent might expect if their child did wrong (Partington, 1984).

Adams (1984) argued that in order to change the situation:

> the power of a teacher generally in relation to corporal punishment will have to be removed by a legal ruling from the European Court, or an Act of Parliament or by powers vested in a local authority (p.26).

Therein lay the essence of the problem which faced the profession, for it is precisely this removal or erosion of teachers' rights to administer corporal punishment which altered their status and which is a central theme of this book. That the European Court was in a position to affect such a decision is discussed in the next chapter.

Notes

1. As cited in Rosen, M (1994) *The Penguin Book of Childhood.*
2. See L J Borstelmann(1983) 'Children Before Psychology: Ideas about Children from Antiquity to the 1800s' in W Kessen (Ed), *Handbook of Child Psychology*, vol 1, New York: Wiley.
3. See for example, De Mause (1974), and P Aries (1962).
4. For more on this theme, see L Gilkey (1965) *Maker of Heaven and Earth.*
5. See *The Times*, 10th August 1986, p5.

6. See also S M Edmund (1996) *The Puritan Family*, New York, Harper and Row, p92.
7. As cited in Scholland (1996) *Shogun's Ghost*. This book provides an historical and contemporary account of corporal punishment within the Japanese educational system. See also Straus (1994) who states that physical chastisement has been in widespread use in most countries of the world.
8. *Tyrer v UK* (1978) European Court of Human Rights Series A, No. 26, 25 April, 1978.
9. As cited in Hill (1897) p183.
10. *Ibid.*
11. For background reading on this period see J Gathorne – Hardy *The Public School Phenomenon, and The Rise and Fall of the British Nanny* (Harmondsworth: Penguin 1977 and 1975). The distinction between schools in Britain should also be noted:
    - 'public' schooling refers to a non-maintained school relying mostly on parents' fees and recognised as a charity. The term 'independent school' can equally well be used here;
    - a private school is fully owned by one or more individuals and run for private profit; and
    - maintained schools, sometimes called state schools in Britain, refers to any school maintained out of public funds. The American 'public school' falls into this category.
12. As cited in Gibson (1978) p65.
13. *Ibid.*
14. *Regina v Hopley* (1860), 2F & F.
15. As cited in Leinster – MacKay 1977, p2.
16. *ibid.*
17. See D. Wardle (1976) *English Popular Education* and S J Curtis and M E Boultwood (1966) *An Introductory History of English Education*.
18. These were defined in 19th century legislation as 'classes who support themselves by manual labour' and included 'masons, carpenters and simple policemen'. A further distinction made before 1870 was the inability to pay school fees of 9d (4p) per week which was considered a main criterion in determining membership of the labouring classes. See Wardle, p.117 for more on this theme.
19. The charity school movement is addressed adeptly in I. Morrish, *Education since 1800*, pp.4-8. See also D Wardle (1976) and H C Barnard (1971) for background information on this issue.
20. The 'Monotorial System' is analysed particularly well by R. W. Rich in *The Training of Teachers in England and Wales During the 19th Century*, (London: Cambridge University Press, 1933).
21. A Tropp, *The School Teachers.*
22. F. Eaglesham's *From School Board to Local Authority* (London: Routledge and Kegan Paul, 1956) is recommended for a fuller picture of the School Board era and the development of education during the latter part of the 19th century.
23. See M E Highfield and A Pinsent *A Survey of Rewards and Punishments in Schools* (London: Newnes, 1952), Ch. 3 for information on school regulations governing the use of corporal punishment.
24. A Tropp, *The School Teachers* p145, fn. 23(1).
25. *Fitzgerald v Northcote and Another (1865)*, 4 F & F 656.
26. *Williams v Eady (1893)*, 10 TLR 41.

27. *Myton v Wood and Others (1980), The Times,* 11 July 1980, p11.

28. *Hudson v the Governors of Rotherham Grammar School and Selby Johnson (1937),* G B Barrell, *Legal Cases for Teachers,* p303, *Yorkshire Post* 248, 25 March, 1937.

29. *Lyes v Middlesex County Council (1962).*

30. *Van Oppen v Bedford Charity Trust (1989).*

31. *Becky Walker v Derbyshire County Council (1994).*

32. For a further discussion on the difference between Common Law and Statute Law see S Brandon, I Duncanson and G Samuel, *English Legal System* (London: Sweet and Maxwell, 1979) and S Brandon, *Criminal Law* (London: Sweet and Maxwell, 1979).

33. *Mansell v Griffin (1908)* KB 947; 24 TLR 431; 52 Sol Jo 376. See also *Beaumont v Surrey County Council (1968),* 66 LCR 580, 112 SJ 704.

34. *Hutt and another v the Governors of Haileybury College and Others (1888),* 4 TLR 623.

35. *Prevention of Cruelty to Children Act,* 1904, c15.

36. *Cleary v Booth (1893),* 1 QB 465; 9 TLR 260; 17 Cox CC 611.

37. *R v Newport (Salop) Justices, ex parte Wright (1929),* 2 KB 416; 141 LT 563; 28 Cox CC 658.

38. *Cook v Attock (1955), Evening Standard,* 13 January, 1955 (unreported).

Chapter 2

Rights, Reasons and the Role of Strasbourg

'Individuals'... rights may require protection, above all, against their own State' (Jacobs and White, 1996, p.5).

The voice of Strasbourg has been heard consistently during the last few decades as judgements handed down by this judidical forum have affected everyday life in Europe. It has been particularly forceful with regard to challenges made to the traditional approach to school discipline by British parents. This chapter provides a framework in which to consider the educational cases examined by the European Court.

In order to accomplish this task, five main areas are discussed: background to the development of human rights legislation; the origins of the European Court and Commission of Human Rights; the European Convention on Human Rights; and the workings of the Court and Commission. Particular attention is paid to the relationship between these two organs which are inextricably linked in the work of receiving and adjudicating applications. Emphasis is placed on the procedure which an individual applicant would undertake in order to seek redress for alleged violation of human rights, since all the major corporal punishment cases taken to Strasbourg were a consequence of individual petitions by British parents on behalf of themselves and their children.

Background

It is useful to consider the established tradition of human rights which led to the creation of such regulatory bodies as the European Court and Commission. Robertson (1982) states that:

'human rights have been cherished through the centuries in many lands... the struggle for human rights is as old as history itself because it is always apparent in the endeavour to protect the individual against the abuse of power by the monarch, the tyrant or the State' (p.9).

Although the principles of human rights have long been recognised, the legislation enacted to protect them has not, until late, found expression in the statute books. Ideas of justice and natural rights[1] were considered by 5th Century Greek philosophers Plato and Aristotle, and the Roman lawyer Cicero. After the Renaissance, states Lloyd (1964), 'the notion gradually gained currency that man possessed certain fundamental rights in a state of nature; and that when civil society came into being, he took over those rights into his newly gained civil status and these still remained protected by natural law' (pp.83-84). Fundamental documents, such as: *Magna Carta* (1215); the *Petition of Right* (1628); *The Bill of Rights* (1689); and the *Habeus Corpus Acts* established the foundations of a tradition that was furthered by the writings of Milton and Locke.

Some countries, such as the United States, provided for human rights through established constitutional arrangements, whilst others have looked to the Common Law. The United Kingdom is a prime example of the latter category. Possessing no written Constitution, she has invoked the Common Law which has developed from common practice and application, and judicial interpretation of what are perceived as accepted norms. Conversely, Europe embraced the tenet of a Civil Law system which descended originally from the Roman Codes.[2] A noteworthy exception to these traditions is Scotland whose legal system is a derived amalgam of Roman Law, moderated with aspects of English Law. The case of *Campbell and Cosans* (1982),[3] described in the next chapter, alludes to this tradition. Lloyd (1972), contends that it is this 'spirit of the civil law' which is partly responsible for the acceptance of the Common Market principle in Europe and other European activities of integration established after the Second World War. This theme is considered more fully later in the chapter.

International law has also contributed to the promotion and development of human rights because, in addition to the evaluation of legal systems for each State, countries have co-operated in common endeavours. Initially, this common concern included such matters as trade, but the foundations were established upon which future human rights treaties could be built. Harris (1973) states that the term 'international law' appears to have been coined by Bentham and that prior to this time it was more commonly known as the 'Law of Nations'. Oppenheim (1953), provides a definition of community law which adds to this discussion. He defines the term 'law' as ' a body of rules for human conduct within a community which by common consent of this community shall be enforced by external power' (p.9).

This is a useful starting point from which to consider the development of international law and later the jurisprudence emerging from the European Convention on Human Rights. Oppenheim adds that from the end of the Middle Ages rules of international conduct were urgently required and that 'writers on the Law of Nations prepared the ground for their growth by constructing certain rules on the basis of religion, moral, rational and historical reflections' (p.17).

It was, however, the establishment of the League of Nations in 1920, contends Harris, with membership 'open' to any State which 'as much as any other single event, marked the beginning of the present system in which international law applies automatically to all states whatever their location or character' (p.12). Further, the original concept of international law recognised the primacy of the Contracting State rather than the citizen, as main subject. As this chapter will demonstrate, the European Convention forcefully challenges the traditional concept of international law by providing for the individual, as well as the State, to be a subject of the discipline. Robertson (1982), explains the importance of such a shift in emphasis whereby international standards regarding basic rights of the individual are to be upheld providing remedies for redress in the event of violation. He continues that such a transformation is a lengthy process and 'much resistance is encountered and many governments seek to shelter behind the classic doctrine of international law and hide their actions behind the cloak of national sovereignty' (ibid.).

After World War I, the League of Nations drafted provisions into its Covenant which perpetuated this spirit of international unity. The main objective was to prevent another worldwide conflict after the horrors of 'the Great War'. The treatment of prisoners of war and war casualties again received attention and eventually there was a gradual swell of opinion that human rights should be the concern of international law. By the 1930s, human rights within international law had emphasised the status of the individual, albeit in a limited number of areas such as slavery, minority rights and humanitarian concerns.

It was the advent of World War II which was instrumental in developing further, international law and the protection of human rights. Robertson (1982) contends that:

> one of the most striking developments in international law since the end of the Second World War is its concern with the protection of human rights... (p.1).

This was particularly evident in the drafting of the *Universal Declaration of Human Rights* (1948), a major outcome of the last war. Its preamble states that it reaffirms 'faith in fundamental human rights, in the dignity and worth of the human person and in the equal rights of men and women'.[4] Robertson (1993) notes the importance of this document, as human rights are mentioned almost for the first time in an international treaty. The First World War treaties had concerned themselves more specifically with minority interest groups rather than to extend the principles of human rights to all people; the Second World War's treaties attempted to go further. The United Kingdom is, along with other countries, a signatory of the *Universal Declaration of Human Rights* which according to Humphrey (1970), ex-Director of the division of human rights in the United Nations Secretariat, 'has now become part of the customary law of nations and is, therefore, now binding on all states' (p.44). However, as S.A. de Smith (1977) emphasises:

> there is indeed something peculiarly exasperating about a broad affirmation of fundamental human rights unaccompanied by any machinery for giving them effective legal protection (p.439).

It was this omission in the UN Declaration, an effective mechanism to protect human rights, which the European Convention sought to provide. The end of the War meant that the time was ripe for fundamental changes, not solely in the enumeration and protection of human rights, but, notes Robertson (1993), in the concept of the nation-state, whereby a new and different system could be established with sufficient controls that challenged the practice of countries hiding behind claims of domestic jurisdiction. The new political order which was to lead to the establishment of a European Court and Commission of Human Rights contained ideas to challenge the traditional notion of state sovereignty and place the individual in a more effective position to seek redress against human rights violations.

The Origins of the European Court and Commission of Human Rights

It is important to see the development of the European Court and Commission of Human Rights within an historical framework, as a desire for political co-operation and greater unity in Europe after World War II. During the post-war era, ideas for European unity and integration were given stronger endorsement, when, Robertson (1963) contends, an unprecedented number of international organisations were established[5]. Convening at the Hague in May 1948, these organisations formed the Congress of Europe, electing Winston Churchill President of Honour. With more than 700 participants, this assembly conveyed a 'Message to Europeans, bursting with the two concepts of 'democracy' and 'human rights' (Beddard, 1993, p.19). The Hague Congress produced a policy document which stated among other things:

> ... we desire a united Europe, throughout whose area the free movement of persons, ideas and goods is restored, we desire a Charter of Human Rights guaranteeing liberty of thought, assembly and expression as well as the right to form a political opposition.[6]

Further, among the political resolutions aired at the meeting was one which suggested that: 'a European Court of Human Rights backed with adequate sanctions should be established to adjudicate in cases of alleged violation of those rights'.[7]

It is against this backdrop of political support for some form of European unification that the Convention was conceived, in what Beddard describes as 'this rarefied atmosphere of European *entente* (p.21). He further speculates whether 'at any time in the history of this Continent, either before or since, such a step could have been taken' (*ibid.*). In order to achieve this unity, notes Robertson (1961), the Hague Congress declared that European states had to establish an economic and political union, and agree to merge some of their sovereign rights. He contends that this merger was 'a revolutionary proposal' causing a departure from the traditional custom and practice of international law which had prevailed for several centuries (p.11).

Amongst the most important of the new European organisations was the Council of Europe: 'basically a political organisation which set up for the first time a democratic assembly representing not the governments but the parliaments of the Member States' (Robertson, 1966, pp.16-17). The Council of Europe's original Member-States comprised: Belgium, Denmark, France, Iceland, Italy, Luxembourg, the Netherlands, Norway, Sweden and the United Kingdom.[8] Article 1 of the Council's Statute stated that the aim of the organisation was to promote greater unity for economic and social advancement. Further, conditions of membership were carefully outlined in Article 3:

> Every member of the Council of Europe must accept the principles of the rule of law and of the enjoyment by all persons within the jurisdiction of human rights and fundamental freedoms, and collaborate sincerely and effectively in the realisation of the aim of the Council.

Robertson (1993) notes the importance of this document, for it went further than previous treaties in its adherence to maintaining human rights as a condition of membership of the Council of Europe. In addition, the Council's Consultative Assembly met to recommend the drafting of a Convention on Human Rights with associated enforcement agencies which would outline how member states were to ensure 'human rights and fundamental freedoms', thereby providing 'a collective guarantee' (*ibid.*, p.4). A procedure for new members was established in Article 4 of the Statute and presently there are 31 Member States within the Council of Europe[9].

The Council today concerns itself with a wide area of subject matters: economic, social, cultural, scientific and legal issues and human rights. The labyrinth of organisations designed to administer them, reflects the eclectic nature of the work.[10] The organs of the Council were devised to include a Committee of Ministers, an executive branch comprising: the Minister of Foreign Affairs of each Member State, or his/her deputy, and also 'the first European parliamentary organ: the Consultative Assembly' consisting of Parliamentary members of the Member-States (Jacobs and White, 1996, p.4).

A serious violation of human rights can result in a member state being requested to withdraw from the Council, under Article 8, and is evidenced by the withdrawal of Greece from the Council in 1969 which followed allegations of human rights violation.[11] The use of this sanction by the Council in order to ensure that Member-States comply with the Statute is, contend Jacobs and White, an innovative device, since traditionally human rights issues lay firmly within the domestic jurisdiction of each country and only became an issue in international law when violation involved another State. Their discussion of this initiative is useful, as traditional notions of international law and State sovereignty have meant that individuals had to rely on the state for protection. Accordingly, *'their rights may require protection, above all, against their own State* – and the values of democratic government require a collective guarantee...' (p.5, emphasis added).

Two important issues from Jacob and White's analysis are pertinent to this discussion. Firstly, the introduction of the right of the individual appeal represented a dramatic departure from the traditional concept of international law, as discussed in the previous section. The cases examined in the subsequent chapter illustrate the fact that having exhausted all domestic avenues of remedy, British citizens appealed to a higher forum which their country, as a member state, is compelled to acknowledge. Secondly, the departure from the doctrine of state sovereignty, in order to indemnify individual human rights has been one of the major thrusts of the Council of Europe's work. At first glance, Article 3 of the Statute appears to be binding on all signatories, and yet decisions handed down by the European Court are not immediately implemented. The case of *Campbell and Cosans* which is analysed in the next chapter, is a prime example. There exists a degree of latitude in a State's interpretation of the Court's decision, 'a certain measure of discretion' (Harris, Boyle, and Warbrick, 1995) or 'a margin of appreciation'.(This theme is referred to in chapter 3.) Presently, it is noteworthy that above all, the fathers of the Council of Europe intended to establish a Convention on human rights which would go beyond pious, well-meaning rhetoric, and for British parents and their children this indeed has been the case.

The European Convention on Human Rights and Fundamental Freedoms

This Convention which we are signing is not as full or as precise as many of us would have wished. However, we have thought it our duty to subscribe to it as it stands. It provides foundations on which to base the defence of human personality against all tyrannies and against all forms of totalitarianism.[12]

The founders of the Council of Europe drafted the Convention for the Protection of Human Rights and Fundamental Freedoms[13] (referred to as 'the Convention'), to reflect their concerns for stronger European unity and to affirm and guarantee human rights after profound and deliberate abandonment of such rights after the last war. The drafters sought to enumerate and define a list of fundamental rights which should be guaranteed in all democratic countries and which would inhibit the return of totalitarianism.

In formulating the Convention, the Consultative Assembly of the Council of Europe was, states Beddard, essentially concerned with two basic questions: what were the rights and freedoms which members of the Council of Europe should guarantee to all people residing in their territories, and how could a collective guarantee be operated. After deliberations, he states, a compromise agreement was made whereby it was decided to include initially only the rights and freedoms traditionally accepted in democratic countries. It was intended to extend the list to incorporate other human rights, but from the outset, given the historical backdrop, 'it was necessary to begin with accepted, widely agreed principles and to guarantee, first of all, political democracy' (*ibid.*). Jacobs and White state that the United Nations Charter was important in international law for establishing 'the principle of respect for human rights' and work in the United Nations has provided a long list of human rights which incorporate two classes of basic rights: social and economic, and civil and political (p.5). It is the latter category which is to be found in the Convention, the former social and economic rights being incorporated into the European Social Charter which was intended to complement the treaty.[14]

The Convention and its Protocols contain human rights and freedoms which, whilst very similar to those stipulated in the U.N. Declaration, are defined and restricted rather differently. Further, a point of departure between the two statements on human rights is according to Brownlie (1981), that 'the Declaration is not a legally binding instrument as such [but serves] as an authoritative guide... to the interpretation of the Charter' (p.144). Conversely, the Convention attempts to provide a form of guarantee for human rights and to obtain a greater commitment from its signatories.

Section 1 of the Convention establishes the civil and political rights to be protected and whilst derived in part from the Universal Declaration, they are delineated more rigorously. Jacobs and White maintain that

> ... for the purpose of an instrument which was to be binding in law, the content of these rights was often made more specific, and the circumstances in which limitations might legitimately be imposed on their exercise were spelt out (p.6).

Article 1 of the Convention reiterates that the contracting state must secure the enumerated rights and freedoms to everyone residing within their jurisdiction. This article is followed by Articles 2-18 which stipulate the guaranteed rights and any limitations which are imposed on them. A brief examination of some of the human rights to be protected under the Convention gives an insight into the nature and scope of the document. Amongst the basic rights outlined include 'the right to liberty and security of person' (Article 5); 'the right to respect for... private and family life' (Article 8) and 'the right to freedom of thought, conscience and religion' (Article 9). Article 2 specifies that 'everyone's right to life shall be protected by law'. Further, the word 'everyone', which permeates the first section of the Convention, does not mention an age limit and is consequently broad and potentially ambiguous. (Chapter 5, which is concerned with 'Children's Rights' amplifies this point.) Article 3 of the Convention has particular relevance to this discussion because of its subsequent application to corporal punishment:

No one shall be subjected to torture or to inhuman or degrading treatment or punishment.

This is particularly important, notes Jacobs (1975) because only in this provision are there no qualifications, restrictions or exceptions to the right guaranteed. Moreover, 'the Convention is not a static instrument, but must be interpreted in the light of developments in social and political attitudes' (ibid., p.36). The dynamic quality of the Convention is well-demonstrated in the Tyrer case,[15] detailed in the following chapter, in which Article 3 was interpreted in light of the norms and values of the 1970s regarding school discipline.

Protocols were added to the Convention, thereby extending the list of human rights to be protected, Article 2 of the First Protocol confirmed in 1957, being particularly pertinent:

No person shall be denied the right to education. In the exercise of any functions which it assumes in relation to education and teaching, the State shall respect the right of parents to ensure such education and teaching in conformity with their own religious and philosophical convictions.

When this protocol was ratified by the United Kingdom in 1952, certain reservations were made concerning avoidable public expense. As shown by the case of Campbell and Cosans, this later article has subsequently proved to have profound implications for the issue of school discipline in the United Kingdom, and is examined in more detail in the next chapter.

In general, 'rights' per se are never absolute but dependent on time, place and circumstance. Within the Convention this reality was recognised and provision made for exceptions, limitations, restrictions and derogations from the proclaimed rights and freedoms. As mentioned earlier, the Convention was drafted during the aftermath of World War II, and was intended to minimise the likelihood of the re-emergence of further totalitarian states. Beddard (1973) notes, however, that: '... the States would not have signed and ratified, even at that time, a document which completely fettered independent action within domestic jurisdiction' (p.42). He notes that a degree of restriction exists even within these items of the articles, so that the only provisions without limitations are the right not to be subjected to torture, or inhuman or degrading treatment or punishment, and the prohibition on holding someone in slavery or servitude.

Given the permissible limitations and derogations from the Convention, it is important to determine what guarantee, if any, is provided by the formal agreement. This issue has been debated widely, and Jacobs and White note that there is a view that member states are obliged to incorporate the text of the Convention, or section 1 at least, into their own domestic law and that whatever approach is used, the human rights guaranteed in the Convention must be upheld. The Convention has not been incorporated into English law; rather the government of the day seeks to ensure that its domestic legislation was compatible with the treaty obligations.

Finally, an area which may seek to limit the guarantee of human rights is that of jurisdiction and the territorial scope of the Convention. Article 1 requires that the Convention be applicable to everyone within the *jurisdiction* of the Contracting State. This particular Article caused difficulty at the time of its inception over the question of whether the Convention should extend to the colonial and overseas territories of the Member-States. To resolve this problem, Article 63 (1) or 'the Colonial Clause' was finally agreed upon, which stipulates:

> any State may, at the time of its ratification or at any time thereafter, declare by notification addressed to the Secretary General of the Council of Europe that the present Convention shall extend to all, or any, of the territories for whose international relations it is responsible.

Robertson (1963) maintains that this was an excellent development resulting in the Convention having application to many parts of the world. A number of member states have extended the treaty to their overseas territories. For example, Great Britain extended the Convention's applicability to 41 overseas territories in 1953, one of which was the Isle of Man.[16] This point is expanded in the next chapter with regard to the *Tyrer* case. In the event that any of these overseas territories acquires independence, the declaration may be nullified in respect of that territory.

To summarise so far, the Convention is an extensive list of human rights and fundamental freedoms subject to certain limitations, restrictions and derogations which are 'legally' permissible. What must also be mentioned, however, is that even within such a limited framework, the Convention seeks to provide remedy if these rights are violated. This is effected by use of its enforcement organs, the European Commission and Court of Human Rights.

The European Commission of Human Rights

The Convention drafters decided that an undertaking by a member state to respect the convention's list of rights was inadequate: remedial measures and methods of enforcement were required. These subsequently found expression in Article 19:

> to ensure the observance of the engagements undertaken by the High Contracting Parties in the present Convention, there shall be set up:
>
> (1) A European Commission of Human Rights [and]
>
> (2) A European Court of Human Rights.

The European Commission of Human Rights ('the Commission'), and the European Court are inextricably linked in their hearing complaints of violations of the Convention. Indeed, the workings of the European Court cannot be appreciated without detailed reference being made to the provisions and the procedures of the Commission.

The composition and procedure of the Commission is established in Section III of the Convention. Under Article 20, membership is based on a number of members equal to the number of states who have signed the Convention. The main function of the Commission is to deal with applications brought against the Contracting States by other countries, under the terms of Article 24. More importantly, however,

> *the Commission may receive petitions* addressed to the Secretary-General of the Council of Europe *from any person*, non-governmental organisation or group of individuals claiming to be the victim of a violation by one of the High Contracting Parties of the rights set forth in this Convention. (Article 25 (1), emphasis added)

A proviso exists here that: 'the High Contracting Party against which the complaint has been lodged has declared that it recognises the competence of the Commission to receive such petitions' (*ibid.*).

Articles 24 and 25 have been considered to be of major importance in the workings of the Convention and before discussing the procedure of the Commission in greater depth, it is instructive to consider further these two provisions. Articles 24 and 25, note Jacobs and White, 'introduced striking innovations by the normal canons of international law' (p.7). A State may bring an action against another country, under article 24, even if it is not directly affected 'purely on humanitarian grounds' (*ibid.*). Article 25, however, has been considered the more important development. Robertson (1966) notes:

> it is the great merit of the European Convention on Human Rights that it institutes a procedure which permits an individual to complain even against his own government. This was a remarkable innovation in international law; so much so, indeed, that some governments hesitated to accept it (p.48).

The United Kingdom agreed to this option of individual appeal in 1966 after long resistance, notes Jacobs (1975). (British parents subsequently went on to utilise this provision for their own grievance against schools, discussed in the next chapter). Retention of the right of petition by the United Kingdom was described by the *National Council for Civil Liberties* as: 'perhaps the key civil liberty issue of the decade'.[17] The Isle of Man, however, withdrew this option in 1976, perhaps anticipating the outcome of the *Tyrer* case.[18] Beddard (1973) considers the Convention is important in international law because of 'the contribution it makes to the status of the individual in the international legal system' (p.1). By 1985, 19 of the 21 Member-States of the Council of Europe had accepted the Court's compulsory jurisdiction.[19] Further, there has been a steady increase in individual applications: from approximately 300 per annum for the first three years of operation [with] an increase since 1967 of up to 50 percent' (*ibid.*, p.5). Articles 24 and 25 differ, however, on the grounds of 'admissibility' which is a major function which the Commission undertakes. As this discussion is particularly concerned with individual application, the procedure for Article 25 is highlighted. The majority of contracting states continue this situation of permitting such appeal, notes Beddard (1993), thus perpetuating the opportunity for individuals to allege violation of human rights against their own country.

To summarise the admissibility procedure of the Commission, following Articles 26 and 27 of the Convention, the Commission decides whether: all domestic remedies have been exhausted; the application is not anonymous; it is not substantially the same as one previously adjudicated; it is not 'manifestly ill-founded' and it is not abusive of the right of petition. (See Figure 1 for a functional flowchart of the Convention Procedure.) Further, Beddard (1980) notes that the trend has been for the Commission to take a more negative and hence more liberal attitude to the issue of admissibility, and that the merits of the application and whether it raises questions of law, are also part of the deliberations.

In cases where the Commission finds the application admissible, Article 28 requires firstly that it ascertains the facts of the case, and secondly that it attempts to secure 'a friendly settlement' by placing itself at the disposal of the parties concerned. If such a settlement is reached the dispute is ended. (This was the result of the *Townend*[20] case detailed later in chapter 3). The function of this agency was summed up by its former President, Sir Humphrey Waldock in 1958:

> The Convention was clearly right... to make the Commission's task of conciliation the central feature of the remedies which it provides. It was not primarily established for the purpose of putting States in the dock and registering convictions against them.[21]

In the event that an amicable solution cannot be reached, the Commission is required to send its report to the High Contracting Parties concerned; to the Committee of Ministers, and to the Secretary General of the Council of Europe for publication (Rule 61). Further, if the case involves an individual applicant, that party is also informed of the report in the event that the dispute will next be adjudicated by the European Court (Rule 76). Finally, within a period of three months after the transmission of the Report to the Committee of Ministers, the Commission considers at a plenary session whether or not to bring the case before the European Court of Human Rights (Rule 70).

It is possible for States as well as the Commission to bring a case before the Court. This contrasts markedly with the right of the individual who, until recently, could not invoke the authority of the Court. When

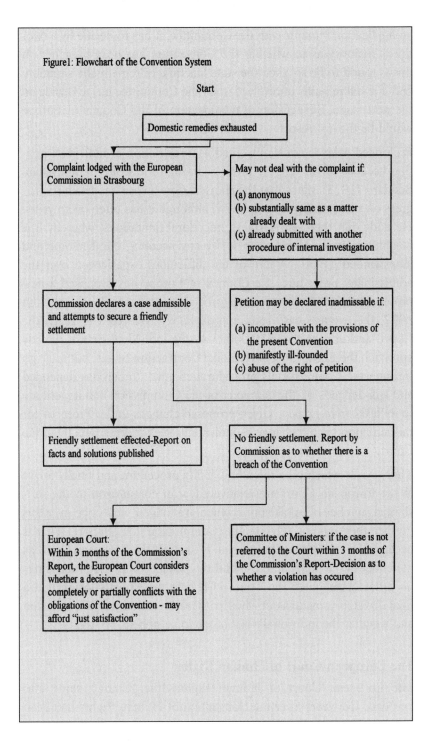

Figure1: Flowchart of the Convention System

Start

Domestic remedies exhausted

Complaint lodged with the European Commission in Strasbourg

May not deal with the complaint if:

(a) anonymous
(b) substantially same as a matter already dealt with
(c) already submitted with another procedure of internal investigation

Commission declares a case admissible and attempts to secure a friendly settlement

Petition may be declared inadmissable if:

(a) incompatible with the provisions of the present Convention
(b) manifestly ill-founded
(c) abuse of the right of petition

Friendly settlement effected-Report on facts and solutions published

No friendly settlement. Report by Commission as to whether there is a breach of the Convention

European Court:
Within 3 months of the Commission's Report, the European Court considers whether a decision or measure completely or partially conflicts with the obligations of the Convention - may afford "just satisfaction"

Committee of Ministers: if the case is not referred to the Court within 3 months of the Commission's Report-Decision as to whether a violation has occured an application remains with the Committee, it has to decide by a two-thirds majority as to whether the Convention has been breached. If this is found to be so, then the state has time to remedy the situation; and if it still remains unresolved, then the Committee has to decide on the next stage. Suspension of membership of the Council of Europe would be the last resort.

Prolonged delay is constantly cited as a restriction of individual petition because of the lengthy process through the Convention system. Beddard (1973) states that the shortest time a case has taken to progress on admissibility is six months, although it has often taken years. He adds that there are certain 'procedural limitations' whereby 'the machinery of the Convention is, by any account, cumbersome and long-winded' (p.50). Aware of the difficulties experienced over the admissibility procedure, the Council of Europe has proposed a new protocol designed to speed up procedures before the Court.[22] In 1997, the average case took approximately five years to reach the Court, and at a cost of £30,000.[23] As the individual cannot directly approach the European Court, unlike Contracting States, but must go through the Commission's procedural channel: 'much has depended and still depends on the character of the Commission and its attitude to its task' (*ibid.*, p.51). Given proposed changes under Protocol 11, this situation should change as individuals seek redress directly to the Court.

Those cases which pass the admissibility procedure and finally arrive at the European Court are relatively few in comparison to the substantial number of applications which are lodged, and once over this hurdle, they cannot rely on the Commission for support. This is because the role of the Commission is to assist the European Court as 'defender of the public interest' and is associated with the proceedings 'in order to enlighten the Court'.[24] It is in the Court's forum that a final decision is made as to whether the Convention has been violated and whether the individual's rights are to be upheld.

The European Court of Human Rights

The European Court of Human Rights (the 'Court') came into existence five years after the Convention of Human Rights had been drafted. In 1955, notes Beddard (1973) the required 'eight declarations of recognition of compulsory jurisdiction were lodged' (p.38). Delay in establishing this judicial forum was due to 'many doubts and misgivings concerning its role in relation to municipal courts' (*ibid.*). As stated earlier, the United Kingdom, for instance, did not recognise the Court's jurisdiction until 1966, fifteen years after having signed the Convention. In contrast to its rather slow and cautious beginning, over 400 cases have to date passed through the qualifying procedure to the Court.[25]

Similar to the Commission, the Court functions by its own set of rules of procedure formulated in 1959, in order to fulfil its obligations under the Convention.[26] The Rules of the Court are divided into two categories: section 1 which deals with 'the Organisation and Working of the Court' and section 2 which refers to the 'Procedure of the Court'. The composition of the Court is stipulated under Article 38.

> The European Court of Human Rights shall consist of a number of judges equal to that of the Members of the Council of Europe. No two judges may be nationals of the same State.

Each member of the Council of Europe has a representative judge in the Court, irrespective of whether all States have signed or ratified the Convention. For example, in 1973 there were 15 members of the Commission and 17 Court judges, even though only 11 states had recognised the Court's compulsory jurisdiction.[27] Beddard states that the reason behind this was that the Court should represent all European States to reflect a true picture of public opinion, and to serve as 'a conscience of Europe' (p.30).

More recent proposals under Protocol II have modified the organisation further whereby the Plenary Court, consisting of all judges, determines matters of procedure and administration; a chamber composed of seven judges will determine the merits of the majority of cases, whilst others will be relinquished to a Grand Chamber of seventeen judges for final judgement. Increasingly the Chamber will take over the role of the Commission in deciding the admissibility of petitions. Cases relinquished to the Grand Chamber are likely to concern serious questions regarding the Convention's interpretation of potential inconsistencies with earlier judgements. Clearly there are likely to be complex arrangements in the transition period between the old and the new court procedures (Mowbray, 1994a). Overall, the proposed changes will effectively abolish the Commission and make the Court a full-time judicial body which both receives and deliberates on cases under the proposed new structure. It is intended that this new system will begin to operate in November 1998 (Government White Paper, 1997).

Under current regulations, Court judges are elected by the Consultative Assembly from the nominees made by each Member-State: of that list of three, 'at least two must be its own nationals' (Article 39). Appointed on the basis of moral character and legal training, Court members are elected for nine year periods of office and are eligible for re-election, according to the requirements of Articles 39 and 40. Protocol II will reduce this to a period of six years in office (Mowbray). Each judge takes an oath or solemn declaration before assuming duties at his/her first Court appearance.

Finally, for the adjudication of each case:

> the Court shall consist of a Chamber composed of seven judges. There shall sit as an ex-officio member of the Chamber, the judge, who is a national of any State party concerned, or, if there is none, a person of its choice who shall sit in the capacity of judge; the names of the other judges shall be chosen by lot, by the President, before the opening of the case (Article 43).

The administration and work of the Court is directed by a President and a Vice-President (rules 8 and 9). In addition, a Registrar is elected by the Court (rule 11) whose main duty is to be 'the channel for all communications and notifications made by, or addressed to, the Court' (rule 14). For the working of the Court, it was decided that it 'shall be at the seat of the Council of Europe at Strasbourg', although 'if it considers it expedient [the Court may] exercise its function in any territories to which the Convention applies' (rule 15). This was requested in the *Tyrer* case, detailed in the next chapter. The plenary sessions of the Court are called 'at least once annually' for which 11 judges are needed for a quorum (rule 16 and 18). A chamber may wish to relinquish jurisdiction in favour of the plenary Court, if a case raises important questions which affects the interpretation of the Convention (rule 48). Finally, a majority verdict is required by the judges for a Court decision and, under Article 51 (2), dissenting opinions are permitted:

> if the judgement does not represent in whole or in part the un-animous opinion of the judges, any judge shall be entitled to deliver a separate opinion.

Analysis of cases in the following chapter includes reference to dissenting opinions which highlight the complexity and difficulty of obtaining consensus. In the event that two written applications, or more, have similar concerns, the Chamber may under Rule 35, 'order that the proceedings in both cases be conducted simultaneously.' (The case of *Campbell and Cosans*, detailed in the next chapter, falls into this category.)

Once in session, the oral hearing is conducted by the President, Vice-President or an elected senior judge who presides over the order in which the various agents, advocates, adversaries, Commission members and 'appointed parties' are to speak (rule 37). To assist in its deliberations, the Chamber may call for expert witnesses and may also 'depute one or more of its members to conduct an enquiry, to carry out an investigation on the spot or to obtain information in any other manner' (rule 38). Finally, the Convention does not empower individual applicants to refer a case to the Court or to appear before it as parties. There has been an important new innovation, in that:

> ... once a case has been referred to the Court by a Government or by the Commission, the applicant may express the wish to take part in the proceedings. If he does so he has, in principle, the right to be represented by an advocate [and] receive legal aid... if necessary.[28]

Now under Protocol II, individuals will for the first time have a right to complain directly to the Court to allege violations of the Convention. This has been described by Mowbray as 'a momentous institutional development' (p.544). Accordingly, it is possible for individuals to have their 'day in court'.

The proceedings are conducted in the official languages of the Court: French and English, one of which is declared to be the 'authentic text'. In the event that a party is unable to make himself/herself understood in either official language, then the use of translations is permissible and all parties can be represented by agents or advisers. A new innovation of 'legal secretaries' to assist the Court has recently been proposed. Further, the Commission delegates 'one or more of its members to take part in the consideration of the case before the Court' and the Court takes into account the report of the Commission (rule 29).

From the individual applicant's situation, therefore, the role of the Commission and its report on the case is crucial. The cases discussed in the next chapter have all undergone what Beddard refers to as 'at least a dozen hurdles' in order to finally come before the Court for adjudication, leaving behind them many others which, for various reasons, did not merit a further hearing. As such, notes Robertson, the Court's role is contingent on: attempts to bring about a friendly settlement having failed; a State or the Commission choosing judicial review; and the country concerned recognising the jurisdiction of the Court. Accordingly he concludes, the majority of the Court's work tends to arise out of individual petitions made to the Commission.

After the hearing and deliberations by the Chamber of judges representative of the Court, or occasionally the plenary Court, a judgement is handed down. This includes the contents of the judgement which includes: the names of the officials and participants; statements of the proceedings and facts of the case; the reasons in point of law and the decision, if any, regarding costs. The Registrar is responsible for publication of the decision and any relevant documents. While the content of the Court's decision is important, what is crucial to Europeans is the *effect* that the decision will have on their lives and the impact of the Court's decisions regarding the use of corporal punishment, which is one of the main themes of this book.

In reaching a judgement, the Court has to decide whether 'a decision or a measure taken by a legal authority or any other authority of a High Contracting Party is completely, or partially, in conflict with the obligation arising from the present Convention' and whether therefore, there has been a violation of human rights (Article 50). With regard to compensation or restitution, this Article further highlights the issue of 'just satisfaction'. To date, over 143 cases have resulted in a financial award and/or costs being made by the Court.[29] Further, in a number of applications, the Court's finding of a violation amounted in itself to 'just satisfaction'. (This was in fact the situation in one aspect of the *Campbell and Cosans* case.)

The decision of the Court is final, and the Convention is categoric that: 'the Contracting states must undertake to abide by the decision of the Court in any case to which they are party' (Article 53). The Court's judgement is transmitted to the Committee of Ministers which has the obligation to 'supervise its execution' (Article 54). On the question of how forceful or binding the Court's decision is, Jacobs and White contend that the individual country is obliged to give effect to the judgement, and failure to comply could result in a country being suspended from the Council of Europe. (The *Campbell and Cosans* case demonstrates also the tardiness of the British government, as a Contracting Party, in implementing the Court's decision, and this point is addressed in greater detail in chapter 3.)

Since the Court's creation, it has adjudicated more than 400 cases[30] which have raised a wide range of concerns. Among these issues are: ill-treatment in Northern Ireland (*Ireland*);[31] Belgian legislation on vagrancy (*De Wilde, Ooms and Versyp*);[32] prison disciplinary proceedings in England (*Campbell and Fell*);[33] and the scope of trade union freedom in Sweden (*Swedish Engine Drivers' Union*).[34] It has been argued that Britain has one of the worst records of violations of the Convention: as of November, 1987 the Court had adjudicated 26 complaints against the United Kingdom, 19 of which revealed that Britain had violated the Convention.[35] Similarly, of the 57 cases referred to the Court against the country in 1993, 31 were found to contain at least one breach of human rights.[36] Alternative arguments suggest that the practice of litigation has a stronger tradition in Britain, and that the failure to incorporate the Convention into domestic law has meant that individuals have been forced to pursue their rights in Strasbourg. It will be interesting to see whether Britain continues to find itself 'in the dock' now that rights are being brought home under proposed constitutional reform.

Summary

Established within the framework of a regional treaty, the Convention and its enforcement agencies, the Court and Commission, were conceived in the aftermath of World War II as a response to the conflict. A specific desire for unity and cooperation between the European States provided the impetus to establish new political orders, the Council of Europe being one such body. Working collectively, the member-states seek to improve the standard of human rights within their territories and the recognition of the right to individual petition contributes to this endeavour. Such an innovation in the application of international law has allowed ordinary citizens to petition against their own country and to look to the Court as the final arbitrator in a dispute. Whilst the individual applicant can only approach the Court through the Commission, issues have been raised which benefit many more individuals. As the definition of human rights changes and expands, the Council of Europe seeks to include more rights. Concurrently, the Court has a vital role to play in interpreting the present Convention and deciding whether human rights have been violated. This is shown by the cases in the following chapter which all relate to the alleged breach of human rights held by British parents and their children with regard to school discipline.

Notes

1. For more information on this theme, see P. Jackson, *Natural Justice* (London: Sweet andMaxwell, 1973) and Lord Lloyd of Hampstead *Introduction to Jurisprudence* (3rd ed., London: Stevens, 1972), ch.3.

2. For further discussion on this theme see F.H. Lawson, *Roman Law and Common Law A Comparison in Outline* (Cambridge: Cambridge University Press, 1952).

3. *Campbell and Cosans v UK* the European Court of Human Rights, Series A Nos. 48 and 60, 25 February 1982 and 22 March 1983.

4. See I. Brownlie (ed) *Basic Documents on Human*, (2nd ed., Oxford: Clarendon Press, 1981).

5. Beddard (1973) *Human Rights and Europe* 1st ed. (London: Sweet and Maxwell) provides more details on these organisations.

6. As cited in A.G. Robertson (1961), *The Law of International Institutions in Europe* p.10.

7. *Ibid.*

8. *See I. Brownlie, Basic Documents on Human, p.320 for member-state's recognition on the right of the individual.*

9. P. Kempee, *A Systematic to the Caselaw of the European Court of Human Rights*, p.IX.

10. The organisation and work of the Council of Europe is well-documented in many texts. Of particular merit are: R. Beddard, *Human Rights and Europe* (2nd ed), and F.G Jacobs, *The European Convention on Human Rights*. See also http://www.coe.fr

11. *Council of Europe, Collected Texts*, p. 608.

12. M. Robert Schuman, as cited in A.H. Robertson, *Human Rights in Europe*, (1st ed) p.5

13. *Council of Europe, Collected Texts*.

14. See D. Harris, *The European Social Charter* (Charlottesville, University Press of Virginia,1984).

15. *Tyrer v UK*. The European Court of Human Rights, Series A, No. 26, 25 April, 1978.

16. *Council of Europe, Collected Texts*, p.603.

17. *The Times,* 14 November 1973.

18. See Gomien (1995) p.79 *Judgements of the European Court* (Strasbourg: Council of Europe)

19. *Council of Europe, Press Release*, (1997) Registry of European Court of Human Rights, April, F-67075, Strasbourg, Cedex.

20. *J. T. Townend Snr. and J. T. Townend Jnr. v UK.*, (Application No. 9119/80), European Commission of Human Rights, Decision as to Admissibility 6 March, 1985; and Council of Europe, Press Release, B(87) 7, 5 February 1987.

21. As cited in Beddard, 1973. p35.

22. Berger (1995) suggests that radical changes under protocol No. 11 will, if ratified by all member-states, abolish the Commission and make the Court a full-time judicial forum both receiving and deliberating on cases under a new structure.

23. See 'Judges Win Power in Historic Bill', (1997) *The Guardian*, October 25, p.1.

24. *Council of Europe, Press Release*, B (85) 1, 11 February, 1985, p.2.

25. Kempee, op.cit. 1996, p.IX.

26. *Council of Europe, Selected Texts*, p. 400-423.

27. Beddard, *Human Rights and Europe*, (1973) (1st ed.) p.30.

28. *Council of Europe, Press Release*, 11 February 1985.

29. Beddard, op.cit. 1993, p.7.

30. Kempee, op.cit. 1996, p. IX.

31. *Ireland v UK*, European Human Rights Reports, 2EHRR, 25 1978.

32. *De Wilde, Oooms and Versyp*, European Court of Human Rights, Series A, No. 12. Decisions of May 28, 1970, Judgement of 18 November, 1970 and No. 14 Judgement of March 1972, on the question of Article 50.

33. *Campbell and Fell v UK*, and 7EHRR, 165 (1984).

34. *Swedish Engine Drivers' Union* case, European Court of Human Rights, Series A, No. 20, 6 February, 1976.

35. Jacobs and White (1996) provide reasons for Britain's long record of being placed 'in the dock' at Strasbourg, p. 23-34.

36. See statistical analysis providing by Farran, 1996, p.392. Beddard (1993) also adds to this discussion, stating that the United Kingdom features second to Italy in being the state against which the greatest number of referrals to the Court have been made.

Chapter 3

The Strasbourg Decisions

The importance of the Convention is that not only is it a statement
of ideals, but it is also practically enforceable (Farran, 1996, p.5).

British parents who failed to gain satisfaction in their domestic
courts seized the opportunity to litigate in Strasbourg. For the
first time, a European forum could settle disputes when parents
felt unhappy about certain matters affecting their child's experience in
school. This chapter presents a content analysis of the major British
cases pertaining to schools and discipline and more specifically, the
question of corporal punishment as a disciplinary sanction[1]. Cases are
presented, where feasible, in chronological order and only the basic
facts of each dispute are examined. The chapter begins with an
examination of the *Tyrer* case,[2] which set a precedent as the first
British case dealing with corporal punishment which completed all the
stages of the Convention system and finally reached the Court. Although the applicants invoked a number of articles in the Convention,
emphasis is placed here on the two provisions consistently invoked
concerning punishment and education.

The Tyrer Case

The reasoning of the Court in the *Tyrer* case about the nature of
corporal punishment was to serve as a crucial first step along a road
strewn with cases of similar concerns, and eventually resulted in a
dramatic shift in educational policy and practice in Britain. This case,
along with that of *Campbell and Cosans*,[3] has provided important
jurisprudence on the issue of corporal punishment.

The case originally evolved from an application lodged with the European Commission by Anthony Tyrer against the United Kingdom of Great Britain in 1972. As detailed in the preceding chapter, the complaints procedure is structured such that an individual applicant must approach the Commission which rules whether the case is admissible for adjudication before it may be presented to the Court. In the Commission's report to the Court, reference was made to the United Kingdom's declaration of 1967 which recognised the jurisdiction of the Court in respect of affiliated territories, such as the Isle of Man, for which it had responsibility regarding international relations and for which it acted as representative in the international forum[4]. This declaration was subsequently renewed in 1972, and thereby held to be in effect when Tyrer's application was lodged with the Commission. As noted in chapter 2, the Isle of Man is a dependency of the Crown yet it retains its own governmental and legal systems. The government of the United Kingdom assumes responsibility for the international relations of the island with regard to the Convention by virtue of Article 63, which extended the European Court's jurisdiction to the Island. The British government reaffirmed, during the hearing of *Tyrer*, that it recognised the Court's jurisdiction in the matter.

The Court was asked by the Commission to decide whether, given the facts of the case, there had been a breach by the United Kingdom under Article 3 of the Convention,[5] which reads: 'No one shall be subjected to torture or to inhuman or degrading treatment or punishment'.

In 1978 oral hearings to decide this dispute began in Strasbourg with a request for an investigation to be carried out on the Isle of Man itself. This was denied since the Court was satisfied that it possessed sufficient information at hand. The case involved Mr. Tyrer alone, a resident of Castletown, Isle of Man who:

> ... being then 15 and of previous good character... pleaded guilty before the local juvenile court to unlawful assault occasioning actual bodily harm to a senior pupil at his school (p.6).

The victim of the assault had reported Tyrer together with three other boys 'for taking beer into the school' (*ibid.*). All four boys were subsequently caned for the offence. In accordance with section 56 (1) of *the Petty Sessions and Summary Jurisdiction Act* (1927), Tyrer was sentenced to receive 'three strokes of the birch' (*ibid.*). The relevant clause of this legislation states that:

> *Any person* who shall *unlawfully assault or beat any other person: shall be liable* on summary conviction to a fine or to be imprisoned *or* instead of, either such punishment, *if the offender is a male child or male young person, to be whipped* (p.7, emphasis added).

Within the context of this legislation, a 'child' is classified as being between 10 and 14 and a 'young person' between 14 and 17. As such, Tyrer fulfilled the age and gender qualifications and, failing to obtain a successful appeal of the decision, the sentence was carried out. Section 10 of *the Summary Jurisdiction Act* (1960) provided for the sentence's execution:

> (a) the instrument used shall, in the case of a child, be a cane, and in any other case shall be a birch rod (*ibid.*).

This statute contains further provisos specifying the actual dimensions of the birch and the conditions under which the sentence should be executed. In accordance with these requirements, Tyrer duly received a medical examination attesting to his physical ability to receive punishment and he was birched by a policeman in the presence of his father and a doctor. The only irregularity appears to be that, contrary to section (b) of the 1960 Act, the beating was administered directly onto the skin without the protection of clothing.

Background to the Case

In the preliminary discussions on the background to the case, particular mention was made in court of a local requirement in the Isle of Man that judicial corporal punishment had been retained despite its abolition in other parts of the United Kingdom. This unique situation was seen as a deterrent 'to hooligans visiting the island as tourists and, more generally, as a means of preserving law and order' (p.10). The policy was reaffirmed in May 1977 when the Tynwald parliament voted almost unanimously for a resolution 'to retain the use of judicial corporal punishment for violent crimes to the person committed by males under the age of 21' (*ibid.*). This sentiment was further substantiated in court by the claim that 'a privately organised petition in favour of the retention of judicial corporal punishment had obtained 31,000 signatures from amongst the approximate total of 45,000 persons entitled to vote on the Island' (*ibid.*). Thus, the Isle of Man submitted, as part of its case, the fact that local custom and tradition supported the practice of judicial corporal punishment, which was entirely within that countenanced by Article 63 (3) of the Convention, namely: that 'local requirements' should have a bearing on the Convention's applicability. Finally, on this issue, the Isle of Man submitted that its legislature was to consider the Criminal Law Bill of 1978 which included provision to restrict the use of judicial corporal punishment for crimes of a more violent nature among which would be omitted, that committed by Tyrer in 1972. The Court was not, however, satisfied with this proposal stating instead that:

> ... there is not certainty as to whether and when the proposal will become law and, even if adopted, it cannot erase a punishment already inflicted. What is more, the proposed legislation does not go to the substance of the issue before the Court, namely whether judicial corporal punishment as inflicted on the applicant in accordance with Manx legislation is contrary to the Convention (p.14).

Accordingly, the Court rejected this part of the Government's submission, and decided instead that the *Tyrer* case should not be removed from the list of impending cases.

In his application to the Commission, Tyrer had alleged that his judicial corporal punishment constituted a breach of Article 3 and no remedies existed to rectify the violation. Further he claimed repeal of the legislation concerning judicial corporal punishment, in addition to personal damages. Tyrer subsequently requested leave to withdraw his application in January 1976 but the Commission refused, since the case raised important questions. He was thus denied his request and he took no further part in the proceedings. The Attorney-General for the Isle of Man argued that the case should be removed from the Court's list in view of the fact that Tyrer, having lodged his application 'when he was under age, had declared after he had attained full age that he wished to withdraw it' (p.12). The Court held that as individuals cannot refer cases to the court themselves, they cannot attempt to have the proceedings discontinued and further, that the regulations require that a friendly settlement be effected at the Commission stage, before a case can be struck off the list, and this had not taken place.

With regard to Article 3, Tyrer had alleged that: 'there had been torture or inhuman or degrading treatment or punishment or any combination thereof' (p.14). This all-embracing claim was examined in detail by the Court. Firstly, the judiciary held that Tyrer's punishment did not amount to 'torture' within the meaning of Article 3, and as interpreted in the case of *Ireland v. UK* (1978)[6] which concerned the ill-treatment of prisoners. Nor was the Court convinced that the level of punishment amounted to being 'inhuman' (p.14). So it only remained for them to decide whether Tyrer's treatment could be classified as 'degrading punishment' (*ibid.*). On this point, the Court was concerned with whether the applicant was not only humiliated by the conviction but also by the form of punishment imposed. Again reference was made to *Ireland*, this time to underscore the point made in the previous chapter that:

> *the prohibition contained in Article 3 of the Convention is absolute*: no provision is made for exceptions and *there can be no derogation from Article 3*' (p.15, emphasis added).

The Isle of Man relied on the context of the punishment in its submission, arguing that in this case judicial corporal punishment 'did not enrage public opinion in the island' (p.15). In response, the Court maintained:

> *it must be pointed out that a punishment does not lose its degrading character just because it is believed to be, or actually is, an effective deterrent or aid to crime control*. Above all... it is never permissible to have recourse to punishments which are contrary to Article 3, whatever their deterrent effect may be (p.15, emphasis added).

Having due regard to the manner of the punishment's execution, the medical examination and the regulations pertaining to the dimensions of the birch used, the Court reached a conclusion unfavourable to the Isle of Man:

> *The very nature of judicial corporal punishment is that it involves one human being inflicting physical violence on another human*

being. Furthermore, it is institutionalised violence that is in the present case violence permitted by the law, ordered by the judicial authorities of the State and carried out by the police authorities of the State... Thus, although the applicant did not suffer any severe or long-lasting physical effects, *his punishment whereby he was treated as an object in the power of the authorities constituted an assault on precisely that which it is one of the main purposes of Article 3 to protect, namely a person's dignity and physical integrity.* The institutionalised character of this violence is further compounded by the whole aura of official procedure attending the punishment and by the fact that those inflicting it were total strangers to the offender (p.16, emphasis added).

Finally, the Court decided that as well as the physical pain experienced, Mr Tyrer was subjected to 'the mental anguish of anticipating the violence he was to have inflicted on him' (p.17) and accordingly held that the element of humiliation had been attained consistent with the notion of 'degrading punishment', and therefore there had been a violation of the Convention.

Under Article 63, the Attorney-General for the Isle of Man maintained that judicial corporal punishment did not render Britain in breach of the Convention. The government submitted that: 'having regard to the local circumstances in the Island... the continued use of judicial corporal punishment on a limited scale is justified as a deterrent' (p.17). However, the Court stated that although Isle of Man residents might be supportive of the use of judicial corporal punishment, it was not convinced that judicial corporal punishment was actually necessary for the maintenance of law and order in the island, noting:

In the great majority of the Member-States of the Council of Europe, judicial corporal punishment is not, it appears, used and indeed, in some of them, has never existed in modern times' (pp.18-19).

They therefore concluded that:

Even if law and order in the Isle of Man could not be maintained without recourse to judicial corporal punishment, this would not render its use compatible with the Convention (*ibid.*).

Accordingly, the Court concluded that there were no local requirements which would render the Isle of Man not guilty of violating Article 3 and as such, Tyrer's allegation that his judicial corporal punishment breached that article was upheld. Finally, Article 50 provides for 'just satisfaction to the injured party'. The Court decided that since Tyrer had withdrawn from the proceedings, his original claim for damages was no longer applicable, and since no other party was involved, compensation was not an issue.

In brief then, the Court decided in the *Tyrer* case: by six votes to one that the applicant's judicial corporal punishment amounted to 'degrading punishment' as countenanced by Article 3 of the Convention; and unanimously that there were no 'local requirements' as contemplated by Article 63 (3) which might affect Article 3's application. Dissenting opinion was given by the elected judge of British nationality, Sir Gerald Fitzmaurice, who argued instead: that the majority decision exaggerated and distorted notions of corporal punishment; that punishment which is institutionalised need not necessarily be considered degrading; and as long as it is administered in private it cannot be considered as inherently degrading where a juvenile is concerned, since the state is acting *in loco parentis* in this situation. The case was however decided in Tyrer's favour, and amounted to an important judgement to the meaning of Article 3. This dispute acted as a significant precedent in applications to the Court on the question of corporal punishment and was followed three years later by another important test case, that of *Mrs X*.

The Mrs X Case[7]

The case of *Mrs X versus the United Kingdom*, originated in a complaint lodged with the Commission in 1977 in which the applicant availed herself of the right to remain anonymous. Mrs X's 14 year old daughter, was attending a grammar school in Cheshire in 1976 when she received: '... three strokes of the cane by the headmistress of her school for having eaten potato crisps' (p.206). The family doctor examined the girl on the same day and noted that:

> ... the caning had left three red weals extending across the buttocks, one of them measuring 14 inches in length, as well as a weal across the right hand which had been inflicted by the whip-

lash effect of the cane, [she] having been obliged to hold her dress up for the caning (*ibid.*).

Further, the applicant complained of 'pain and discomfort' suffered by her daughter for several days after and bruising marks which remained for two months. Mrs X alleged that this corporal punishment amounted to degrading treatment and punishment and that she had no effective remedies under UK law. Finally, she alleged that the refusal of the education authorities to guarantee that her child would not again be subjected to corporal punishment violated her right as a parent under Article 2 of Protocol No.1.

Background to the case

Mrs X initially complained to the District Education Officer about the caning incident and in 1977 he responded that no action would be taken about the complaint. Further, the Commission heard that: 'the Cheshire Education Commission does not prohibit corporal punishment in its schools and lays down certain guidelines for its infliction' (p.206). One of these requirements was that a second teacher be present when corporal punishment is carried out: this was not observed in the present case. In addition to a complaint to the Local Education Authority, Mrs X, along with her daughter, lodged a complaint with the local police. Consequently the police conducted a thorough inquiry with a view to prosecuting the headmistress, but the Director of Public Prosecutions decided not to pursue the case.

The next stage of Mrs X's complaint was to instigate a private prosecution, the hearing of which took place in the Magistrate's Court in 1976. During these deliberations, her daughter's past school conduct was examined and, overcome by distress, she was unable to continue. Subsequently, the case was dismissed. By then the dispute had attracted a great deal of publicity and 'provoked a number of obscene anonymous letters addressed to [the girl] as well as the use of her name and her case in a pornographic magazine preoccupied with flagellation' (*ibid.*). Mrs X referred to these matters in 1977 when she lodged a complaint with the Commission claiming that such response was 'the natural and inevitable consequence of attempting to initiate any litigation in such cases' (p.207). As such, the applicant's complaint involved not only issues concerning Article 1 of Protocol 1 and

Article 3 of the Convention, which concern education and punishment, but also to Article 26 which refers to the efficacy of pursuing available domestic remedies.

In deciding whether the case of Mrs X was admissible, the Commission began by examining Article 2 of Protocol 1:

> no person shall be denied the right to education. In the exercise of any function which it assumes in relation to education and to teaching, the State shall respect the right of parents to ensure such education and teaching in conformity with their own religious and philosophical convictions.

The government argued in this instance that the complaint was 'incompatible with the provisions' of this article since the terms 'religious' and 'philosophical' could not be interpreted as covering preferences 'in the matter of disciplinary punishment at school' (p.208). Further, they contended that the complaint was 'manifestly ill-founded' because Mrs X had failed to indicate 'any religious or philosophical convictions which were offended by the corporal punishment of her daughter' (p.208). However, this part of the application was considered to be admissible.

Next, the government relied on Article 26 as part of its argument why Mrs X's case should be declared inadmissible, by claiming that domestic remedies had not been exhausted. The government submitted that 'Mrs X had failed to bring a civil action for assault against the headmistress and to proceed with the private prosecution' (p.209). The Commission noted initially on this point, that the law requires not only that domestic remedies be used, but also that they 'are sufficient in the sense that they are capable of redressing their complaints' (*ibid.*). With regard to having recourse to civil proceedings, Mrs X had been advised by her counsel that this course of action would have little likelihood of success under the English legal system because

> ... in view of the girl's past conduct the Court would probably find that she 'richly deserved the punishment' and that the caning was not 'accompanied by excessive force' (p.210).

As noted in chapter 1, before 1987 a teacher was unlikely to be convicted of assault under English law if the corporal punishment administered fulfilled certain criteria, one being that the punishment was reasonable and moderate. The Commission concluded that Mrs X was not obliged to pursue the private prosecution and was thus satisfied that the domestic remedies available did not fulfil the require-ment, implied by Article 26, that they are sufficient and capable of providing redress. Accordingly, the application was held to be admis-sible under this article, leaving Article 3 of the Convention as the last resort for the government.

Mrs X alleged that the caning of her daughter was contrary to Article 3 which states that no one should be subjected to torture or to in-human or degrading treatment or punishment. The government's main contention on this issue was that the application was 'manifestly ill-founded' as the girl's punishment 'did not constitute degrading treatment or punishment' as countenanced by Article 3, but the Com-mission was unpersuaded.

The application of Mrs X having been declared admissible, the Com-mission were faced with the task of attempting to secure a 'friendly settlement', under Article 28. In the absence of a 'friendly settlement' a case may be passed on to the Committee of Ministers or the Euro-pean Court, as noted earlier. But in the case of Mrs X, a 'friendly settlement' was secured in December 1981 by means of a payment of £1200 by the Government, described as 'an ex-gratia payment together with costs'.[8] More importantly, however, a letter from the Department of Education and Science was circulated to Local Educa-tion Authorities which stated that: 'Authorities will wish to be aware that the use of corporal punishment may in certain circumstances amount to treatment contrary to Article 3 of the Convention'.[9]

Stephen Sedley, a High Court judge and a leading authority on law and education in Britain, interpretated the memorandum thus:

> behind the settlement... lay a recognition that ever since the Tyrer case the writing had been on the wall and that the UK Govern-ment would probably lose if it fought the case out, particularly given the excessive character of the beating.[10]

The Campbell and Cosans Case

The case of *Campbell and Cosans* originated in applications made by Mrs Grace Campbell and Mrs Jane Cosans against the United Kingdom in 1976. On October 6, 1979, the Commission ordered 'the joinder' of the two applications under Rule 39 of the Commission's Rules of Procedure.[11] (As noted, this is performed when cases raise similar concerns.) Both Mrs Campbell and Mrs Cosans alleged a violation by the United Kingdom of its obligations under Article 3 of the Convention and Article 2 of Protocol No.1. In addition, both applicants resided in Scotland and had children of compulsory school age. At issue in both cases was the use of corporal punishment as a disciplinary sanction in the Scottish maintained schools which their children attended. It was further noted that due to practical and financial reasons, no alternative schooling existed for the children other than the maintained sector.

Background to the Case

Mrs Campbell's son Gordon was seven years old at the time of her application to the Commission and attended a Roman Catholic primary school within the jurisdiction of the Strathclyde Region Education Authority. The school used corporal punishment as a disciplinary measure but there was dispute as to whether this sanction applied to children below the age of eight. Mrs Campbell had requested a guarantee from the Strathclyde Regional Council that Gordon would not be subjected to corporal punishment: this request was refused. Whilst in the school until July 1979, Gordon Campbell did not receive physical chastisement.

Mrs Cosans' fifteen year old son, Jeffrey, was attending a High School in Cowdenbeath in the Fife Region Education Authority area when on September 23, 1976 he was informed that he would be receiving corporal punishment from the Assistant Headmaster on the following day. Jeffrey had broken school rules since he 'tried to take a prohibited short-cut through a cemetery on his way home from school' (p.7). Jeffrey reported to school but, upon his father's advice, refused to accept corporal punishment and as a result was given a school suspension until he was prepared to alter his decision. His suspension from school began officially from October 1st, 1976 and a subsequent meeting on the 18th October with the regional Senior Assistant Director of Education failed to effect a resolution of the problem. His parents both expressed their disapproval of the disciplinary measure. The suspension was lifted on January 14th of the following year, since it was considered that nearly a term's suspension 'constituted punishment enough' (*ibid.*). This was made contingent, however, on the fact that amongst other things, Jeffrey would adhere to the disciplinary regulations of the school. Once again Jeffrey's parents registered their disapproval of corporal punishment and their wish that he should not receive it whilst a pupil in the school. This was interpreted as a refusal to accept the conditions of adherence to school rules and consequently the suspension was not lifted. In a rapidly-evolving 'Catch 22' situation, Mr and Mrs Cosans received notification that their son's non-attendance at school could warrant prosecution. Jeffrey ceased to be of compulsory school age on his birthday on 31 May 1977 and never returned to the school. He had been absent since 24 September of the previous year, a period of approximately eight months.

The background of the case of *Campbell and Cosans* involves discussion firstly of the status of teachers-at-law when they administered corporal punishment, and secondly of Scottish education law. We have seen that teachers did not normally risk charges of assault precisely because they were *in loco parentis* under the auspices of the Common Law. Thus they could administer corporal punishment providing that it fulfilled four main criteria: that it be given in good faith, that the child's age and circumstances be taken into account, that it be such as a reasonable parent might use and that it be consistent with school policy.[12] The Court summed up the situation as it stood in 1982 and which reflected that of English law:

> Teachers in both state and other schools are, by virtue of their status as teachers invested by the Common Law with power to administer punishment in moderation as a disciplinary measure. Excessive, arbitrary or cruel punishment by a teacher or its infliction for an improper motive would constitute assault (p.8).

In the two Scottish schools concerned, corporal punishment was administered by use of a leather strap or 'tawse' on the pupil's palm, either in front of the class or, for more serious offences, in the headmaster's room by the headteacher or deputy (*ibid.*). The legislation governing the conduct of the two schools was the *Education (Scotland) Act* (1962), repealed without substantial modification by the *Education (Scotland) Act* (1980). More specifically, section 29 (1) of this statute states in its powers concerning education, that education authorities shall have regard to pupils being educated according to their parents' convictions as far as is compatible with reasonable public expenditure.

Further, the Court heard that agreement had been reached in principle that '... the teaching profession should be encouraged to move towards the gradual elimination of corporal punishment as a means of discipline in schools' (p.9).

Endorsing this view was the report of the *Pack Committee* (1977), which had been appointed by the Secretary of State for Scotland to investigate discipline in Scottish schools. It carried recommendations that 'corporal punishment should, as was envisaged in 1968, disappear by a process of gradual elimination rather than by legislation' (*ibid.*). As such, Scottish Authorities were pursuing a policy which would result in the diminution and eventual ban of corporal punishment.

A further piece of Scottish legislation pertinent to the deliberations was the *Schools General (Scotland) Regulations* (1975). Provision 4 of these regulations stated that a pupil may be excluded from school by an education authority if 'the parent of the pupil refuses or fails to comply, or to allow the pupil to comply, with the rules, regulations or disciplinary requirements of the school' (*ibid.*). This was in keeping with the situation faced by Jeffrey Cosans. Finally, as in the *Tyrer* case, public opinion was invoked to substantiate the government's argument that the use of corporal punishment was well-supported:

> Its continued use by teachers is... favoured by a large majority of Scottish parents and, according to the Pack Committee's report, [by] pupils, who even prefer it to some other forms of punishment (*ibid.*).

It was these aspects of Scottish legislation which had led Mrs Campbell and Mrs Cosans to seek redress from the European Court, having previously exhausted the domestic remedies available. Both applicants thus claimed that the use of corporal punishment in the schools attended by their children amounted to a violation of the Convention and that there was a failure to respect their *philosophical convictions* against the use of physical chastisement. Further, Mrs Cosans submitted that her son's suspension from school 'violated his *right to education*'.

The Court's adjudication of the case began with an examination of Article 3 of the Convention which, as mentioned in the earlier dispute, was pivotal to the *Tyrer* case. Both mothers claimed that there had been a violation of this article which prohibits various types of ill-treatment. Since neither Jeffrey Cosans nor Gordon Campbell had in fact received corporal punishment, it was therefore decided that the Court did not have to concern itself with 'an actual application of corporal punishment' (p.12). An important qualification to this statement was made, however:

> the Court is of the opinion that, provided it is sufficiently real and immediate, *a mere threat of conduct prohibited by Article 3 may itself be in conflict with that provision.* Thus, to threaten an individual with torture might in some circumstances constitute at least inhuman treatment (*ibid.*, emphasis added).

Whilst the Court believed that 'the system of corporal punishment can cause a certain degree of apprehension in those who may be subject to it,' it was not convinced that Gordon Campbell and Jeffrey Cosans had been in a situation which amounted to 'torture' or 'inhuman treatment' as countenanced by Article 3. That being decided, it remained for the judiciary only to decide on the clause 'degrading punishment'. In this part of the proceedings guidance was sought by reference to the *Tyrer* case. It was held that whilst Jeffrey Cosans 'may well have experienced feelings of apprehension or disquiet when he came close to an infliction of the tawse... such feelings are not sufficient to amount to 'degrading treatment' within the meaning of Article 3' (p.13). This finding was also held applicable for Gordon Campbell. In conclusion, therefore, the Court did not accept the allegation that there had been a violation of Article 3.

The next two legal arguments regarded Article 2 of Protocol No.1 which contains 'the right to education' and respect of parents' 'philosophical convictions'. Both Mrs Campbell and Mrs Cosans alleged that the second sentence of this article was violated because of 'the existence of corporal punishment as a disciplinary measure in the schools attended by their children' (p.14). The government objected on a number of counts to this allegation, submitting instead that matters relating to discipline lay outside the scope of this article.

The Court recognised, in response to this, that in many instances discipline was left to the individual teacher who, under the auspices of Common Law, traditionally had a right to administer corporal punishment within certain stated guidelines. Despite the principle of *in loco parentis*, however, the Court held that the State had assumed responsibility for 'formulating general policy' for maintained schools such as those attended by Gordon Campbell and Jeffrey Cosans. Moreover, the Court felt that the involvement of central and local authorities in the development of a 'Code of Practice' for corporal punishment, and its policy towards the elimination of corporal punishment alluded to earlier, fuelled the argument that the State was indeed engaged in matters of discipline.

Further, the government maintained that the views held by Mrs Campbell and Mrs Cosans relating to corporal punishment, did not amount to 'philosophical convictions' *per se*, and that the term was not broad enough to include matters relating to school discipline. The Court did not accept this submission either, deciding instead that the term 'philosophical convictions' amounted to 'such convictions as are worthy of respect in a democratic society... and are not incompatible with human dignity; in addition, they must not conflict with the fundamental right of the child to education'. It was felt that: 'the applicants' views relate to a weighty and substantial aspect of human life and behaviour, namely the integrity of the person, the propriety or otherwise of the infliction of corporal punishment and the exclusion of the distress which the risk of such punishment entails' (p.16).

The government had also pleaded on this point that the obligation to respect the applicants' 'philosophical convictions' had been achieved because of the adoption of a policy eventually to abolish corporal punishment, whilst concurrently respecting the views of parents who approved of the retention of this form of disciplinary sanction. Finally it was argued that Britain had satisfied the terms of the reservation made to Article 2 of Protocol No.1, ratified in 1952 that, when responding to its obligations, unreasonable public expenditure, should be avoided.[13] Whilst it was agreed that the establishment of separate schools for children of parents who objected to corporal punishment would be incompatible with the need to avoid unreasonable public expenditure, it was concluded that more could have been done.

> The Court does not regard it as established that other means of respecting the applicants' convictions, such as a system of exemption for individual pupils in a particular school, would necessarily be incompatible with the provision of efficient instruction and training, and the avoidance of unreasonable public expenditure (p.18).

(This option was used as the cornerstone of the proposed *Education (Corporal Punishment) Bill* (1985),[14] discussed in chapter 7.) It was found that Mrs Campbell and Mrs Cosans had been victims of a violation of the Convention and their philosophical objections to corporal punishment had not been respected.

The first sentence of Article 2 of the first Protocol was also allegedly violated according to Mrs Cosans in that her son was denied '*the right to education*'. It was submitted that since Jeffrey Cosans had been suspended from school because he had refused to accept corporal punishment, his access to education was thereby denied him. Despite the fact that it had now been established that there had been a violation of the second sentence of the article, the Court felt that the first sentence had to be examined on its own merits. This was because of 'a substantial difference between the legal basis of the two claims, for one concerns a right of a parent and the other a right of a child (p.19). The Court went on to decide:

> His return to school could have been secured only if his parents had acted contrary to their convictions, convictions which the United Kingdom is obliged to respect under the second sentence of Article 2... [and] there has accordingly also been, as regards Jeffrey Cosans, breach of the first sentence of that Article (*ibid.*).

Having thus decided on Article 3 and all of Article 2 of Protocol No.1, the Court held unanimously to delay discussion on the question of compensation and 'just satisfaction' for the applicants.

The issue of just satisfaction in the *Campbell and Cosans* case, within the meaning of Article 50 was decided by the Court on March 22, 1983. Mrs Campbell's costs in respect of legal expenses and other expenses were accepted in part, to be paid by the United Kingdom. Significantly, Mrs Campbell claimed for an undertaking by the government 'that her children would not be subjected to any form of corporal punishment at schools within the United Kingdom's jurisdiction' (p.14). In response to this claim, the government indicated that as of August 1982, the Strathclyde Regional Council had decided to abolish corporal punishment in its area and that they were: 'actively considering the implications for the whole of the United Kingdom' (*ibid.*). The ramifications of the *Campbell and Cosans* case were to have a direct impact on British teachers, as manifested in the *Education (No.2) Act* (1986), discussed later in this chapter.[15]

In brief, the Court held unanimously in the *Campbell and Cosans* case: that no violation of Article 3 was established. By six votes to one it held that, as regards Mrs Campbell and Mrs Cosans, there had been a breach of the second sentence of Article 2 of Protocol No.1 concerning parents' 'philisophical convictions', and by six votes to one that Jeffrey Cosans had been denied 'the right to education'. Again, a dissenting view was held by the elected judge of British nationality, Sir Vincent Evans, who stated that he was unable to support the majority decision, for in his view, inclusion of corporal punishment under the rubric of 'philosophical convictions' was to distort the true meaning of the word. However, the applicants' rights were found to have been breached due to the presence of corporal punishment as a disciplinary sanction in Scottish schools and their legal costs were accepted in part. Further, Jeffrey Cosans' suspension from school for refusing to accept corporal punishment was upheld as a violation of the Convention, and he was awarded payment for 'moral damages' of £3,000[16].

It was the *Campbell and Cosans* decision by the Court which led to a spate of similar claims being lodged with the Commission. In reference to the *Tyrer* case, Lord Denning had stated:

> The logical consequence... is this. If the case of any child who is beaten at school is now taken to the European Court the chances are 99 to 1 that the Court, will hold that it is a degrading punishment, contrary to the Convention, and that therefore we are dis-

obeying the Convention in that way... it is 99 to 1 that when the next decision comes from the European Court of Human Rights it will condemn all corporal punishment in schools as being degrading.[17]

After the judgement in *Campbell and Cosans* Lord Denning's prediction was more likely in that two new grounds were added: parental objections to corporal punishment must be respected, and a pupil could not be debarred from receiving education because his parents held such convictions. The pressure group *The Society of Teachers Opposed to Physical Punishment* (STOPP), provided parents with support for having their philosophical objections to physical chastisement made known to school authorities, as shown in figure 2. The *Townend* case (1987)[18] developed further the Convention's jurisprudence in the area of corporal punishment and was resolved during the time that Britain finally introduced legislation to abolish the practice in maintained schools.

The Townend Case

An application was lodged in 1980 by the father of a 15 year old boy who refused to accept corporal punishment and was subsequently suspended from a comprehensive school in Rotherham. The background to the case reveals that Townend Jnr. was involved in a disagreement at school with a fellow pupil on December 10th, 1979. The Commission's report describes how

> ... a teacher entered the classroom and told the two boys that if they wished to argue, they could fight it out properly there and then. Thereupon, the two boys proceeded to fight in the classroom in front of the teacher and othe members of the class (p.3).

The boys claimed that they did not receive a reprimand after this event, nor were they reported to senior management in the school. The government disputed this, stating instead that both boys were 'warned at the end of the lesson as to their future conduct' (*ibid.*). A similar incident occurred the following day when the same class of pupils was under the charge of the same teacher.

A fight erupted involving Townend Jnr. and three other boys. They were ordered to report to the Second Master to receive corporal

Figure 2

Copy of 'Parents Form' withdrawing Permission for Corporal Punishment to be Administered to their Children

To the Headteacher/Chairperson of the Governors/Local Education Authority.

Name and Address of School:

I, ..., wish to inform you, in the light of the ruling of the European Court of Human Rights, that I forbid the school authorities, and any teacher employed by them or serving under them, to use physical punishment on my children.

Signed: Names of child/ren:

Address: 1.

                                     2.

                                     3.

                                     4.

Date:

(Special thanks to Martin Rosenbaum, 'Society of Teachers Opposed to Physical Punishment' for permission to reproduce this form.)

punishment; all four subsequently failed to attend. Mr Townend advised his son not to submit to the cane, and he telephoned the school that he did not wish his son to be corporally punished. Within one hour of the call, Townend Jnr. had been suspended from school by the headmaster. This was followed by a letter stating that the boy would 'remain suspended from school until he submitted to the proposed punishment of two strokes of the cane' (p.4).

The government's response to this was that these incidents were 'the mere application of reasonable physical force' and required to keep the pupil 'under control' (*ibid.*). Mr Townend claimed that there had been occasions when he had previously refused to allow his son to be caned and a maximum of two weeks suspension had ensued. Moreover, the return to school had not been subject to any agreement to receive corporal punishment. Finally, Mr Townend claimed that he was on record as having withdrawn his consent for his son to be physically chastised, but he was not opposed to other disciplinary sanctions being implemented. The question of home tuition being supplied for the pupil was raised but this service was not subsequently extended to him by the local authority.

Background to the Case

The government's record of Townend's school experience differed markedly from that of his father. Three occasions were cited between 1978 and 1979 when the pupil received corporal punishment, all of which were documented in the school punishment book. At the third such incident the pupil 'initially refused to be caned, but was eventually caned in the presence and with the agreement' of his father (*ibid.*, p.5). Further, the government countered that there was in fact no record of Mr Townend's objection to corporal punishment prior to December 11, 1979, the date of the second fighting incident. Moreover, it was claimed that the pupil had received only one suspension from school 'when he was re-admitted after having apologised for his indiscipline' (*ibid.*).

A second meeting was convened on February 26th 1980, for all parties involved in the dispute after which Townend's suspension from school was continued. Subsequent to this meeting Mr Townend received a letter on March 4th, 1980 from the local Director of Education, stating that the Education Committee and Schools Sub-Committee had decided to support fully the governing body of the school that Townend be allowed to return to school only if he was prepared to submit to the punishment prescribed by the headmaster. It is unclear whether such punishment would include physical chastisement, but it appears that it was interpreted as such by the applicants, since Mr Townend's son did not return to school. Consequently, 'he was deprived of education for the final term of his schooling' (p.5). The pupil alleged that as a result he was 'unable to sit school leaving examinations, which he would otherwise have taken' (p.6). As in the case of Jeffrey Cosans Townend found himself without any examination qualifications after leaving school and experienced great difficulty obtaining employment. Under recent education law, examined later in chapter 4, suspensions which exclude pupils from taking examinations are now limited.

What is particularly interesting about the legal arguments emerging from the *Townend* case is the allegation that

> the proposed corporal punishment... and the school's authorised
> use of corporal punishment to which he would have been subjected
> if he had returned, are contrary to Article 3 of the Convention
> (p.6, emphasis added).

Accordingly, not only the *threat* of corporal punishment, but its very existence within the spectrum of school punishments were claimed to be violations of the Convention. Further, Mr Townend claimed that, under Article 2 of the First Protocol, his philosophical objections to corporal punishment had not been respected, and his son asserted that his school suspension amounted to a denial of *'the right to education'* under this provision.

The government argued that the *Townend* case was analogous to *Campbell and Cosans* in that 'there is no question of the threat of corporal punishment constituting 'torture' or 'inhuman treatment,' nor that Townend 'was humiliated in the eyes of others to the requisite degree' which might amount to 'degrading treatment' (pp.9-10). The applicants in Townend submitted, however, that contrary to the situation in *Campbell and Cosans*, 'the threat of corporal punishment... was real and immediate, although no actual punishment was inflicted' (p.12). Further, they alleged that Townend was 'humiliated and debased in the eyes of the other boys who were present when the Second Master stated that he intended to give each boy two strokes of the cane on the hand' (p.12).

In addition, the applicants believed that there had been a breach of Article 3 on previous occasions when the pupil had received corporal punishment and, when encouraged by a teacher to engage in fighting with another pupil. Finally, it was argued that Townend had been humiliated and debased 'in the eyes of his fellow-pupils, the teacher... his opponent' and indeed 'in his own eyes' (p.12).

Citing the *Tyrer* case as authority, the Commission stated that the test of 'degrading treatment or punishment' is whether 'the person concerned has undergone, either in the eyes of others or in his own eyes, humiliation or debasement attaining a minimum level of severity, to be assessed in view of the particular circumstances of the case' (p.130). The Commission concluded that in the *Townend* case, this level of humiliation was not found. The absence of any medical evidence indicating adverse psychological effects further reinforced this viewpoint. Thus, this part of the application was considered to be 'manifestly ill-founded' within the meaning of Article 27 of the Convention.

Mr Townend's *'philosophical convictions'* against corporal punishment were not accepted by the government. His presence at one of the earlier canings of his son was, it was claimed, tacit confirmation of his approval of corporal punishment. The government submitted that it was incumbent upon Mr Townend to make clear his objection to corporal punishment with the Local Education Authority, and if he 'did hold relevant philosophical convictions concerning the use of corporal punishment, he failed effectively to make those views known' (p.11).

The Commission, however, concluded that whilst Mr Townend's objections to corporal punishment were disputed by the government, it was satisfied that they did indeed exist. After the two occasions of fighting involving Townend Jnr., he had clearly expressed his view to the local education authority and further, he 'refused to withdraw these objections even when he was informed that criminal proceedings would be instituted against him for not returning his son to school' (p.15). By citing *Campbell and Cosans* the Commission believed that the infliction of corporal punishment as a condition of admission to the school, also raised issues requiring determination. Accordingly, it was concluded that the Townend case evoked questions of law which could only be determined by examination of the merits of the dispute, and the case could not be declared 'manifestly ill-founded' as the government had hoped (p.15).

In keeping with the rules of the Convention system, the Commission then placed itself at the service of the contesting parties of the *Townend* dispute with the aim of effecting a 'friendly settlement'.[19] This was achieved in February 1987 under the terms of which ex gratia payments of £3,000 and £200 were awarded to the pupil and his father respectively, the applicants also receiving costs. What is particularly noteworthy about the *Townend* settlement, unlike similar cases taken to Strasbourg, is that the Commission acknowledged the provisions of new UK education law as ensuring respect for human rights. The relevant provision is section 47 (1) of the *Education (No.2) Act* (1986), which states:

> where, in any proceedings, it is shown that corporal punishment has been given to a pupil by or on the authority of a member of the staff, giving the punishment cannot be justified on the ground that it was done in pursuance of a right exercisable by the member of the staff by virtue of his position as such.

This effectively took away teachers' Common Law right to use physical chastisement and their traditional defence in law. Further, paragraph 8 of the statute states that a person cannot be 'debarred from receiving education... by reason of the fact that this section applies in relation to him'. By the time *Townend* reached the 'friendly settlement' stage of the Convention procedure, seven years had elapsed and the *Campbell and Cosans* judgement had been handed down. The government had in the interim introduced legislation effectively abolishing corporal punishment, from August 15th, 1987. This derived from the government's need to reconcile domestic law with its treaty obligations under the Convention which continually upheld the rights of British parents. They, in turn, were given on-going support from the 'Society of Teachers Opposed to Physical Punishment' who kept the issue in the public arena. This organisation has been replaced by 'End Physical Punishment of Children Worldwide', highlighted in chapter 6, which has adopted a broader base opposing all physical chatisement of children.[20]

Unlike the *Townend* case there remained cases awaiting judgement in Strasbourg, in which pupils were not merely *threatened* with corporal punishment but actually *received* it, and the parents of these pupils cited among other things Article 3 of the Convention. The Court has yet to adjudicate a case which involves the actual infliction of school-based corporal punishment in a state or maintained school and consequently no definitive interpretation of this clause has been handed down that would indicate whether this sanction in general or in certain circumstances constitutes a violation of the Convention. Until this occurs, it remains uncertain whether the practice of corporally punishing pupils in schools is a contravention of human rights within the context of Article 3. *Tyrer* is unmistakably the lynchpin of the corporal punishment cases, for prior to this judgement, the issue of young persons receiving physical chastisement had not been addressed in the Strasbourg forum. Moreover, the case is cited and relied upon by subsequent litigants who anticipate that the Court's decisions in future cases will reflect similar reasoning.

Other Cases

There were allegedly over 30 cases involving issues of corporal punishment and school suspension which were lodged with the Commission; the majority of which were registered after the Court's ruling on the *Campbell and Cosans* case in 1982. Statistics supplied by the *Society of Teachers Opposed to Physical Punishment* (STOPP) in its June 1983 newsletter add further to this figure:

> Thirty four 'corporal punishment' cases have now been submitted to Strasbourg. Twenty two of the cases (fourteen beatings and eight suspensions for refusing to be beaten) relate to incidents that took place after the 25 February 1982 (p.5).[21]

There does, however, appear to be some discrepancy over these figures. Whilst *STOPP* and Hansard reports have consistently cited a total of over 30 cases since 1982, my research in Strasbourg revealed fewer. In April, 1986, for example, only 12 such cases were found to be registered and in July 1987, 21 cases concerning corporal punish-

Figure 3

Statistics of Corporal Punishment Cases Taken to Strasbourg

As of October, 1985:

Cases Resolved:

Tyrer v UK

Campbell and Cosans v. UK

Mrs X v. UK

Cases declared admissible. *Townend v. UK*

Mrs and Ms X v. UK

Durairaj v. UK

Cases pending:

Under Article 3

i) Caning of an eleven year old Chesterfield boy;

ii) Caning of a twelve year old South London boy;

iii) Caning of another twelve year old South London boy;

iv) Caning of a fourteen year old South London boy;

v) Caning of another fourteen year old South London boy;

vi) Caning of an eleven year old boy;

vii) Caning of a fifteen year old Durham boy;

viii) Caning of a thirteen year old Durham boy;

ix) Caning of an eleven year old Hereford boy;

x) Caning and slippering of a fourteen year old East London boy;

xi) Caning of a fifteen year old Bedfordshire boy;

xii) Caning of an eleven year old Hampshire boy;

xiii) Caning of a thirteen year old Gloucester boy;

xiv) Tawsing of a twelve year old Lancashire girl;

xv) Caning of a fourteen year old Rotherham boy;

xvi) Caning of a thirteen year old Kent boy;

xvii) Caning of a thirteen year old South Wales boy.

Figure 4

Summary of the Main Strasbourg Decisions Relating to Corporal Punishment

As of October 1985:

The Tyrer Case (1978)

Facts of the Case:
Fifteen year old Isle of Man boy birched after assault on fellow schoolboy, by order of a Manx court.

Main Articles of Convention:
Article 3: 'no one shall be subjected to torture or to inhuman or degrading treatment or punishment'.

Forum:
Commission and Court

Decision/Solution:
Judicial corporal punishment amounted to 'degrading punishment'.

Award:
Applicant withdrew from case in 1976 and, therefore, no damages awarded.

The Mrs X Case (1981)

Facts of the Case:
Fourteen year old schoolgirl caned by headmistress in an English grammar school.

Main Articles of Convention:
Article 3 and Article 2 of Protocol No 1.

i)   'no person shall be denied the right to education' and

ii)   The state shall respect parents' 'philosophical convictions' in relation to education.

Forum:
Commission

Decision/Solution:
A 'friendly settlement' effected.

The Campbell and Cosans Case (1982)

Facts of the Case:
Allegation of violation of Convention due to threat of corporal punishment as a disciplinary sanction and the suspension of 15 year old schoolboy for refusing to accept such punishment in Scottish school.

Main Articles of Convention:
Article 3 and Article 2 of Protocol No 1.

Forum:
Commission and Court

Decision/Solution:
i)   a breach of respect for parents' 'philosophical convictions' with respect to Mrs Campbell and Mrs Cosans and,

ii)   violation of the 'right to education' as regards Jeffrey Cosans.

Award:
i)   £940 in respect of legal costs and expenses to Mrs Campbell,

ii)   Approximately £8,500 in respect of legal costs and expenses to Mrs Cosans, and

iii)   £3,000 to Jeffrey Cosans in respect of pecuniary and non-pecuniary loss.

The Townend Case (1987)

Facts of the Case:
Suspension from an English secondary school for refusal to accept corporal punishment.

Main Articles of Convention:
Article 3 and Article 2 of Protocol No 1.

Forum:
Commission

Decision/Solution
A 'friendly settlement' effected.

Award:
i)   ex-gratia payments of £3,000 & £200 to pupil and father respectively & costs,

ii)   Commission acknowledged that provisions of the education (No2) Act (1986) ensures respect for human rights.

ment were pending before the Commission (see Figure 3 for further statistical breakdown). The disparity between these numbers may be accounted for by those litigants whose knee-jerk reaction to failure within the British legal process, is to register their *intention* that they will be applying to Strasbourg, but for some reason ultimately fail to do so. The British figures may be further bolstered because some applications may have been in the process of being lodged in Strasbourg; a percentage of which may not have come to fruition. Further, it is possible that one application may have dealt with more than one child. Nevertheless, a substantial number of corporal punishment cases made their way through the Convention system in the 1980s.[22] What the cases do all share, as with the four previously discussed, is reliance on the same articles within the Convention relating to human dignity and the right to education. Figure 4 provides a summary of the major findings detailed in the chapter.

Summary

Several British parents litigated in Strasbourg after having failed to gain satisfaction in domestic courts. Through the cases of *Tyrer, Campbell Cosans*, and *Mrs X*, they successfully challenged the use of corporal punishment claiming that it constituted 'degrading punishment' and contravened their 'philosophical convictions'. Furthermore, exclusion from school for refusing to accept the sanction was held to be a denial of 'the right to education'. Since the abolition of corporal punishment in maintained schools outstanding cases have been resolved in clusters, in which the govenment has tended to make out-of-court settlements.[23]

Legislative reform during deliberations in the *Townend* case effectively meant that for children in the maintained school sector, and on the Assisted Places Scheme in non-maintained schools, debate over the issue of physical chatisement as a disciplinary sanction was redundant. Cases pending in Strasbourg since then have tended to be lodged on behalf of children in non-maintained schools, such as *Roberts-Costello v. UK*,[24] and the Court continues to be a focus for advocates of children's rights. This issue is elaborated further in chapter 6. At this point it is important to examine the alternative approaches to corporal punishment which form the basis of the next chapter.

Notes

1. The case of *Handyside v. UK*, (The European Court of Human Rights Series A, No. 24, 24April 1976) was an exception in that it concerned obscene publications for school use rather than corporal punishment.

2. *Tyrer v. UK*, The European Court of Human Rights, Series A, No. 26, 25 April, 1978.

3. *Campbell and Cosans v. UK*, The European Court of Human Rights, Series A, Nos. 48 and 60, 25 February, 1982 and 22 March, 1983.

4. *Council of Europe: Collected Texts* (Strasbourg, 8th ed., 1972), p.603. Interestingly, judicial corporal punishment is still legal on the island. See *The Independent* (1997) 'Girl of 12 Thrown into Jail on the Isle of Man, 7 June, p.3.

5. *Council of Europe, Collected Texts*, p.3.

6. *Ireland v. UK*, The European Court of Human Rights, Series A, No. 25, 29 April, 1978 p. 66-68, para. 167 and 174.

7. *Mrs X v. UK*, (Application No. 7907/77), The European Commission of Human Rights, Decisions and Reports, Vol. 14, June 1979. See also 140th Session Minutes, DH (79)6, 31 October, 1979, p.11. And Decision as to Admissibility, 12 July, 1978.

8. *Childright*, No. 15, March 1985 and No. 39, July/August, 1987.

9. Department of Education and Science, Memorandum, 1981, as cited in *Childright*, No.15, March 1985, p.14.

10. *Childright*, No. 15, March, 1985, p.14.

11. *Council of Europe, Collected Texts*, p.310.

12. See J Partington: *Law and the New Teacher*, (London: Holt Rinehart and Winston, 1984), p.109 for elaboration on this theme.

13. *Council of Europe, Collected Texts*, p.27.

14. *Education (Corporal Punishment) Bill*, 1985, Bill 57.

15. *The Education (No. 2) Act*, 1986, c.61.

16. See J Andrews: 'Just Satisfaction Under the Convention', *European Law Review* (Vol. 18, 1983), p.286, for more on this point.

17. *Society of Teachers Opposed to Physical Punishment News*, June/July, 1985.

18. *J T Townend (Snr.) And J T Townend (Jnr.) V. UK*, (Application No. 9119/80), The European Commission of Human Rights, Decision as to admissibility, 6th March 1985; *Council of Europe, Press Release*, B(87)7, 5 February, 1987.

19. *Council of Europe, Human Rights News* (Press Release), B(87)7, 5 February, 1987.

20. The 'Society of Teachers Opposed to Physical Punishment' (STOPP) disbanded in 1988 having achieved its central goal of the abolition of physical chastisement in British state schools. Some of its members have now jointed 'End Physical Punishment of Children Worldwide' (EPOCH), an organisation which opposes all physical chastisement of all children in all contexts. (Personal communication, from Martin Rosenbaum, 14 December 1997).

21. *STOPP News*, June/July 1983, p.5.

22. These include:

    Mrs X and Ms X v. UK (Application No. 9471/81), The European Commission of Human Rights, Decision as to admissibility, 13 March, 1984, 166th Session Minutes 5-16 March,1984, DH(84)4, 9 May 1984.

    Durairaj v. UK (Application No. 9114/80), The European Commission of Human Rights Decision as to admissibility, 11 October, 1984.

    S J and A v. UK (Application No. 10592/83), Council of Europe, Human Rights News C (86) 8, 23 January, 1986.

The Studley Case, STOPP, Britain's Violent Teachers: A Dossier of Beatings Reported to STOPP, 1982, p. 12-14.

Sams v. UK ibid., p. 14-15.

Arnold and Gray v. UK, ibid., p. 15-17.

STOPP, Newsletter, June/July 1983, p.3.

Z v. UK, STOPP, Britain's Violent Teachers, p. 17-18.

Brant v. UK Case, ibid., p. 3-4.

Sweeting v. UK Case, *STOPP Newsletter,* June/July 1984, p.3.

Hanvey v. UK Case, *ibid.*, p.3-4.

Blencoe v. UK, STOPP Newsletter, June/July, p.4-5.

Lund v. UK ibid., p.6.

23. See *Council of Europe, Press Release,* B(87)27, 21 August, 1987 and *Times Educational Supplement,* 2 October, 1987.

24. *Roberts-Costello v. UK,* (1993), The European Court of Human Rights, 89/1991/341/414. Series A, No. 247, 25March 1993. See also Mowbray (1994b) for an insightful discussion of this case in 'Corporal Punishment in Private Schools', *Journal of Forensic Psychiatry,* Vol. 4, No. 3, pp. 546-550.

Chapter 4

Sparing the Rod: Alternative Approaches to Discipline in Schools

While it is a myth that corporal punishment is the only form of discipline that some children understand, it may unfortunately be true that it is the only form of discipline that some educators understand (Hyman and McDowell, 1979).

The abolition of corporal punishment left some teachers wondering how to tackle discipline problems and how to respond when pupils challenge your authority with the reply 'you can't make me.' New times require new techniques. With the demise of corporal punishment, alternatives have been and are being developed. At the same time teacher authority in schools needs to be maintained rather than undermined or thrown into jeopardy. This chapter is necessarily wide-ranging, beginning with a philosophical examination of key concepts concerning school discipline and what we mean by words like 'punishment', 'discipline' and 'control', and how this relates to the 'authority' of the teacher. Within this philosophical context, alternatives to physical chastisement are then considered. So this leads to the proposal for a framework for good practice underpinned by principles of social justice and the current legal situation. The chapter concludes by highlighting the implications for school policy in the shift away from corporally punishing children.

Philosophical Considerations
Punishment
Although there is clearly an overlap between the terms 'punishment', 'discipline' and 'authority' in common usage, they are conceptually

different. 'Punishment' is often related to such terms as 'sanction', 'penalty', 'chastisement', 'correction' and 'control', and 'control' is frequently confused with the term 'discipline'. Peters (1966) distinguishes between the latter term and punishment by stating that 'discipline... is rooted in a learning situation' and conveys the notion of 'submission to rules of some kind of order' (p.267). Such rules may be self-imposed or externally imposed by those in authority. Conversely, ''punishment'... is a much more specific notion which is usually only appropriate when there has been a breach of rules' (*ibid,* pp.267-68).

Definitions of 'punishment' have also conceptualised the word as being associated with physical pain. For example, 'punishment' is defined as: 'the intentional infliction of pain by someone in authority on someone as a consequence of a breach of rules' (*ibid.,* p.268).

This traditional view of punishment as being linked with pain carried with it notions of legitimacy. Wilson (1974) describes this as 'the infliction of pain which it is *right* that one should have to suffer for moral wrong doing' (p.93). Similarly, Moore (1982) notes:

> the root notion in punishment is that it requires the intentional infliction of pain on someone who has committed an offence. This infliction of pain must, strictly, be undertaken by someone who has been given a right to do so, someone in authority 'de jure' (p.84).

The majority of teachers in Europe can no longer regard themselves as being in authority to inflict pain intentionally by virtue of 'a right to do so.' Accordingly, the nature and purpose of punishment has been changed so that pedagogic punishment meets new social norms and conforms to the legal guidelines.

Traditionally, ideas about punishment have been centred on three main areas: retribution, deterrence and reform.[1] 'Retribution', notes Bean (1981), requires that punishment be equated to the crime. At its simplest this theory encapsulates the idea of 'an eye for an eye', and is seen by its critics as characteristic of a barbaric system. Secondly, 'deterrence' serves as an example to prevent others committing the same offence. Finally, the reformative or rehabilitative theory of punishment has become particularly prevalent in discussion of modern day penal systems, the aim being the reform of the offender into an acceptable member of society. Thus it is considered the most progressive and legitimate of the theories of punishment.

A further model, this time proposed by Moore, adds the terms 'psychological' and 'juridical', both of which have relevance to school discipline. The 'psychological' model involves 'conditioning or negative reinforcement', which we will explore later in this chapter; whilst 'juridical' refers to punishment inflicted by someone in authority, as a result of wrongdoing. The 'someone in authority' within an educational context is normally the teacher or headteacher. Moore contends that whilst several paradigms have application in schools, 'the juridical model is the only one morally defensible' (p.31). He adds:

> the juridical model is thus relevant to teaching in the sense that it stands behind the activity of teaching. Its purpose is that of securing the condition under which successful teaching can be carried on. But juridical punishment is appropriate only because the rules which have been broken are known rules (p.33).

As there is an 'imbalance of power' between teacher and pupil, notes Royce (1984), there needs to be scrutiny of punishment policy to assess whether in fact the position of power is abused. A further justification of punishment is found in the theory of Utilitarianism. Bentham wrote:

> all punishment is mischief; all punishment in itself is evil. Upon the principle of utility, if it ought to be admitted, it ought only to be admitted in as far as it promises to exclude some greater evil'.[2]

The Utilitarian approach suggests therefore that punishment can be justified to augment the well-being of a community. Docking (1980) notes that support for the Utilitarian view 'lies in its social expediency and its unique deterrent power. It is essentially a means to an end and not an end in itself' (p.203). Similarly, Burns and Hart (1970) contend that Bentham's conception of punishment is essentially forward looking in that it seeks to protect society, rather than backward-looking in order that offenders be chastised for past misdemeanours. Punishment is not mischief in that it has no purpose: rather it can be used to motivate members of a community and encourage positive behaviour which is in the interest of everyone.[3]

Finally, Bradley (1927) adds a warning that:

> punishment is punishment only where it is deserved. We pay the penalty because we owe it, and for no other reason; and if punishment is inflicted for any other reason whatsoever than because it is merited by doing wrong, it is a gross immorality (pp.26-27).

Pedagogic Punishment

There are similarities and differences between punishment of adults under the penal system and pedagogic punishment of children. Bradley states that pedagogic punishment or chastisement of children by parents and teachers, is different from judicial punishment since the former permits 'greater latitude of particular consideration of the individual case' (p.31). The analogy between judges and teachers lies in the fact that both authorities are concerned with imposing punishment on an offender or culprit. Peters elaborates further:

> the rules of school approximate to the rule of law as, to a large extent, they are issued by those in authority and enforced by sanction ... [and] ... the teacher is in a position of the judge and the probation officer combined. He [/she] can both administer rules impartially and follow up necessary punishments (pp.287-288).

Furthermore, teachers can be expected to know the children they punish whilst the legal justice system is administered by strangers. (The judicial corporal punishment administered in the *Tyrer* case highlights this point as the fifteen year old pupil was birched by a police official unknown to him.) Moreover, teachers assume a responsibility for children both morally and intellectually, and school based punishment aims to be both formative and reformative.[4] Bradley adds 'pedagogic punishment' is substantially different from adult punishment since juveniles cannot be held responsible for actions in the same way as adults can and their punishment should therefore be more in the nature of improvement (p.31).

Whilst it has been, and still is, debatable whether a punishment need be corporal, punishment *per se* is a common feature of the pedagogic process. To justify the use of punishment in the school as a means of preserving order, Docking contends that distinction must be made between whether punishment 'as an institution' is justified; and secondly, whether a teacher is justified in punishing 'a particular child for a particular offence' (p.205). If these two criteria can be satisfied, a third justification is required as to the form and extent of punishment. Further, he states that the punishment system in a school constitutes part of the 'hidden curriculum' whereby 'the child may perceive the values of the school more in terms of how misdemeanours are dealt with than what is actually said' (p.211).

Research into education has provided support for the view that punishment can be justified in schools in order to maintain social order and reduce the problem of pupil indiscipline. The *Plowden Report* (1967) states that:

> punishment will be defended solely as a means to order... a punishment must be understood by the child and be seen to be just and to this extent accepted by him (p.270).

Likewise, Rutter *et al.* (1979) contended in their report into secondary school education and its effect on pupils that 'obviously a certain amount of firm disapproval, and also punishment, is necessary in the control of disruptive behaviour (p.186). Stenhouse (1967) cautions however, that without justification of the need to maintain social order, 'punishment is just a sophisticated form of revenge' (p.183). Moreover, he contends that 'collective punishment' in schools can be justified only when 'each member of the class has committed the same offence or broken the same rule... [since]... the class cannot be regarded simply as a corporate entity... which is responsible for the individual members comprising it' (p.190). The principle of collective punishment has, nevertheless, been upheld on occasions by the courts as in *R v. Jeffs* (1955).[5] Furthermore, punishment must be related to values of fairness and justice (Smith, 1985). Bean, in his study on juvenile punishment recommended that 'punishments be fair and above all must be seen to be fair' (p.147). The incorporation of principles of social justice into school discipline policy is highlighted later in this chapter.

Beyond management and control, further justification of school-based punishment lies in the desire to establish in children the principles of morality. Kay Shuttleworth emphasised this objective in 1841, writing:

the punishment of children in all schools ought... to be addressed to the conscience of the child rather than to the public opinion of the school... The object of all moral education is to awaken the conscience (pp.7-8).

The same theme is echoed in this century by writers like Ewing (1929) who talks about getting children 'into good habits', and Docking who contends that the right to punish arises from 'the rightness of moral principles' and that punishment should lead to pupil awareness of what is morally right rather than what is socially expected (p.211). He contends further that 'improvement' is therefore the general theme underpinning philosophical arguments justifying pedagogic punishment. This is supported by the assumptions, notes Bean, firstly that 'children are amenable to discipline'; and secondly, that there is a need to safeguard the future of society (pp.116-117). His third basis for this line of argument is that 'pedagogic punishment protects by providing stability for the child, for it provides boundaries to the child's wilful nature. It protects him by helping to establish his place in the universe' (p.118).

Finally, punishment in schools is justified by the need to prepare children for the realities of life beyond the classroom. In the words of Royce:

> the institutionalisation of punishment at school is said therefore to be a way of preparing the young for, and getting them used to, the institutionalised system of punishment to be found elsewhere, namely the non-school punishment system (p.86).

Objections to punishment at school

So far we have discussed the concept and justification of punishment, but there are counter-arguments as to its applicability to children. Bentham contended that whilst punishment might be relevant to children on some occasions, he deliberated over whether children were too young to appreciate future consequences. Marshall (1984) goes one step further by stating:

> whilst it can be argued that it is most difficult, if not impossible, to conceive a society without some rules which are socially sanctioned, it is not obvious that these rules must apply to children,

and it is far from obvious that if it is claimed that children are obliged to follow such rules that this is moral obligation' (p.104).

Likewise, Royce is not convinced that punishment as preparation for future adult life is justification itself, for children are already held responsible for their action within the penal system, commensurate with their age and maturity. (This theme is addressed more fully in chapter 6.) Moreover, he suggests that 'what is most challenging is the idea that all punishments should be removed from teachers' repertoire of inducements to learning' (p.94). This is because:

> ... parents who are in favour of their children being educated in schools may well hold philosophical convictions against their children being punished at all, and not just against their being beaten (*ibid.*).

'Philosophical convictions' against corporal punishment have already been expressed via litigation in Strasbourg as detailed in the previous chapter, but to date no case has been adjudicated by the Court in which a parent objected to punishment *per se*. Royce proposes as one alternative to school-based punishment the removal of disruptive pupils from the normal school system and 'the creation of more suitable learning environments' (*ibid.*). Clearly, this may still constitute 'punishment' to the child and parent. He concludes that 'children should not be required to submit to institutions which conscript them yet cannot function without punishing them' (*ibid.*).

The 'morality of compulsion', notes Wilson (1971), is at the heart of school discipline as schooling is compulsory. This adds further weight to the inadequacy of the *in loco parentis* doctrine for, although parents may acknowledge that their child must attend school compulsorily, they may not automatically delegate their right to punish the pupil, physically or otherwise.

To summarise, the term 'punishment' traditionally implied the intentional infliction of pain on an offender against their will in response to a misdemeanour or moral wrongdoing. Legitimate authorities exist, such as judges and teachers, who are empowered to make pronouncements and impose punishment. In the school context, such punishment is justified by the need to maintain social order which will facilitate learning, to inculcate the principles of morality, and to prepare children for the realities of life beyond the classroom. Whilst 'punishment' has denoted pain, the term may also be employed to suggest a disciplinary sanction which is not necessarily physical chastisement. Various forms of punishment exist, and whilst the focus in schools has traditionally been corporal punishment, a spectrum of alternative sanctions can be utilised in schools as discussed later in this chapter.

Discipline and Control

Next we broaden this philosophical discussion beyond the term 'punishment' to explore related words often used interchangeably: discipline and control. There are conceptual differences between these words, and Slee (1995) argues that careful definition and analysis of their underlying assumptions encourages an awareness of the implications for school policy.

The word 'discipline' can be employed in two senses within educational settings. One relates to academic disciplines or subjects, the other to issues of school management. The latter is not necessarily negative but refers to a way of getting things done in school, or what Slee refers to as 'educational orderliness'. Legitimacy and logic rest within such a conceptualisation, especially if, as he advocates, the meaning of rules assumes greater moral authority if their form, content and application is the subject of negotiation between teachers and pupils about school policy on the issue.

Discipline can also be perceived as development of the individual, promoting self-actualisation and empowerment. This is along the lines of Dewey, who wrote in 1916 that 'a person who is trained to consider his actions, to undertake them deliberately, is in so forth disciplined. Discipline is positive' (p.129). This contrasts markedly with the connotation of discipline as used to subordinate, to compel obedience and 'to cow the spirit' (*ibid.*).

Ideally, Wilson (1971) argues, discipline should be seen as a recognition of a need for order and working together, and in such situations 'punishment and reward are educative, rather than mere inducements to toe the line' (p.94). Further, both discipline and control are forms of order, 'but the order in each case is of a logically different kind' (p.77). He sees discipline as part of an educative order, whereas control can be self induced or externally imposed.

Support for alternative, non-corporal punishments are based on encouraging a sense of self-discipline within the pupil, rather than seeing discipline and punishment as synonymous (Cryan, 1995). Hyman and D'Allessandro (1984) suggest that 'we must view discipline as motivated by a set of internal controls, not by fear or harm' (p.37).

In drawing a distinction between discipline and control, Slee argues persuasively that educational theory on discipline should demonstrate consistency between teaching objectives, curriculum and school management. Otherwise, disciplinary procedures are reduced to 'a mechanistic euphemism for behaviour modification' and the educational value of the system is compromised (p.18). So discipline can be justified within the school context as something to be encouraged within the pupil as a positive attribute to benefit the individual and the educational community, 'whereas control assumes a conflict of interest, disagreement concerning goals, and is tangential to the aims of education' (Slee, p.28).

When discipline is associated with negative notions of discipline there may develop within schools what Ritchie and Ritchie (1981) call 'the power politics of authority,' where 'the teacher becomes a police officer rather than a pedagogue' (p.84). Within this situation of teacher and pupil as adversaries, the disciplinary system can lead to alienation.

> This often corroborates the conviction of the pupils that education is something which is imposed on them from outside by the custodians of a coercive corporation (Hirst and Peters, 1970, p.124).

Finally, Schostak (1983) provides a powerful analogy which illustrates this point:

> social control creates a complex and sticky web enmeshing those who think they control, those who think they are controlled and those who resist. Deviance arises as tears warp and break the web (p.15).

Despite a general rejection of corporal punishment today there is still concern over the imbalance in power relations in educational settings.

A movement away from physical chastisement to non-corporal alternatives does not necessarily signal a philospohical shift in the conceptualisation of authority, discipline and control. For example, Slee argues that 'suspension was to do what corporal punishment could not: maintain a docile school body in schools' (p.59).[6]

Exploring the terminology of discipline and control causes us to question the very basis of education, not only the legitimacy of sanctions but the nature of the institution and processes of schooling. We need to ask:

> does the school discipline policy act to shield irrelevant curricula, inadequate teaching, the absence of pupil democracy in the school; or the failure of the labour market to ensure a meaning for schooling (*ibid.*, p.22).

A broader concept of discipline may encourage teachers to think beyond controlling, regulating or punishing, and instead to re-position the issue as one concerning curriculum, teaching and school organisation. This is more in line with what Slee calls 'a principled theory of discipline consistent with educational aims' (p.22). Such a movement draws on earlier notions of discipline as proposed by Dewey (1916), Hirst and Peters (1970) and Wilson (1971), and incorporates ideas of democratic rather than authoritarian school governance, towards what Crittenden (1991) describes as 'ethical discipline'. Importantly, teachers need to question the extent to which disruptive behaviour can be dismissed as the responsibility of the pupil, or whether in fact 'the emphasis on punishment is a symptom of something amiss in the larger learning system' (Short *et al*, p.95), or what Connell *et al* (1982) refer to as 'the pathology of the institution'.

Finally, social and legal changes have led to a challenge to traditional notions of authority. How does the concept of authority relate to the associated terms of discipline and social control, and how does it derive legitimacy when applied to pupils in schools?

The Concept of Authority

The authority of the teacher has in the past been linked closely with the right to administer corporal punishment as a disciplinary sanction. Teachers relied upon the special position they held under Common

Law by acting *in loco parentis* to carry out physical chastisement subject to school regulations, but without recourse to parental approval. As a result of the European Court's jurisprudence, discussed in the previous chapter, the British government was compelled to address the issue and statutory enactment has now removed teachers' traditional right to chastise their pupils physically. This has modified their status in law and by association their authority in the classroom. The discussion now moves to consideration of the authority of the teacher with reference to its philosophical meaning and the challenge to teacher authority which the abolition of corporal punishment might suggest in the light of new social norms.

Linguistic analysis of the word 'authority' suggests ambiguity and complexity. The word derives from the Latin 'auctoriat' meaning 'bearing' or 'presence' and, notes Peters (1966), was frequently employed in reference to the 'demeanour' of a dignitary. He further suggests that the word has an 'aura' about it and is appropriately used in legal systems and communities, such as schools in which teachers are given the right to decide what is correct and to apply rules for enforcement (p.239). The concept of 'authority' is also 'inseparably connected with a rule-governed form of life... [and] this presupposes some sort of normative order that has to be... maintained and perpetuated' (p.238). Additionally, 'authority' denotes 'producing... originating... and inventing in the sphere of opinion' (*ibid.*, p.239). Of these two interpretations, the former is concerned with the function of social control and those in authority who may employ disciplinary sanctions, and the latter meaning denotes an authority or someone with expertise in a particular field or area of the curriculum. Both meanings of 'authority' are appropriate to teachers and both are open to challenge, for in performing this dual role, distinct qualities of competence are required. It is the authority of the teacher in the sense of being placed in the position of disciplinarian and social controller with which this section of the chapter is concerned.

Beyond this distinction, the concept can also be classified in terms of 'formal' and 'actual' authority. The difference lies in authority formally confirmed and authority in practice. Accordingly, notes Moore (1982), the teacher will normally have authority 'de jure' subsequent upon appointment, but teachers need also to have authority 'de facto' if there is not to be chaos in the classroom (p.85).

What is central to the notion of authority is 'being able to get orders obeyed simply by giving them'(*ibid.,* p.83). Entwistle (1970) and Bantock (1970) discuss the notion of 'authority' in terms of negative and positive connotations. In the former sense, authority can develop into authoritarianism or 'authority for its own sake' while in the latter case, the imposition of authority can still allow individuals to develop and come to self-actualisation. The constraint which authority can automatically impose is considered by some to be an offence to the issue of liberty, but John Stuart Mill considered that children were a special category in which it was morally justifiable to restrict their freedom. Authority is usually taken to be the antithesis of liberty and the difficulty, contends Schofield, lies in striking a balance between the two extremes for 'if we move too far in either direction... we create a situation in which 'licence' not freedom emerges' (p.271).

When a person's authority is challenged he/she may resort to the imposition of sanction, so the concept of 'authority' is often associated with that of 'power'. Schofield states that as authority can be imposed 'there is always, at least in the background, a suggestion of physical power or force to give backing to the authority' (p.261). This is in keeping with the traditional concept of authority whereby behind the voice of the teacher, notes Peters, there was often the cane. He distinguishes further between 'power' as denoting ways 'in which an individual subjects others to obey his will by physical coercion' and 'authority' which involves 'the appeal to an impersonal normative order or value system which regulates behaviour basically because of acceptance of it on the part of those who comply' (p.239). Thus 'authority' implies a sense of something being 'right', 'correct' or 'legitimate'; accorded to an individual of special status in the community, who may support their 'authority' by the use of sanctions.

Authority in education has a particular significance. The school is an institution whose major aim is to educate, to help bring out a child's ability and to encourage the notion that study is worthwhile. Further, schools are concerned with passing on a community's culture and instilling modes of behaviour, all of which requires the pupils' participation in the process. The school setting may be described as 'authoritative' and the teachers who represent the authority have legal obligations for which they are answerable to the community. Peters suggests that authority by itself may be ineffective and may need to be backed up to bring about minimum conditions in which learning can take place. Likewise, Bantock argues the case for restricting freedom on the basis that education and learning cannot take place in an undisciplined and unrestrained 'free' environment. The justification for authority in school would seem therefore to be located in the *raison d'être* of the institution itself and the need to instill order to ensure that learning can take place. Entwistle (1970) contends nevertheless that:

> teachers cannot expect to have authority 'ex-officio'; and even if they expect it, the existence of disorderly classrooms demonstrates that in fact they manifestly cannot rely upon the authority rituals of the school (p.64).

Furthermore, there is the question of accountability. Schofield describes the situation thus:

> Society recognises that, as the result of special training and education, certain people are worthy of the status of teacher. But, in return, the society which awards them status makes strict demands about the way the teacher behaves (pp.267-268).

Accordingly, teachers have to justify their actions and their use of authority to impose punishment, and to limit the freedom of pupils. We also have to be prepared to analyse critically the concepts we use and the way in which we treat pupils even if, as Smith (1985) points out, there is no shortage of people who regard such questioning as itself subversive. In exercising their authority, teachers traditionally may have chosen to use extrinsic sanctions rather than intrinsic methods of discipline, corporal punishment as opposed to relying on pupils' self-discipline. However, change in the legal context has removed this option for the majority of teachers in this country and accordingly alternatives to corporal punishment have been developed.

Alternatives to Corporal Punishment

Alternatives to corporal punishment have always existed and have been used to varying degrees in schools. The abolition of physical chastisement by law in Britain, may have prompted some schools finally to relinquish the cane, but for others change came about by a belief in the efficacy of alternative sanctions, or the realisation that

Figure 5: Alternative Sanctions to Corporal Punishment

Punishments
- Verbal reprimand
- Standing outside the classroom
- Withdrawal of privileges
- Extra work – academic
- Making reparation
- Time-out – removing a pupil from the situation
- Temporary segregation of individual within the school
- System of demerits
- Intervention by Pastorial Tutor/Year Head/Guidance Counsellor
- Detention-informally during school day
- Detention – official with parental knowledge and consent
- 'On report' system whereby behaviour is monitored with or without parental knowledge
- Pupil/Student Court
- Threat of parental involvement
- Isolation with a member of the Pastoral team
- Withdrawal from normal teaching groups
- Isolation within a different year group
- Isolation in a unit in the school
- Temporary exclusion
- Permanent exclusion
- Off-site units of education

Strategies to increase desired behaviour
- Participation in extra curricular activities
- Verbal reasoning
- Positive reinforcement/praise
- Use of rewards
- Token economy where stamps etc. are earned for good behaviour and traded for rewards
- System of merits
- Counselling services
- Peer support programmes
- Pupil/Studentcouncils – involvement in decision-making process
- Behaviour plans/contracts with or without parental involvement
- Behaviour modification approaches e.g. the Behavioural Approach to Teaching Secondary Children (BATSAC); Behaviour Reflective Relationship (BRR); Positive Discipline (PD)
- Valuing of pupils' work eg through display
- Letters of commendation eg from Year Head to parents.

abolition was inevitable[7]. However, the legislation which removed corporal punishment from British state schools in 1986 was silent as to what should replace it and schools have been working on alternatives during the last decade with guidance provided in some cases from local authorities[8]. Furthermore, there has also been a growing literature on school sanctions and how teachers should respond to questions of discipline and punishment. What follows is an overview of some of the main alternatives to corporal punishment. The list of strategies in figure 5, is indicative rather than exhaustive. Indeed Maurer (1984) enthusiastically claims in a publication that there are *1001 Alternatives to Corporal Punishment*. Here the focus is on the main options available as discovered through the literature and through working with teachers.

Listing some of the alternatives to corporal punishment suggests sanctions which are feasible. This spectrum of responses ranges from verbal reprimand to permanent exclusion. Although wide-ranging, the sanctions could be divided as falling into a *disciplinary model of practice*; and a *pastoral model*. In the former the traditional responses such as writing lines, detention and exclusion feature significantly. Alternatively the latter is rooted in the pastoral care system with a focus on positive reinforcement, support and counselling aimed to increase desired behaviour. In some schools there is an overlap between the two paradigms incorporating aspects of both approaches. Neither is without problems and next we examine some of the issues emerging from these polarised models.

The pastoral care model of discipline draws heavily on psychology and behavioural learning theory. This suggests that positive reinforcement as opposed to punishment will encourage good discipline. The principle is that you reward good behaviour and, using strategies to strengthen desirable actions, ignore the bad conduct. When ignoring indiscipline is impossible, punishment is used sparingly and immediately, and must always be accompanied by explanation so that the children know why they are being punished (Skinner, 1968, Meacham and Wiesen, 1989, Kelly, 1987, Rumbold, 1992, Colmar, 1991, Tulley, 1995). If punishment is used punitively and unsparingly, the theory is that children will not necessarily change their behaviour, but will try to avoid getting caught.

Within the pastoral care model of school discipline there are a number of strategies. From the alternatives listed in figure 5, some of the main ones are the *Positive Teaching: the Behavioural Approach* and the *Behavioural Approach to Teaching Secondary Aged Children* (BATSAC). Developed by Weldall and Merrett (1989), these emphasise positive teaching methods for dealing with poor behaviour in the classroom. Accentuating the positive and addressing teacher, as well as pupil, behaviour is seen as the key to creating a less stressful school climate and encouraging effective teaching. The approach is also disseminated through teaching kits, for example the *Behavioural Approach to Teaching Package* (BATPACK). Similarly, the *Behavioural, Reflective, Relationship* (BRR) approach advocated by McPhillimy (1996) involves the use of techniques such as reward and punishment within a positive pupil-teacher relationship. Finally, *Assertive Discipline* is a theory based on an American system which again has a commercial basis producing packaged material. The major thrust of this approach is towards creating rights in the classsroom (Canter and Canter, 1976). There is focus on establishing rules of behaviour, setting limits and recognising teachers' rights to uninterrupted lessons and to parental support. This approach has been adopted by schools in Britain, and is based on a system of positive and negative consequences to enforce the regulations (Martin 1994). Similar ideas are expressed in guidelines produced by local authorities in Britain, such as Nottingham County Council's *Children's Behaviour in Schools* (1994).

The awarding of rewards and privileges features as characteristic of many disciplinary policies and has a long tradition in schools. Derbyshire County Council, for example, list rewards as including: merit systems and competitions; public mention and acclaim; specific privileges; and the recording of achievements in pupil profiles (1993, p.13). Further afield in Australia, for example, the New South Wales Department of Education (1989) recommends award cards, notes to parents, merit certificates and awards for the whole class. Conversely, withdrawing privileges is a strategy which can be used to serve as punishment. One of the problems concerning the withdrawal of privileges, however, is its efficacy for older children. From their research in New Zealand, Ritchie and Ritchie found that:

the secondary school systems really had very few privileges to bestow or withdraw, and thus had often to rely too heavily upon punishments (p.90).

The challenge lies in identifying suitable, non-patronising rewards for older pupils to help motivate good behaviour.

There may be an over-dependence on inappropriate and unimaginative sanctions, what has been described as 'an arid set of traditional techniques', such as detention systems, lines or punitive tasks such as... cleaning the blackboard' (*ibid.*). Further, there is a danger of over-using, mis-using or potentially abusing a particular sanction. As detailed earlier in chapter one, corporal punishment was allegedly over-used in some schools, often to the same pupils (STOPP, 1982). Similarly,

> schools that set up... only a time-out room, find, not surprisingly that everything untoward that happens turns out to be a 'time-out' problem. No wonder the room becomes crowded! (Tasmania Department of Education, 1990).

Furthermore, whatever sanctions are employed in schools they need to be negotiated by the school community with a view to ensuring consistency among teachers. Without relating discipline to a set of agreed principles and procedures, 'it could be a matter of chance whether a misbehaving student were sent to a guidance officer, to a self-esteem group, or have a suspension' (*ibid*).

Punishments may also follow trends, such as the establishment of off-site teaching units, also highlighted in figure 5, to accommodate pupils referred with behavioural problems. This was a feature of the 1970s[9]. Financial support makes the further development of these uncertain. Currently, there appears to be excessive use of exclusion as a disciplinary sanction here[10] and elsewhere, such as in New Zealand.[11] Likewise, in Australia, Slee reports increases in suspension from school when corporal punishment is removed as an option.[12] More alarming still is the possibilty of 'medicalisation and the classification of indiscipline as sickness' which has recently manifested itself in diagnosing behaviour in terms of Attention-Deficit Syndrome.[13]

Whether rooted in an authoritarian model or related to a pastoral approach and behaviour modification, discipline may still remain a problem for school communities. This is because these strategies or responses do not strike at what may be causing dissaffection and in-discipline. A number of authorities point to the inadequacy of the curriculum, raised earlier in the chapter, in engaging pupils with the learning process:

> Disruptive behaviour occurs when demands that are reasonable for most of the class are quite unreasonable for those who lack the capacity, background or skills to deal with them (Ritchie and Ritchie, p.90).

Similarly, strategies for managing behaviour requires schools to tailor teaching and learning to meet individual needs (Derbyshire County Council, 1993; Parker-Jenkins and Irving, 1995; Slee, 1995; TES, 1997c). The introduction of the National Curriculum in 1989 seriously weakened schools' ability to respond to individual difference. Accordingly, we need to view pupil behaviour within a broad perspective of what happens in schools for '... in the long run the issue of discipline is intimately related to the design of the curriculum' (Ritchie and Ritchie, 1993).

School climate also has a bearing on school discipline and the use of sanctions. Research suggests that systems which have moved on from a dependence on punitive techniques, to positive reinforcement, praise and verbal reasoning have more success (Rutter *et al*, 1979). In a movement away from an authoritarian to a democratic climate, consideration needs to be given not only to pupil representation and the opportunity for their voice to be heard regarding the disciplinary policy, but to the messages conveyed tacitly through teaching approaches, and the informal curriculum. The Elton Report (1989) noted that:

> When we visited schools we were struck by the differences in their 'feel' or atmosphere. Our conversations with teachers left us convinced that some schools had a more positive atmosphere than others (p.88).

From the discussion so far a number of issues have emerged and I would argue that no one strategy can be recommended as a response to discipline problems in schools. Nor is there a blueprint which can be disseminated from central or local government and be equally successful for all schools. For policy to be effective, the school community must have input and ownership of a plan which is responsive to the needs and views of its members (Tattum, 1989, Thompson and Sharp, 1994). Schools vary, pupil composition varies and cross-cultural issues also need to be considered in devising policy which is appropriate. Consequently, there is no quick panacea for the problem, rather a spectrum of responses from disciplinary models of practice countenancing what we could describe as 'zero tolerance'[14] of any infraction of the rules, to pastoral care models rooted in a school ethos of positive reinforcement.

Answers to the question about alternatives to physical chastisement are multi-faceted and complex. The solution rests not just in a mechanistic list of punishments, or what I would call the 'sanction chain' which come into play according to the severity of the offence. To articulate sanctions in this way is to engage in exercises of gate-keeping, containment and social control. What is required is a repositioning of discipline and punishment into the centre of the educational agenda where the issue can be related to school environment, curricula offering, pedagogical style and the pastoral care system. Furthermore, exploring alternatives is not about undermining the authority of the teacher or abandoning discipline; it is about developing ideology which includes democratic principles, and empowerment. As discussed earlier in this chapter, the concept of discipline relates to punishment but this does not mean solely physical punishment. The movement away from corporal punishment to alternative disciplinary sanctions also signals a philosophical shift in the way we conceive of behaviour. Slee recommends critically evaluating 'the nature of authority in schools [and] what discipline may mean beyond control, management and punishment' (p.59). Perhaps more radical still is the proposition that 'teacher' and 'punisher' need not necessarily be the same person. For example, we might borrow from the French system where there is a separation between academic and pastoral tutor. The latter category, classified as 'pion', assumes responsibility for pupil discipline.[15] In Britain, there has been a long tradition of the 'teacher' being *in loco parentis* in the broadest sense, as discussed earlier in chapter 1, with both academic and pastoral care responsibilities. Whilst the individual teacher cannot have authority imposed for himself/herself, we might look to how a broader, more comprehensive counselling system might support the educator. Finally,

> No list of principles, no handbook of advice by psychologists and others, can replace the professional support that teachers can give each other (Ritchie and Ritchie, p. 87).

We need to recognise the value of providing opportunities for teachers to network and the importance of support through pre-service and in-service training. These and other points have important policy implications but before exploring them further, we should look at the legal context in which school discipline takes place.

The Legal Situation

Although corporal punishment is now unlawful in Britain for pupils whose education is provided by a local authority or those on an Assisted Places Scheme, the law recognises certain instances when the use of physical contact may still be necessary e.g. in order to avoid injury to the child, other people, or to property (Education No2 Act, 1986, section 47(3)). It is also the duty of the headteacher under the 1986 Act to determine measures regarding behaviour, which may include the formulation of rules and provisions for enforcing them (section 22). This is with a view to promoting self-discipline among pupils with 'a proper regard for authority'. Where the school is linked to the local education authority, the headteacher also has an obligation 'to prevent the breakdown or continuing breakdown of discipline in the school' (section 28). Policy should be subject to wide consultation and participation including both teaching and non-teaching staff, and be set out in written form (DfEE Circular 8/94). Behaviour and discipline go hand-in-hand, and in some schools the issues are conceived within a broad framework of 'policy on behaviour'. Either way, information on sanctions and rewards should be stipulated in the school prospectus for parents. Regulations governing detention, for example, carry implications concerning parental notification and other details in order to avoid complaints which potentially may constitute 'false imprisonment'.[16] Interestingly, a current Education Bill which seeks to strengthen the aim of schools in dealing with indiscipline and poor behaviour by pupils contemplates 'giving schools the power to detain pupils after school without the consent of their parents'. Such a move is a potential minefield, and case law has demonstrated the problem of pupils leaving school at irregular times.[17]

Further legal obligations relevant to this discussion are that head teachers and teacher governors of the governing body have a central role in ensuring that there is consistency between the governing body's written statement, and the school policy. Given recent cases of disagreement between headteacher and governing body over discipline policy, for example over exclusion, this need for consistency is clearly obvious. Finally, local authorities are required to provide pupil referral units, which have tended to be established as an alternative to home tutoring (NUT, 1993) and retain young people within an educational system (Lovey, 1992). More recently there have been suggestions that schools themselves establish units within the school to avoid pupils having to be excluded.

As well as legal underpinning, effective sanctions utilised as alternatives to corporal punishment carry resourcing implications. *The Elton Report* into pupil behaviour in 1989, highlighted the needs of children with emotional and behavioural difficulties, and most importantly made recommendations on adequate expenditure for staffing levels. Furthermore, there has been government recognition of this need.

> Teachers should not be blamed for failures in maintaining good order and discipline if the necessary support systems within the school for providing practical advice and help are absent (DfEE Circular, 8/94).

However, the impact of the *Educational Reform Act* (1988) and Local Management of Schools means that support systems are often inadequate. For example, off-site units which flourished in the 1970s have become vulnerable in the 1990s because of the question of who is to pay for them (Lovey). Counselling and referral of pupils may be required, which comes within the remit of the *Children Act* (1989), placing an obligation of liaison and cooperation between education authorities and social services – but again funding is an issue. And there is a general legal obligation on the local education authority as employer for ensuring a safe environment at school under the *Health and Safety at Work Act* (1974) which concerns the welfare of both staff and pupils. This may require an increase of staffing levels to provide satisfactory working conditions and an improved staff-pupil ratio.

Towards a Framework of Good Practice

Requiring alternatives to corporal punishment has led to examination of the nature of schools, power-relations and the shift away from the emphasis on punishment towards self-discipline and behaviour which supports a positive learning environment.

A number of key principles emerge which help inform what policy on school discipline should incorporate. Drawing on behavioural psychology, punishment should be *immediate* and *effective*. It is not always possible but the closer the punishment is to the time that the act was performed, the more effective it is in inhibiting further acts. In order to achieve this it must be very clear what the school's position is on the offence and the scope, if any, for flexibility in responding to it. *Consistency* in practice is also a factor of importance, in order to diminish situations where a single offence prompts varying degrees of response from different teachers. To that I would add that policy should be *fair*, based on principles of proportionality, and appropriate to the offence. For example, corporal punishment was typically used more frequently on boys than girls. If it had not been abolished by virtue of the influence of the European Court of Human Rights in Strasbourg, it is likely that it would have been found to breach domestic legislation in the form of the *Sex Discrimination Act* (1975). The alternatives to corporal punishment must also be seen to be fair, and used in an equitable manner regardless of gender, social class or ethnicity. This is echoed by the National Union of Teachers (1993) which recommends that behaviour policies be linked to the school's equal opportunities strategy. Finally, policy must be set on a proper legal footing: corporal punishment is unlawful for schools but detention, for example, can also be challenged as potentially constituing unlawful imprisonment.[18]

In reconsidering the power relationship between teachers and children there is also scope for pupil advocacy within a democratic model of school management. As the earlier section of this chapter highlighted, the exercise of authority and power is seen as an intrinsic and in-separable part of the teacher's role, but the misuse or abuse of such power needs to be considered. It has been suggested that 'teachers have to give up being judge, jury and executioner and frequently at the same time counsel for the defence and prosecution as well' (Ritchie and Ritchie, p.89).

In practice this would require opportunity for the pupil's voice to be heard in an acceptable manner and forum and, where appropriate, with support mechanisms. In many American states, for example, school principles receive training to ensure that in discipline cases, 'due process' has taken place and students have been allowed to give their side of the story (Miles 1997). This is not advocated for every single misdemeanour which takes place in the classroom but for more serious cases where the offence can lead to loss of privileges or ex-clusion. The Courts here so far always accepted that it would be im-practical to abandon the dual role in dealing with minor mis-demeanors in school. Collectively, these principles would promote fairness in the system for both pupils and teachers, ensuring a more predictable and consistent response to problems.

Beyond this, the discipline policy of the school should be collectively decided upon with input from representatives of teachers, school governors, pupils and parents. As stated in the introduction, it is ironic that schools talk about 'whole school policy' yet rarely do they incor-porate the views of pupils. Practically this would require negotiated discipline policies in co-operation with pupils, perhaps through a pupil/student council. Policy also needs to have monitoring and evaluation built in to assist in the long-term goal of developing an environment in which everyone can work. In rejecting fear, threat or coercion, characteristic of corporal punishment, a culture of mutual respect and mutual reliance needs to be fostered in which the rights and responsibilities of *all* members of the school community are given recognition. This could be expressed in a Code of Conduct, agreed by school managers, teachers and representatives from pupils, parents and non-teaching support staff. (Under the *South African Schools Act*, (1996), for example, such codes are now compulsory, outlining discipline policy and the regulation of good conduct).[19] Formulation of a code of conduct, addressing rules and sanctions, should be based on principles of rights and responsibilities which are owed to and *owned by* all members of the school community. (The concept of 'rights' is explored more fully in chapter 6). It also places *accountability* on all members who should not be assuming rights without being answerable for their actions. Some of the worst cases of indiscipline among pupils of late has been characterised by an emphasis on the 'right to education' with very little said of the responsibility to fellow pupils and staff to ensure that the learning process can take place, and in a safe environment.[20]

Guiding Principles on School Discipline

From the discussion so far, policy on discipline should be formulated in such a way that it is:

• immediate

• effective

• consistent

• lawful

• justice-based

• accountable

Implications for School Policy

A shift in school discipline requires a reconceptualisation of policy formulation and evaluation. Furthermore, moving beyond a punitive, authoritarian model of discipline carries with it significant implications for school management.

• School discipline should be seen as a management issue for and within the school as a whole. This requires seeing school discipline as a holistic model, rather than a single-issue strategy, and obtaining effective support from the school governing body.

• Policy on discipline relates to the wider context of school climate and culture and the fostering of an ethos in which all members of the school community are valued.

• Principles of social justice should underpin disciplinary policy, to ensure that sanctions are seen to exist within a firm but fair democratic system, and that there is clarity and consistency in both school rules and classroom rules.

- There needs to be a shift away from perceiving discipline as a narrow set of regulations to contain and control, to one which locates the concept more broadly in the curriculum, pedagogy and organisation of the school.

- Teachers require both pre- and in-service education on an alternative ethos of behaviour management, reinforced by training and networks.

- Adequate assessment of children's problems with appropriate follow-up counselling needs to be available for schools, and finally

- The cane was cheap; its replacement is not. Alternatives to corporal punishment carry implications in terms of resourcing, staffing and training.

Conclusion

Teachers may fear loss of status and authority as a result of the removal of corporal punishment. Indeed there has been a call from politicians for its return[21] and some teachers may mourn the demise of this disciplinary sanction. Yet generally speaking, teaching associations have not as corporate bodies called for its return, the majority view now being that we have moved on from the arid rehearsal of whether physical chastisement should or should not be used in schools, and instead recognise that the sanction belonged to a bygone age, and that exploring alternative approaches is the only way forward. Added to this is the need for on-going support for teachers in the form of resourcing and training. Responsibility for pupil behaviour still falls predominantly on teachers during the school day and their involvement in policy formulation, and their support in implementation, is vital. Employing alternative sanctions to corporal punishment is not about abandoning discipline, it is about reconceptualising it within a framework of non-physical sanctions, underpinned by broader interpretations of what should be going on in schools. Neither is it about undermining teacher authority. It is about establishing rights and responsibilities for everyone in the school community.

Many schools in Britain have spent the last decade exploring alternatives to physical chastisement, and some have addressed broader issues concerning school ethos and management. Elsewhere the struggle to abolish corporal punishment goes on, as discussed in the next chapter, with some countries only recently removing the practice, and still others not persuaded, that an overall ban is necessary.

Notes

1. For more on the classical theories of punishment, see Bean (1981) *Punishment: A Philosophical and Criminological Inquiry.*

2. See Bentham, J. *Theory of Legislation* (1840); *Principles of Morals and Legislation* (1970) edited by Burns and Hart.

3. Wilson (1971) takes exception to Bentham's maxim that all punishment is 'mischief' and argues persuasively that it has a part to play in society.

4. See Longford for more on this theme in *The Idea of Punishment* (1961).

5. *R V Jeffs* (1955) *The Times* 11 January. There is also the general 'law of common purpose' for use with mob rioting for example (Craig v Bentley).

6. Slee (1995) uses Foucault forcefully throughout his examination of power relations in schools from an Australian perspective. See M Foucault (1979) *Discipline and Punish: the Birth of the Prison*, Harmondsworth; Penguin Books.

7. Hansard Parliamentary Debates, Houses of Commons, Vol.102 No 154, July 22nd, 1986, p232.

8. *Ibid.* p 248

9. For more on this subject see Lovey (1992) *Teaching Troubled and Troublesome Adolescents*, chapter 2 and 3 of which examines special education units.

10. Hansard reports figures of 10,344 secondary pupils and 1,608 primary pupils in year 1995-6 (*Childright* 1997 No. 142, p.220). See also Derbyshire County Council (1997) *The Exclusion of Pupils from Schools* Report of the Chief Education Officer 29 January;

    Leicester County Council, *Report of the Director of Education; Exclusion of Pupils from Schools* (1966);

    The National Union of Teachers (1992), Education for Disaffected Pupils 1990-1992;

    Derbyshire County Council (1997) *The Exclusion of Pupils from Schools*; and Offices for Standards in Education (1996), *Exclusion for Secondary Schools 1995/6*, London HMSO.

11. For more on exclusion rates in New Zealand see Ritchie and Ritchie (1993).

12. For discussion on exclusion rates in Australia see Slee (1995).

13. For more on this theme see Moghadam and Fagan (1994) *Attention – Deficit Disorder.*

14. 'Zero tolerance' is a concept devised in New York and associated with criminal offences. Increasingly, the term is being used to denote a refusal to tolerate any misdemeanors. Presently it is being contemplated as policy with police divisions e.g. Merseyside. See Bratton W., Pollard, C., Orr J., Mallon R., Dennis , N (Ed) (1997). *Zero Tolerance: Policing a Free Society*, London; Institute of Economic Affairs. See also, *The Guardian* (1997b) 'Why the Jury is still Out, on Zero Tolerance', December 9, p.2.

15. The word 'pion' is slang for 'surveillant' and refers to someone in an administrative position who supervises pupils moving around the school, between lessons and in the library etc: they may also handle punishment of pupils.

16. Detention as unlawful imprisonment was raised in litigation in the 19th Century.

17. See for example *Hutt and Another v The Governers of Harleybury College* (1888).

18. *Ibid.*

19. For more on this legislation see The South African Department of Education (1997), *Understanding the South African Schools Act*, Pretoria; Department of Education.

20. For more on this theme see 'Anarchy Rules Okay' (The Ridings School). *The Sunday Times* (1996), 3rd November, p.14.

21. See Parker-Jenkins, M (1996) 'A Simple Solution That Never Worked', *Times Educational Supplement*, November 15, p.26.

Chapter 5

International Perspectives

State parties shall take all appropriate legislative, administrative, social and educational measures to protect the child from all forms of physical.....violence, injury or abuse.... while in the care of parent(s)..... or any other person who has the care of the child (United Nations Convention on the Rights of the Child, 1989, article 19).

The European Court in Strasbourg regarded Britain as being seriously out of step with Western Europe in the 1980s over school-based corporal punishment. Indeed, not only had the practice ceased in the majority of states in this continent, but some countries such as Iceland, claimed never to have used the sanction. [1] Beyond Europe, however, the punishment has varied usage and Britain has not been alone in demonstrating reluctance in giving up physical chastisement of pupils. This chapter considers corporal punishment as a disciplinary sanction within a spectrum of European States. It then considers South Africa which has recently outlawed the practice; the United States in which half the country has moved to abolition; and Australia which, except for one state, is a 'cane-free' zone. These three countries also serve as a useful basis of analysis since they share similar historical traditions concerning school discipline, and their courts have handled litigation regarding the nature and extent of the sanction. Without over-simplifying the practice in such large and diverse countries, the intention is to describe briefly traditional patterns of disciplinary policy and to identify emerging trends concerning corporal punishment of pupils.

European Developments

Britain became the last country in Western Europe to end physical chastisement in schools, as of August 1987, when the 1986 Act was implemented. The country's position *vis-à-vis* the rest of the continent was frequently raised during adjudication in Strasbourg of the British corporal punishment cases. For example, in the case of *Mrs X and Ms X* (1981),[2] the Court was informed of commonly accepted standards among other member-states of the Council of Europe, and was told that 'the United Kingdom now stands in splendid isolation in permitting this form of punishment'.

The use of corporal punishment in Europe was commonplace, although the schools were based on different educational systems.[3] For example in Germany there were rigorous regulations regarding its use (Newell 1972). Removal of the practice throughout the Continent has however, been taking place for over two hundred years – in Poland (1783), Italy (1860), Belgium (1867) and France (1867).[4] Other countries followed suit in this century such as Portugal (1950), Spain (1967), Germany (1970); with Ireland being the last country before Britain to move to abolition in 1982.[5] Likewise the practice was banned in Russia and all states in Eastern Europe by 1972 (Newell). As noted school-based physical chastisement is not universal. Further, whilst countries like Britain were very reluctant to give up the practice, other European countries have moved beyond the school to abolishing corporal punishment in the home.

The Nordic Circle of Denmark, Finland, Sweden and Norway have been particularly vigorous in challenging parental chastisement. Sweden's *Parenthood and Guardianship Code* (1979), for example, states that:

> the parent or guardian should exercise the necessary supervision in accordance with the child's age and other circumstances. The child should not be subjected to corporal punishment or other humiliating treatment.

Interestingly, this legislation employs the concept of 'degrading treatment' as does the European Convention on Human Rights. Likewise, the foreword to the Finnish *Child Custody and Rights of Access Act* (1983) states that the child 'shall be brought up in spirit of understanding, security and love. He shall not be corporally punished or otherwise humiliated.'

Not all parents in Scandinavia share these sentiments on child-rearing for, ironically, a group of Swedish parents lodged a complaint at Strasbourg in 1979, contending that their 'religious and philosophical convictions' were not being recognised by virtue of Swedish legislation *forbidding* parents from corporally punishing their children. The *Blom*[6] case ultimately failed to progress beyond the Commission stage of the Convention system, as it was concluded that:

> the actual effects of the law are to encourage a positive review of the punishment of children by their parents, to discourage abuse and to prevent excesses which could probably be described as violence against children.

By 1996 six countries within Europe had prohibited all physical chastisement of children, and the Council of Europe has encouraged its member-states to do likewise (EPOCH, 1996). The European pressure for reform places physical chastisement within a broader context of efforts to reduce family violence in general.[7] For example, in a Council of Europe Committee of Ministers recommendation (1985) it was stated that:

> it is the very assumption that corporal punishment of children is legitimate that opens the way to all kinds of excesses and makes the traces or symptoms of such punishment acceptable to third parties (*ibid.*, p.7).

Thus far Britain has rejected extending the ban on corporal punishment to the home. Instead the government has defended 'reasonable chastisement' of children by parents. The United Nations Committee report on the Rights of the Child (1995) stated:

> The United Kingdom position represented a vestige of the outdated view that children were in a sense their parents' chattels. In the Scandinavian countries stricter legislation had resulted in fewer cases going to court than in the United Kingdom.[8]

Overall the aim has been to pass law which changes attitudes to children rather than to intervene in family autonomy and prosecute parents. Despite conflicting views over child rearing and the use of physical chastisement, legislative reform in Scandinavia has clearly emphasised the rights of the child before those of the parent.

Within Europe, Scandinavian countries have taken a lead in promoting child welfare. The Swedish pressure group, *Radda Barnen*, for example, fights for children's rights around the world providing aid and advocacy, and is supported by over 100,000 members and 50,000 sponsors (EPOCH, 1996). This group participated in the drafting of the *United Nations Convention on the Rights of the Child*, as well as promoting implementation of Sweden's law outlawing parental chastisement. The group sees the UN Convention as fundamental to its work in promoting children's rights within and beyond Europe. Similarly, the organisation End Physical Punishment of Children (EPOCH) which was highlighted in the previous chapter, co-ordinates a worldwide alliance from its base in Britain which is aimed at ending all physical chastisement of children through education and legal reform. Generally, the focus in western Europe has been on extending rights to children, having now dispensed with corporal punishment in schools.

South Africa

Corporal punishment is currently being abolished in South Africa, which outlawed school-based physical chastisement in 1995 by a departmental circular pending the implementation of the *Schools Act* (1997). This brings the country into line with European states who have rejected the sanction and ensures statutory underpinning of the decision. Historically, indigenous African education was in evidence prior to the arrival of the Dutch in 1652, and was characterised by an emphasis on the inculcation of values, such as respect for authority. The development of formal education was associated with the development of separate or apartheid schooling. Although initially concerned with 'religious conviction', the basis soon shifted to one of 'racial distinction' (Van Zyl, 1997, p.55). The history of education in South Africa has been predicated on the fact that black, Indian, 'coloured' (mixed-race), or white children have not generally been taught together (ibid.). Education was influenced by the British, the Dutch and the Afrikaners who shaped and developed separate educational systems for these different groups.[9]

Corporal punishment has been a traditional feature of school discipline throughout South Africa, as well as detention and exclusion, with policy reflecting the British model (Squelch 1997). Regulations were expressed through administrative legislation detailing where it could be used, by whom and to whom (Olmesdahl, 1984; Staatskoerant, 1990; Edulaw, 1995a). Additionally, as with the British experience, reliance was placed on Common Law which provided guidance on the test of reasonableness in its use, and requirements concerning the child's age, mental and physical state, as well as the nature of the misdemeanour and the teacher's motivation in using physical chastisement. Abuse of the sanction was also recorded in South Africa, when teachers and headteachers ignored the regulations, and both civil and criminal litigation ensued. For example, in *S v. Meewis* (1970),[10] a teacher was found guilty of assault after hitting a boy repeatedly for writing out a sum incorrectly on the blackboard.

Abolition of corporal punishment in South Africa came about within the context of constitutional change. In this case, the *Bill of Rights* (1996) provided the impetus for extending human rights to school children. Section 12(1) of the Constitution states similar provisions as that contained in article 3 of the European Convention on Human Rights. The South African article stipulates that:

> Everyone has the right to freedom and security of the person, which includes the right not to be treated or punished in a cruel, inhuman or degrading way.

As with the Strasbourg document, corporal punishment is not specifically identified, but in the spirit of the times and the general advocacy for increased human rights in South Africa, it lends itself to the school context. Accordingly, abolition of physical chastisement has been conceptualised in South Africa within the context of human rights (Squelch, 1997). This philosophy has underpinned the corporal punishment cases adjudicated in Strasbourg. Likewise, advocacy of child welfare in Europe has taken place in debates on extending human rights to children.

Currently, the apartheid system is being dismantled. Under the 1993 Constitution, nine non-racial provincial departments have replaced the former ethnically-based structures. This has been reinforced by the Constitution of the Republic of South Africa and the *South African School Act* (1996) which are geared towards providing non-racially based education in the country (van Zyl). It is in this climate of political change and support of human rights that the issue of punishment in schools has been addressed.

Despite a movement towards abolition, support for retaining corporal punishment in South Africa has been expressed by teachers, administrators and parents, with a fear that removing the sanction will erode control and authority in the classroom (*Edulaw*, 1995b). This is a common concern identified throughout this discussion and appears to be characteristic of individual members of the teaching profession in general rather than specific to any one school system.

Controversy over the use of physical chastisement in South African schools continues to be part of the political climate. Indeed, attention has focused on juvenile and judicial punishment broadly, expressed clearly in *S v. William and Others* (1994).[11] In this case concerning adolescent offenders, it was argued that 'juvenile whipping' constituted 'cruel and inhuman' punishment and was unconstitutional. In the final judgement, the penalty was held to be a breach of the Constitution and this was followed by an announcement that corporal punishment in schools and other educational institutions was to be abolished (*Edulaw*, 1995b). Education departments were thus required to draw up new legislation governing the practice. For example, the Gauteng *School Education Bill* (1995) in Section 22 states that no one may administer physical chastisement 'to a learner at any public school or private school', and contravention of this provision may lead to a fine or imprisonment. Furthermore, during its deliberations in *S v Williams* reference was made to the British cases of *Tyrer*,[12] and *Campbell and Cosans*,[13] detailed earlier in chapter 3, and the American case of *Ingraham v Wright*[14] which we will review in the next section. This is because in the absence of their own precedents, South African courts are obliged to consider international case law and be persuaded by it findings.[15]

Nationwide abolition of corporal punishment has taken place as a result of the *South Africa Schools Act* (1996). Section 10 of this Act states that: 'No person may administer corporal punishment at a school to a learner.'

This includes both state and independent schools. South Africa has gone further than the UK, USA, and Australia in imposing an abolitionist measure on all schools (Squelch 1997). In the light of constitutional reform, South African teachers have been instructed to inform parents and pupils of the new regulations governing the practice, and to develop alternative disciplinary sanctions. On my visit to South African schools during the first year of abolition, I was told by head teachers that change will take time, as 'old habits die hard.' And there are tremendous problems in many of the 30,000 schools in the country, especially of overcrowded classrooms. The shortage of resources generally, let alone funds for developing alternative sanctions, may well mean that the cane still remains in many schools. I also discovered disagreement among teachers over what constitutes corporal punishment, and it is by no means clear that the law is intended to make illegal *all* acts of physical chastisement of pupils. At a time of major political upheaval, teachers are thus having to respond to new legislation governing school discipline, and to absorb new concepts concerning children's rights which challenge previous patterns of behaviour in the classroom.

United States of America

Here a teacher's right to administer corporal punishment has traditionally been recognised, and the American Supreme Court has upheld teacher authority in this matter. Unlike Western Europe, physical chastisement is still legally permissible and just under half of the American states permit teachers to make use of the sanction.

The traditional authority of American teachers mirrors that of their English counterparts:

> under the Common Law rule governing the use of corporal punishment in public schools, teachers may impose reasonable but not excessive force to discipline a child (p.714).[16]

Historical evidence suggests that as with British schools, detailed earlier in chapter 1, there was a perceived connection between the concept of 'sin' and child-rearing, and a belief that children were born evil as well as ignorant. It was assumed that religion could be used to steer children away from such sin. Parents were initially entrusted with responsibility for instructing children in traditional religious values, and schools continued this mission 'underscoring the social and religious necessity of conformity and restraint through rote memorisation and recitation' (Ryan, 1994, p.72). Moreover, 'this Puritan regard for conformity and restraint also included the use of corporal punishment' (*ibid.*).

Significantly, a motto used in schools at the time reinforced the view: 'better Whipt, than Damn'd' (Morgan, 1966, p.103). This ideology also found expression in the formal school curriculum, for example, the letter 'F' in the alphabet was accompanied by the saying: 'The Idle Fool Is Whipt in School' (Ford, 1962, p.8). Further documentation reveals 'memoirs and stories of floggings, beatings, humiliations and sadism in the colonial American tradition' (Hyman, 1990, p.35). Earlier attempts to challenge the excessive use of corporal punishment such as the *Children's Petition* of 1669 and 1698, discussed in chapter 6, were unsuccessful. However, Ryan notes that:

> increasing sensitivity in England and America during the 18th Century to the abuses of corporal punishment provided the foundation for reform efforts in classroom management during the 19th Century (p.73).

As with Britain, reform came about in the 19th Century but 'although the Declaration of Independence ignited the birth of the Republic, the liberties guaranteed to its citizens did not include freedom from the lash to school children or to adults' (*ibid.*).

Today, legislative change has improved the position of adults, but children are still vulnerable to physical chastisement. Despite a gradual shift in educational philosophy, 'reports of flogging, paddling and boxed ears continued throughout the 19th Century in both urban and rural schools' (Kaestle, 1983, p.66).

It is the notion of 'paddling' which appears to characterise the approach to corporal punishment in the United States and the term is used interchangeably and synonymously with corporal punishment. The 'paddle' is a thick wooden plank which has traditionally been used as an instrument for disciplinary punishment and applied to a child's posterior (Hyman, 1988). As with the practice of physical chastisement in Britain, regulations governing the practice have been developed by schools. Such was the popularity of the sanction in the 19th Century that only New Jersey saw fit to bring an end to the practice in 1867: the rest of the country was left to determine policy on an individual state basis, in keeping with other matters concerning education. Furthermore, as Bauer *et al* (1990) note, New Jersey's abolition of corporal punishment 'did not exactly light a spark igniting similar legislation in other areas,' for it was to be over a hundred years before the next state Massachusetts, followed suit in 1972 (p.286).

Approximately half of the American states have thus generally appeared reluctant to abolish the practice of administering corporal punishment despite substantial research challenging its efficacy or appropriateness as a disciplinary practice. At the end of the Second World War, the *Nation's Schools Survey* indicated that 87% of school superintendents supported its use (Ryan). By 1985, only 8 states had banned the practice (ibid.); and in 1990, the figure was said to be 11, leaving three-quarters of the states still 'legitimizing the use of corporal punishment.' (Bauer *et al*, p.286). Currently, the figure is given as 27 out of 50 states, suggesting that it is retained by just under the majority (EPOCH, 1996). It is difficult to get a clear picture of the situation, but I found from my research that although some states have enacted legislation to abolish the sanction, it has been expressly allowed by 22 states, while others permit discretion to school boards or head teachers.[17]

This reluctance to dispense with corporal punishment across America is based in part on custom, and practice. Ryan points to entrenched social norms and conventions.

> Those teachers who continue to use the paddle regularly and openly, do so in general because the larger community expects and approves of such behaviour (p.77).

Hyman and McDowell (1979) caustically state it is not that corporal punishment is the only thing that some children understand; rather it is the only form of discipline some teachers understand! Likewise, Bauer *et al* maintain that despite substantial evidence cautioning against the use of physical punishment, it has not been highly successful in adjusting views shared by teachers, parents, administrators and state legislatures across the country who still condone the practice.

Overall, therefore, the practice has been supported by tradition (Hyman *et al*, 1979), by parents (Kelly, 1985), by the judiciary (1977), and by some state governors (Miles 1997).

Ingraham v. Wright (1977)

The case of *Ingraham v. Wright* (1977) is of particular interest because it was a major test case raising concerns over schools, discipline and children's rights with special reference to corporal punishment. In the dispute, the judiciary was called to adjudicate on whether severe and excessive corporal punishment of pupils was unconstitutional. The case was originally filed in 1971 by James Ingraham and Roosevelt Andrews in the US District Court of Florida and included a class action brought on behalf of all children in the Dade County Schools. The defendants called to respond to these allegations were the principal, W.J. Wright, two vice-presidents and the superintendent of the Dade County school system. Ingraham et al. did not argue that all acts of corporal punishment were unconstitutional but alleged that those of an excessive nature were a violation of the 8th Amendment of the US constitution:

> Excessive bail shall not be required nor excessive fines imposed, *nor cruel and unusual punishment inflicted*' (emphasis added).[18]

The key issue in the case was, states Piele (1979),

> whether corporal punishment as a principle is inherently inconsistent with the tests of constitutional law and thus whether school officials throughout the nation have the authority to administer corporal punishment in any degree at all (p.92).

It was also argued by the plaintiffs that the corporal punishment meted out was so excessive as to violate the concept of 'human dignity' and the right to 'due process.' (The principle of human dignity was reaffirmed in the European Court's decision in the *Campbell and Cosans,* and *Tyrer* cases discussed in chapter 3.) By a five to four decision the Supreme Court ruled that corporal punishment administered in American schools as a disciplinary sanction did not constitute 'cruel and unusual punishment', and that the pupils punished were not protected by the 8th Amendment as it had relevance only to criminals. Further, it was felt that sufficient remedies existed under Common

Law and general safeguards provided by the open nature of a school, to ensure against the misuse of teacher authority. In reaching this decision, the Court rejected the suggestion that corporal punishment was not in accord with 'the dignity of man' and contemporary values regarding the use of punitive sanctions. Finding for the school, the Court instead stated that the concept of reasonable physical chastisement represents

> the balance struck by this country... between the child's interest in personal security and the traditional view that some limited corporal punishment may be necessary in the course of a child's education (p.733).

Thus, by a slim majority, the Supreme Court upheld the teacher's authority to administer corporal punishment in this landmark case, and as the USA is not a party to the European Convention, *Ingraham et al.* had no further redress.

The decision prompted wide debate about discipline and children's rights. Bauer *et al* point to this case as representative of a general trend whereby American courts have been unsupportive of attempts to abolish corporal punishment.

> They were unswayed by or unaware of the scientific evidence pertaining to this matter. Support for corporal punishments appears pervasive in US society. Clearly, cultural traditions have been more influential than research findings in determining public policy (p.294).

Alexander and Alexander (1985) state that in challenging the legality of corporal punishment in American public (state) schools three main arguments have been raised. Firstly, psychological and social concerns demonstrating that society has now progressed beyond using physical chastisement; secondly that this form of punishment is 'cruel and unusual' as countenanced by the 8th Amendment; and thirdly, that 'procedural due process of law' should be provided if the sanction is to be administered (p.293). *Ingraham* is still the leading case in America on school-based corporal punishment, and continues to be cited in subsequent litigation.

Contradictions within recent trends in the use of corporal punishment in America make it difficult to provide a clear picture. Surveys from the *Office of Civil Rights*, for example, suggest that the use of physical chastisement is steadily declining, yet Hyman (1990) maintains that this agency severely underestimates the extent of usage. Accordingly, whilst the OCR figure is approximately 1.5 million per year, he places the number in the region of two to three million incidents. This is because 'impromptu shoves, slaps and kicks' are not officially recorded. (Disagreement over what constitutes corporal punishment was also raised earlier with reference to the South African context.) Likewise, Ryan points to the fact that the figure in America is likely to be underestimated because school districts with an enrollment fewer than 1,500 pupils are not always included in the statistics. Added to this, Bauer *et al* claim that there are occasions when the act has been carried out illegally in states which have, in principle, outlawed the practice and where documenting incidents could lead to legal consequences. (This point was raised in chapter 1 with regard to the British situation.)

Children's rights advocates continue to lobby on the issue within the country (Keaney, 1995; Straus and Kantor, 1994; Straus, 1990). Adah Mauer for example, organised the American pressure group End Violence Against the Next Generation, whose main purpose is the collection and dissemination of information about school-based corporal punishment. Likewise, advocacy has been pursued through the National Centre for the Study of Corporal Punishment and Alternatives in the School. They work, note Bauer *et al*, to encourage top-down changes, hoping that the attitudes and practices of legislatures and judicial officials will percolate down to principals, teachers and parents. In the meantime, 'spare not the rod' supporters in the United States retain the upper hand in the face of state sanctions and federal tolerance through *Ingraham* (p.296). America's position on this matter is regarded by some; as 'an outstanding exemption in the industrialised world' (*ibid.*, p.294). The picture is not entirely bleak, however, as despite judicial tolerance and state authorisation of the practice, school policy based on positive rather than punitive sanctions, as noted in the previous chapter, have been developed in American school districts across the country.

In the United States, a gradual shift away from corporal punishment has taken place in some states, 'although the United States as a whole has not joined the community of countries abolishing corporal punishment' (Bauer *et al*, p.286).

Anti-corporal punishment lobbyists in America have shifted their attack since the *Ingraham v. Wright* case. Teaching associations, local school boards, and state legislatures have been encouraged to instigate legislation and regulations which would prohibit or discourage the use of corporal punishment (Hyman and Wise, 1979; Bauer *et al*, 1990; Dubanoski *et al.*, 1983). The issue of corporal punishment in American schools became more a political than a judicial concern. The opposite can be said of the British situation, for Strasbourg served as a catalyst for educational reform and Westminster imposed the change via legislative enactment, all of which lay beyond the power of the teaching profession or local government authorities to prevent.

Without benefit of Strasbourg there has not been the legal authority or compulsion to move to abolition of the practice across the country. There is no legal obligation to do so, but the European Court could provide moral authority and may be cited as persuasive authority by litigants who wish to bring about reform to this aspect of education. Rodley (1984) believes that in the *Tyrer* case, for example,

> the implications of the Court's ruling are not confined to Western Europe... since the ruling related to a standard which is universal, not just regional. As such this ruling is powerful authority for the scope of standards elsewhere.

Those advocates who call for equal treatment of children, irrespective of habitat, may point to the British punishment cases adjudicated in Strasbourg as proof that a child has an inviolate right to the dignity and integrity of the physical person, free from any form of physical chastisement. In the absence of appeal to the Strasbourg Court, supporters of abolition in North America, like the Parents and Teachers Against Violent Education, the National Coalition to Abolish Corporal Punishment in Schools and People Opposed to Paddling Students Incorporated, can only lobby and work for the enactment of legislative reform at the local and national levels, and look to landmark decisions by the American Supreme Court in cases such as *Goss v Lopez*,[19] *Re Gault*,[20] *Re Winship*[21] and *Tinker v Des Moines*,[22] that have enhanced the legal status of children and given judicial recognition to some of their rights, especially that of 'due process'(Bishop and Miles 1998). Whilst the US Supreme Court in the *Tinker* decision concluded that students do not shed their rights at the school gate, there is still limited constitutional protection for pupils (Miles 1997).

Continuing interest in the children's rights movement and the work of interested groups in North America suggest that the matter is not over. Canada also permits the practice in some provinces, but section 12 of the Canadian *Charter of Rights and Freedoms* stipulates 'everyone has the right not to be subjected to any cruel and unusual treatment or punishment.' Conceivably, corporal punishment could be challenged in Canada as unconstitutional given the expansive wording of 'treatment' as well as 'punishment', and could be applied in non-criminal contexts. The Canadian Charter is potentially stronger than the Eighth Amendment of the US Constitution and could be invoked widely, since in all provinces, except British Columbia, corporal punishment as a disciplinary sanction is still legally possible. It should be said that while all rights and freedoms in the Charter are subject to such reasonable limits prescribed by law as can be demonstrably justified in a free and democratic society, according to section one, it seems unlikely that a Court would ever rule a practice it found to be 'cruel and unusual' to be 'reasonable and justified.'

In Britain, physical chastisement has not been defined primarily in terms of human rights, but has remained essentially an educational issue. The absence of a written constitution in this country has meant that human rights have not been explicitly protected in any comprehensive rights document, as they have been in Canada and the US. The situation began to change in the aftermath of the Second World War, as detailed in chapter 2, when the UK became a signatory to a number of declarations. It would seem appropriate to view the issue of corporal punishment in North America within a broad framework of human rights, rather than as an educational issue alone, enshrined in tradition and custom, galvanising political strategies for effecting educational reform. State legislative action since the *Ingraham* case has rendered over half of the states now outlawing corporal punishment in schools. Although the Supreme Court did not interpret the Eighth Amendment as prohibiting this kind of sanction, there has been an increasing trend to place restrictions on its use or abolish it completely. As such, a national standard may emerge through legislative reform rather than by Supreme Court decree.

Predictions remain speculative as to whether the North American judiciary will choose to become actively involved in regulating school policy and use human rights documents as a catalyst for reform. The Supreme Court of Canada has shown a willingness to interpret the Charter in a broad and purposive fashion. A new and dynamic course of constitutional jurisprudence, akin to that demonstrated by the US judiciary in the 1960s, could greatly propel the notion of pupil rights, but the American judiciary may have lost the impetus of the 1960s when it led the way in extending constitutional guarantees to pupils (as discussed in the next chapter). Children in Europe are being regarded as having a status before the law worthy of equal protection and until the political or judicial will is formulated or regained to bring about similar reform in America, a fundamental disparity will exist between the rights of children living on either side of the Atlantic.

Australia

Along with America and South Africa, Australia inherited many of the British traditions concerning schools, discipline and teacher authority. Historically, corporal punishment was in evidence in state schools, and case-law helped to test the extent to which the sanction could legally be administered in Australian institutions. Thus, all three countries discussed in this chapter share a similar basis for analysis, and they have all experienced the controversy surrounding the use of corporal punishment and the educational debates concerning the alternatives. What is of particular interest here is the added dimension of re-introducing the sanction, which New South Wales contemplated at the time of abolition.

Education in Australia has from the 19th Century been a matter of state control, with each of the six states developing policy independently. Whilst differing in some details over schools and curricula, they share similarities in practice and administration (Maclain and Smith, 1971), and educational provision followed the Westminster model with a Minister of Education responsible to Parliament at federal or Commonwealth level (Birch, 1976). Law affecting education takes place at both national and local level, and as with the British system, corporal punishment has featured as a traditional sanction in the Australian classroom.

Australian colonies after 1850 established elementary school systems to respond to the need to increase educational provision:

> it was believed that social and moral improvement would result from literacy and instruction in useful knowledge, and it was expected that the social fabric would be strengthened as the masses learned to imitate the middle classes in diligence, responsibility, and respect for authority (*ibid.,* p.1).

Further, within the public school systems created, there tended to be centralised control of schools, teacher training and school discipline. At the turn of the century 36% of Australians lived in New South Wales and out of a population of approximately 1.3 million people, 240,000 pupils were on public school enrolment (*ibid.,* p.2). In these foundation years, Australian schools responded to a pattern of steadily increasing immigration with over 2 million European migrants after the Second World War leading to just over a million pupils enrolled in Australian schools. By 1965, the figure was nearly 2.5 million (Maclain and Smith). What is particularly noteworthy about the development of education in Australia is the challenge it has faced to provide provision in a large, sparsely populated continent through a centralised system of state education.

The expansion of education in Australia has been piecemeal, with primary schools established in the 19th Century, followed by an expansion of schools at secondary level, with large numbers of denominational and independent schools offering alternative provision. Whilst education in Australia has been a state responsibility, as stated earlier, Commonwealth involvement has taken place particularly in the post-1945 period. Finally, Mitchell (1975) maintains that the public perception of teachers changed little between the late 19th Century up to the 1960s, as they were seen as 'authoritarian and commissioned to inculcate the Victorian values'(p.15). This came about, in part, as a result of their duty to maintain discipline according to state regulations.

Traditionally, discipline in Australian schools has consisted of four types: corporal punishment, detention, suspension and exclusion; and all states are recorded as having used physical chastisement (Birch). Regulations governed usage: for example, in West Australia it was stipulated that 'corporal punishment may be inflicted for offences against morality, for gross impertinence, or for wilful and persistent disobedience' (ibid., p.49).

There has tended to be general agreement, within the states, that this disciplinary sanction should only be used for serious cases of insubordination; that the principal or his/her delegate should be responsible for administering the sanction; and that the event should be recorded (ibid.). The actual instrument used has, however, varied from state to state. It was stated that

> corporal punishment shall be administered by a strap in Victoria, by a cane on the hand in New South Wales and Western Australia, by either means in Tasmania... [and] the Queensland prescription is... a form which is not 'degrading, irregular or unnecessarily severe' (ibid.).

There was no mention of an instrument to be used in South Australia. Interestingly, a gender differential existed whereby only boys were noted in the Queensland regulations; it was entirely forbidden for girls in Victoria and South Australia, and limited to those over twelve years of age in Western Australia and New South Wales. Whilst legal for girls in Tasmania, corporal punishment was permissible only in exceptional cases of overt defiance of teacher authority (ibid.). (This point on gender inequality in the application of corporal punishment as a sanction is discussed later.)

Case law in Australia, as elsewhere, has also helped to determine the nature and extent of corporal punishment in schools. In *Smyth v. O'Byrne* (1894)[23] concerning the conviction of a teacher for an alleged assault on a pupil, a Queensland court made reference to English precedents for guidance.

> A schoolmaster may, in respect of school offences, misbehaviour, disobedience, idleness and the like, lawfully inflict moderate and reasonable corporal punishment (p.126).

Generally, the courts in this state gave attention to 'the manner, mode and severity of the punishment in determining reasonableness' (Birch, p.68). In *Connor v. MacDonald* (1912)[24] a student teacher was found

to be in breach of school regulations which restricted the use of corporal punishment to the school principal or delegate. Similar points
were raised in chapter 2 when looking at the British historical and
legal tradition governing teacher authority. Likewise, a teacher's
authority to use corporal punishment for a misdemeanour going to or
from school was also recognised by the Australian judiciary in *Craig v.
Frost* (1936).[25] As mentioned above, corporal punishment in Australian schools was in some states restricted to use on boys only. This
prohibition for girls was a feature of *King v. Nichols* (1939)[26] in which
a female pupil was slapped by a teacher in breach of school rules. As
the punishment was judged to be warranted and reasonable, the case
was dismissed although costs were not awarded due to the violation
of regulations governing the practice.

Whilst corporal punishment cases such as these were only examined
in Queensland, Birch contends that they served as persuasive
authority for the Supreme Courts of other Australian states. Also, during the latter half of the 20th Century, the question tended to become
academic as Australian states moved to abolition of the practice.
Recent state education policy in Australia relating to corporal punishment has thus become a response to enquiries into school discipline
and broader socio-political debates about the nature of schooling and
the positioning of pupils *vis-à-vis* teacher authority. Roger Slee
(1995) has written authoritatively on the changing theories and practices of discipline and his work is particularly useful here for chronicl-
ing the demise of corporal punishment across Australia.

In Western Australia, an enquiry was convened by the Director-
General of Education to determine the nature and extent of disciplinary problems in the state. The *Dettman Report* (1972) was 'the
most extensive government inquiry into student discipline in Australia'
looking at the broad social context of schooling and avoiding the
examination of discipline in the narrow sense of 'correction' (p.123).
This enquiry found that the majority of the problems faced by Western
Australian teachers at high school level were similar to those faced by
their predecessors, but that there was now 'a tendency to question the
authority of the teacher' (p.124). Significantly, this was the first
Australian government report to recommend the abolition of corporal
punishment, a point reiterated in the *Beazley Report* (1984) and

Louden Report (1985). Whilst there was support for abolition at this time, there was also resistance by teachers because of the fear of inadequate resources to provide alternative sanctions. Divergent views on the issue and reluctance to see an end to corporal punishment was also shared by some politicians who claimed 'the community favours its retention' (p.129). (A similar argument was raised in the *Tyrer* (1978) case, over support for judicial corporal punishment in the Isle of Man.) Furthermore,

> the teachers' union was unequivocal. They would not support abolition until such time as the resources to maintain control in schools were in place (*ibid.*).

However, major reports on discipline and child welfare produced from this state during the 1970s and 1980s opposed traditional sanctions of discipline and control. Abolition of corporal punishment in Western Australia subsequently took place in 1987, the same year as the ban in Britain came into effect. However, unlike the British experience this was immediately followed up with amended guidelines for suspension and school discipline (*ibid.*).

Victoria similarly shifted to elimination of corporal punishment and the Labour government moved ahead with speed for 'rapid formal abolition of corporal punishment' in 1983 (*ibid.*, p.131). This was accompanied by the *Maddocks Report* (1983) which contained provision for re-shaping policy in line with principles based on cooperation, and conflict resolution; and towards a democratic ethos of school management as highlighted in the previous chapter, 'suggestive of a break with the past punitive models for controlling aberrant young people in schools' (p.132). However, there seems to be an element of contradiction here, since a compromise was proposed, as in Britain's *Corporal Punishment Bill* (1985),[27] which permitted parents to opt formally to have their children exempted from corporal punishment and 'those students whose parents did not pursue this option were exposed, often by default, to corporal attention' (*ibid.*, p.132). As with the experience in some American states, discussed previously in this chapter, evidence from research was not by itself persuasive.

Again teachers were reported to be resistant to change, and an enquiry in 1991 into teachers' views in Victoria on the issue revealed their

desire 'to retain the upper hand in power relations in schools', parti-
cularly among secondary school educators (Lewis, Lovegrove and
Burman, p.137). Neither were these sentiments felt by teachers in
Victoria alone, for generally,

> observation of other states and territories reveal the rehearsal of
> old themes. The abolition of corporal punishment lies at the heart
> of states' debates about discipline and regulations... it symbolizes
> the power relationship between students and teachers (p.139).

Abolition in Victoria came about in 1983, 'Corporal punishment was
to be struck from the punitive arsenal and schools were to substitute
suspension as the measure of the 'last resort' (Slee, p.134). This has
now replaced corporal punishment as cause for concern. Numbers are
rising, partly because of the abolition of corporal punishment and also
because of modifications to suspension procedures which have
enabled schools to exclude pupils more easily. However, there are
other reasons pointing to the increase in rates of suspensions in
Australia, or exclusions in Britain, in the aftermath of abolishing corporal punishment which have been noted in the previous chapter and
are explored in the conclusion. At this point we shall continue examining the pattern of abolition across Australia.

Like Victoria, New South Wales moved to abolition in 1987 under a
Labour government, supported by the political pressure exerted by the
Executive of the New South Wales Teachers' Federation and lobbying
from Parents and Teachers Against Violence in Education (Slee).
Abolition was seen within the general context of reducing family
violence, which is how the issue has been conceptualised in parts of
Europe. Two years later, however, the *Fair Discipline* Code (1989)[28]
authorized schools to reintroduce the disciplinary sanction if there
was sufficient community response. This time both boys and girls are
eligible and regulations limit use of the cane to four strikes a day for
any one pupil (*Sydney Morning Herald,* 1988). This suggests a rather
confusing and contradictory political climate in which abolition of
corporal punishment was, and still is, taking place in New South
Wales, due in part to a change to a liberal government and possible
attempts at popularised policy, (*Sydney Morning Herald,* 1989a). A
survey conducted at this time into the effectiveness of the Code
revealed, however, that the reality of abolition of corporal punishment

was likely to be accepted since: 'results from the teachers' surveys and the public meetings indicated a very low level of support for corporal punishment' (Conway, Tierney and Schofield, 1991, p.36).

However, a different result was discovered when parents were surveyed, since 'almost half the parents supported this discipline measure for *other* people's children' (*ibid.*).

The option of reintroducing corporal punishment in the Code was subsequently removed in the *Education Reform Amendment* (School Discipline) Act (1995). Abolition now has application for all state schools; and it is a requirement of registration for private ones (*Sydney Morning Herald,* 1997a). Some religious schools have strongly opposed this regulation, citing biblical support, for the need to use physical chastisement (*Sydney Morning Herald,* 1997b).

The politics of corporal punishment reveal that pressure group lobbying, as in Britain, also contributed towards a climate conducive to abolition in Australia, but in keeping with the traditional pattern of educational development in Australia, the centralist control of states was significant. Consequently,

> all states were responsive to local lobbies... but discipline policy was shaped at the centre and delivered as instruction to schools... Abolition was typically seen as an imposition to be resisted (Slee, pp.141-142).

Phasing out the practice was an approach adopted by South Australia beginning, initially, at primary level while at the same time exploring alternative sanctions during the 'cultural shift' as abolition took effect, through to secondary school level in 1991 (*ibid.*, p.142). Schools also received copies of guidelines on policy, an implementation kit and for networking purposes, a *Directory of Schools with Good Practices.*

Likewise, Queensland joined the majority of Australian states, moving to abolition by 1995, and accompanied with support for practitioners.

> Teachers would be provided with in-service education on alternative methods of school discipline; [and be] given two extra student-free days during the year which would be devoted to student behaviour management (ibid., p.143).

This contrasts markedly with the experience of British teachers who were given no specific guidance but were instead expected to develop policy on alternative sanctions within the course of other educational imperatives thrown up by a barrage of educational reform at the time.[29] Significantly, the Director-General of Education in Queensland admitted that even with the availability of the cane there had been on-going problems of behaviour which justified more resources and support for teachers (Scott, 1992).

Finally, Tasmania followed the example of other Australian states by investigating the problem of discipline in schools, this time in the form of *Student Behaviour of Serious Concern* (1990). This was accompanied by a move towards a more inclusive and comprehensive policy which rejected one single strategy as an answer to school discipline and, instead, contemplated an holistic examination of the school culture in order to develop a supportive environment (Slee). However, abolition of corporal punishment in this state has still not been legally achieved as a motion calling for an end to the practice was recently defeated. It thus remains available if agreed by a school community although take-up is not great. This is due in part to the fact that the Tasmanian branch of the Australian Education Union is advising its members that corporal punishment may be in contravention of child protection legislation, and that it will not provide legal support for any teacher challenged over the use of physical chastisement.[30]

Unlike Britain, reform in Australia was initiated by political rather than judicial will. This was accompanied by government reports and pressure group lobbying supportive of change. In the movement towards abolition of corporal punishment in Australian schools, individual states engaged in policy-making on discipline which was invariably perceived as threatening the traditional authority of teachers. Schools were encouraged to look beyond a narrow concept of control and instead engage in broader debates concerning school culture, power relations and democratic models of school management. In some cases, despite progressive policy on corporal punishment there was still an inclination to rely on punitive mechanisms such as suspension, as teaching associations and school communities needed to feel assured that authority was still in place before a policy shift could occur. However, many Australian schools have gone on to explore alternative disciplinary sanctions which encompass concepts of self-discipline, and democratic participation.

Conclusion

The underlying trend in international developments in the field of human rights suggests that the child is to be afforded equal protection to adults under the law. This trend carries with it major implications for child welfare and family law. The dignity and integrity of the person will continue to be at the forefront of the debate on children's rights, especially since judicial corporal punishment has been decreed inappropriate for adults. The Strasbourg Court has demonstrated its unwillingness to accept school-based corporal punishment and has seized the opportunity to bring Britain into line with the social policy of the rest of Europe, as noted earlier in this chapter.

Similarly, recent developments in South Africa have led to abolition, and America and Australia have both moved closer to a nation-wide ban. There is clearly discernible an international dissemination of legal norms which can serve as a mechanism of social control, responsive to changing popular ideologies, and influencing social policy and practice.

Ironically, at a time of concern over violence in society and the general rejection of corporal punishment as a disciplinary sanction, counter arguments have been raised. In America, there have been calls for a return to old-fashioned discipline in schools (Cryan, 1995); and in Britain, members of the former Conservative government have proposed the return of the cane in schools (Parker-Jenkins, 1996). This flies in the face of work being done to ensure the physical integrity of pupils and to move away from punitive measures.

Asserting the rights of the child, distinct from and sometimes in conflict with those of the parent as well as the teacher, is becoming more commonplace in European courts. There have been attempts to forge a link between physical chastisement and child abuse which clearly sits uncomfortably in the school milieu. Corporal punishment is contrary to the philosophy underpinning recently developed notions of children's rights, which is discussed next.

Notes

1. Maurer (1984) *1001 Alternatives to Corporal Punishment* p.5.

2. *Mrs X and Ms X v UK* (1981) Application no. 9471/81) European Commission of Human rights, Decision as to Admissibility 13 March 1984; 166th Session Minutes 5-16 March 1984 DH 984); *Childright* (1987) No. 42, Nov-Dec, 5.

3. See King (1969), Cook (1974), Elvin (1981) and Mallinson (1980) on the histories of education in Europe.

4. Maurer (1984) p.5.

5. *Ibid.*

6. *Blom v Sweden (1982)* (Application No. 8811/79) Report of the European Commission of Human Rights, decision as to Admissibility 13 May 1982.

7. See for example *Council of Europe Committee of Ministers Recommendation*, R1985/44; *Council of Europe Conference on the Evolution of the Role of Children in Family Life* 1994.

8. As cited in *EPOCH* (1996), p4.

9. See also Bonner, P., Delius, P. And Posel, D. (Eds.)(1993) *Apartheid's Genesis 1935-1962*, Braamfontein; Wits University Press.

10. *S v. Meewis* (1970) (4) SA 532 (T).

11. *S v. William and others:* (1995) (3) SA 632.

12. *Tyrer v. UK* (1978) European Court of Human Rights, Series A, No. 26, 25 April

13. *Campbell and Cosans v. UK* (1982) No's 48 and 60, 25 Feb 1982 and 22 March 1983.

14. *Ingraham v. Wright* (1997) US Supreme Court Reports 430 (annotated 51).

15. *Constitution Act* (1996) section X.

16. *Ingraham v Wright* (1977). US Supreme Court Reports 430 (annotated 51).

17. Bloom, S (1995) 'Spare the Rod, Spoil the Child: A Legal Framework for recent Corporal Punishment Proposals', *Golden Gate University Law Review*, Vol. 25, No 1, p.369.

18. *Ingraham v. Wright* (1977) US Supreme Court Reports 430 (annotated 51).

19. *Goss v Lopez* (1975) 419 U.S.

20. *Re: Gault*, U.S. Supreme Court. Report (annotated) vol 18, (U.S 387).

21. *Re: Winship* (1970) U.S. Supreme Court Reports vol.25 (U.S 397).

22. *Tinker v Des Moines*, U.S. Supreme Court Reports (annotated vol.21 (U.S. 393).

23. *Smyth v. O'Byrne* (1984) Ex Parte O'Byrne, 5 Q.L.J. 125, pp. 126-127.

24. *Connor v McDonald* (1912) 6 Q.J.P. 119.

25. *Craig v. Frost* (1936) 30 Q.J.P. 14018.

26. *King v Nichols* (1936) Q.J.P. 171.

27. *Corporal Punishment Bill* (1985), London: HMSO, Bill 57.

28. *Fair discipline Code*: Guidelines for Discussion by Government School Communities (1989), New South Wales: NSW Dept. Of Education.

29. The abolition of corporal punishment in Britain came into effect one year before the *Education Reform Act* (1988) which had major impact on schools with the introduction of the National Curriculum. This ended a decade of educational legislation which called for changes in the delivery, organisation, management and funding of schools. See Jeffs (1995) for more on this theme.

30. I am indebted here to research student Michael McIntyre of McQuarrie University, New South Wales who confirmed this data on Australia as of January 1998, and to the Tasmanian branch of the *Australian Education Union*, for explaining the situation regarding the current use of corporal punishment in the state.

Chapter 6

Children's Rights

Children may be smaller than we are, but their rights must weigh as heavily as our own' (Leach 1994 p.224).

Should children's rights weigh as heavily as those of adults? What effect do such claims have on other members of society; and what should be the extent of children's rights in school? An underlying theme of the British corporal punishment cases taken to the European Court is that of 'children's rights'. The Court's juris-prudence has been important for what it implies of children's rights, particularly with regard to the school context and the authority of the teacher. This chapter explores the growth of the children's rights movement; the concept of 'the child' and childhood; the basis upon which entitlements are justified and the notion of 'rights' applied to children. Finally, the discussion focuses on the challenge which children's rights present to teachers and the implications this raises for schools.

The Growth of the Children's Rights Movement

The children's rights movement is an international feature of the 20th century,[1] but its roots can be traced to earlier times. The *Children's Petitions* of 1669 were, in a sense, an attempt to single out children as a special need category and specifically to call for restricting corporal punishment by teachers. The anonymous author of the first petition claimed that:

> The man who is not able to awe and keep a company of youth in obedience without violence and stripes, should judge himself no more fit for that function, than if he had no skill in Latin or Greek'.[2]

Although early attempts to challenge physical chastisement failed, the issue did not disappear and concern over children's welfare continued. Pioneers of the 19th century such as Lord Shaftesbury and writers such as Kingsley and Dickens aimed to awaken the nation's conscience by highlighting the plight of children in Britain and calling for shorter hours and improved work conditions for young children in factories. Whilst these developments were more in the name of children's best interests rather than their 'rights', they laid the foundation of a movement which was to modify the traditional status of children *vis-à-vis* adults.

Early writings on children's rights demonstrate interest in the cause. More (1799) had anticipated the movement towards the recognition of 'the rights of youth, children and babies', as a natural progression of entitlement.[3] Siogvolk (1852) asked the question: 'The 'rights of man' and the 'rights of woman' have been discussed 'ad nauseam'; but who vindicates the rights of children?' (p.32).

Julie Valles (1979) dedicated her autobiographical novel:

> to all those who died of boredom at school or who were made to cry at home, who during their childhood were tyrannised by their masters or thrashed by their parents.[4]

In *Children's Rights,* Wiggin (1892) argued that 'a multitude of privileges, or rather indulgences, can exist with a total disregard of the child's right' (p.4) and concluded that 'the child has a right to a place of his own, to things of his own, to surroundings which have some relation to his size, his desires and his capabilities' (p.15).

Throughout the 20th century there has been increased concern over children's rights but not until the 1960's did the movement gain momentum and fresh impetus was provided by pupil and student militancy. Freeman (1983a) notes that 'the real impetus to children's rights is contemporaneous with the liberation and student movements of the late 1960s' (p.19). Wringe (1981) concurs that the student unrest in Britain's universities during this time had repercussions in schools, and cites as an example: a strike mounted by the Schools' Action Union in a London comprehensive school resulting in the suspension of pupils.[5] Other instances of such activity included a strike by pupils at Holland Park Comprehensive,[6] a school demonstration attended by 2,500 pupils in 1972[7] and the establishment of the National Union of School Students with the declared aim of achieving 'a greater degree of democracy in schools and ultimately a say at national level in discussion-making' (*ibid.*). Pupil militancy was supported by the development of underground literature used to publicize the issue of Children's Rights.[8] Another publication was *The Little Red School Book* (1971), translated from the Dutch, which advised children about how they could influence their own lives. With particular regard to school punishment the authors suggested that pupils 'demand your rights but be polite' (p.71).

To see the thrust for children's rights simply as a 'downward seepage' of unrest at university level is to underestimate the cause, for a number of factors were present. Wringe suggests firstly the importance of adult writers such as A.S. Neill,[9] who advocated the notion of school democracy. Similarly Firestone (1970) made clear the connection between the liberation of women and that of children, their oppressions being mutually reinforcing and entwined. Secondly, the early 1970s was important for the beginning of the 'de-schooling' debate in which writers addressed the nature of institutionalised education. Jonathan Kozol captured the essence of the mood in his book *Death At An Early Age* (1968). Archard (1993) notes the rejection of established authority and that of the school as a central institution of authority in its own right, and the means by which 'ideologies of deference to authority and hierarchy' transmitted to the young were being challenged (p.46). A third element in the children's rights movement was the support for pupil as well as teacher input into the school curriculum.[10] A fourth strand was that provided by The National Council for Civil Liberties (NCCL) which issued a series of discussion papers in 1971[11] entitled *Children Have Rights*, one of which highlighted the unsatisfactory situation of the legal position of children in relation to school authorities and the powers and responsibilities of head teachers. Finally, the NCCL passed an executive resolution in 1972 calling for active campaigning on three specific rights for school children: the abolition of corporal punishment, greater democratic participation of children in the educational process, and the right of children to determine their personal appearance in school.[12]

Reaction by teaching associations to the children's rights movement tended initially to be non-supportive. The National Union of Teachers expressed its concern over the weakening of teacher authority and the Assistant General Secretary of the National Association of School-masters claimed that: 'agitation for children's rights was based on the false premise that 'children from an early age are capable of determining what is good for them'.[13]

The only teaching association declaring itself in favour of children's rights was the left-wing splinter group of the NUT, Rank and File, which fully supported the idea of children participating in school democracy.[14] Although the 1960s and 1970s saw increasing support for recognising children as persons in their own right, there were differing views. For example, in the House of Lords debate on the *Protection of Minors Bill* (1973),[15] Lord Hale maintained that, 'generally speaking, most people are in favour of children' (p.932).

What is remarkable about this statement is that in the 1970s it needed to be said at all. It may well be that 19th century attitudes still have currency and that it cannot automatically be assumed that children in Britain are well-liked or preferred above animals. Indeed cruelty to children became a criminal offence in the country sixty years after similar legislation protecting animal rights.[16] Criticism of this ambivalent attitude is a recurring theme of the children's rights movement.

Across the Atlantic the movement also gained momentum in the 1960s, with state laws highlighting the issue of child abuse and the special needs of children. By the 1970s, notes Margolin (1978), the notion of children's rights entered debate. Gross and Gross (1977) state that this 'shift is subtle but important' since a need denotes 'dependency', and a right denotes 'equality' (p.317) and they contend that 'we have tended to err on the side of protecting children, often to the degree of infringing their rights' (*ibid.*). By the 1970s, the movement for children's rights was taking form in the United States as young people were perceived to be 'the most oppressed of all minorities' (*ibid.*, p.1.). The movement covered a wide range of issues, and in schools, for example, compulsory attendance and lack of choice within the curriculum were key areas of concern (*ibid.*, p.3.). Initially, states Margolin, 'children in trouble' were the focus of attention but then interest grew to include children in 'intact' homes' (p.445). He concludes that in America, the children's rights movement has been largely concerned with the notion of 'due process', school desegregation, school discipline and freedom of expression.[17]

The cases of *Re Gault*,[18] *Tinker*,[19] *Re Winship*[20] and *Ingraham v Wright*,[21] noted in the previous chapter address some of these issues, and in a piecemeal manner human rights were gradually extended to American children.

International Treaties on Children's Rights

International recognition of children's rights has been expressed in the form of charters and declarations throughout the 20th Century. Chanlett and Morier (1968) state that 'the concept that a child has rights is of relatively recent vintage', for until 1914 the focus had been on 'the duties of children to parents and society, but never any question of rights they might be entitled to' (p.4). In the aftermath of the First World War, organisations were formed to help with relief, one of which was Eglantyne Jebb's Save the Children dealing with the problems of minors (*ibid.*). This was followed by the Save the Children International Union in Geneva 1920 and four years later Jebb presented to this organisation a charter specifically concerned with children's rights. This 'Declaration of the Rights of Geneva' was adopted on September 24th 1924 by the fifth Assembly of the League of Nations. It embodied in the broadest sense the 'basic principles of child welfare, leaving appropriate action to each country, within its needs and resources' (*ibid.*, p.4). In 1934 the League of Nations confirmed the principles of the Declaration, one of which pertained specifically to education.

> The child must receive a training which will enable it to earn a livelihood, and must be protected against every form of exploitation.[22]

The Universal Declaration of Human Rights (1948)[23] was silent about children's rights and it was not until 1959 that the situation was rectified. The preamble to the new document, entitled *the United Nations Declaration of the Rights of the Child*[24] states in its preamble that 'by reason of his physical and mental immaturity' the child requires 'special safeguards and care, including appropriate legal protection before as well as after birth' (*ibid.*, p.6). As a general principle the document states that 'mankind owes to the child the best it has to give' (*ibid.*). Principle One declares that the child should enjoy 'the rights set forth' and the preliminary statement calls for 'parents ... voluntary organisations, local authorities and national governments to recognise these rights and strive for their observance by legislative and other means' (*ibid.*). Ten principles are proclaimed within the document, number seven of which specifies that 'the child is entitled to receive education, which shall be free and compulsory, at least in the elementary stages'(*ibid.*, p.7). Principle two provides that

> *the child shall enjoy special protection*, and shall be given opportunities and facilities, by law and by other means, to enable him *to develop physically in a healthy and normal manner and in conditions of freedom and dignity. In the enactment of laws for this purpose the best interest of the child shall be the paramount consideration* (*ibid.*, p.6, emphasis added).

It is noteworthy that as far back as 1959, declarations of children's rights were written in terms of child-rearing in 'conditions of dignity'. This theme is echoed more recently in several of the Strasbourg decisions discussed in chapter 3.

Whilst the 1959 Declaration of the Children's Rights highlights 'rights and freedoms', it only expresses 'principles'. Freeman (1983a) describes these as deliberately vague as to what rights children should have, and as to who should bear the correlative duties. In fact, the 1924, 1948 and 1959 declarations of children's rights are noteworthy 'by their simplicity of language' and inadequate enforcement (Chanlett and Morier, p.7). Similarly, Bel Geddes (1977) states that for the most part principles concerning the rights tend not to be legal documents, they rarely have enforcement; the European Convention is a notable exception. Instead they provide an ideal situation in which they may say 'too little about means and a lot about ends'.[25] Freeman (1983b) describes many of the documents of children's rights as containing 'blueprints rather than reasoned arguments' (p.19).

In the 1970s a variety of documents were written demonstrating the continued desire to recognise and promote and also to enforce rights.

The Advisory Centre for Education (ACE) published a *Draft Charter of Children's Rights* in 1971, convinced that 'more than any other group, children need special protection and special facilities' (p.105). (Whether children do in fact need 'protection' or 'rights' is a controversial point considered later.) ACE also contends that 'our society does not readily recognise children's rights' and that greater effort is needed to rectify the situation (*ibid.*). Accordingly, the proposed draft was intended to provoke discussion of 'the way we treat children and the way we *should* treat children' (*ibid.*). In 1972 the NCCL issued a 'Bill of Rights for Children' which included a range of rights from 'the right to receive parental love' to the right to be recognised 'as a person.' Similarly Foster and Freed published an American *Bill of Rights for Children* (1972) with a main concern not to remove from children 'moral and legal obligations but... to enhance their sense of responsibility' (p.344). In Canada the Berger Commission (1975) advocated a Bill of Rights for children which would provide enforcement and legal obligations,[26] and the decade culminated in the International Year of the Child in 1979.

The drafting of the *United Nations Convention on the Rights of the Child*[27] started in 1978 and was completed in 1989, containing many principles expressed in earlier documents and representing what is currently 'world consensus on the status of the child' (Freeman, 1992, p.70). The importance of education is recognised in Article 15(1) which calls for: 'the right of the child to education... with a view to achieving the full realisation of this right on the basis of equal opportunity.' Of particular relevance here is the second subsection of this article which adds:

> States Parties shall take all appropriate measures to ensure that school discipline is administered in a manner reflective of the child's dignity (15(2)).

The article clearly echoes the language of the European Court in the cases of *Campbell and Cosan*[28] and *Tyrer*[29]. Further, Article 10 of the document provides for

> the right of the child to freedom of thought, conscience and religion... [and]... the liberty of the child and his parents... to ensure the religious and moral education of the child in conformity with convictions of their choice' (10(3)).

Once again the jurisprudence of the European Court is reflected in the sentiments of this provision with regard to educational rights. Conflict could arise out of this article, however, if the convictions of the child are not compatible with those of the parents. It is also unclear which party's rights in such a dispute, should take primacy. It is believed that the UN draft will go further than previous documents in that 'it sets out positive rights for children as individuals'.[30] Franklin describes it as 'the most significant policy development intended to promote children's rights' (p.16), and John (1995) sums it up as containing entitlement to prevention, provision, protection and participation. Finally, as with the *European Convention on Human Rights* there have been calls for the *UN Declaration of the Rights of the Child* to be incorporated into domestic law (Freeman, 1992). In 1991 Britain eventually ratified the document subject to a number of reservations, such as the placement of young people in custody with adults.

In addition to international declarations of 'children's rights', there are a range of European charters, such as the *European Convention on Human Rights*,[31] which have particular relevance to minors. The Children's Legal Centre contends that the Convention 'provides unique protection for the fundamental rights and freedoms of children and young people'.[32] This is evidenced by the cases discussed in this book but it is noteworthy that invariably the litigation is instigated at the behest of the parent.[33] A variety of European declarations concerning children's welfare have been established and in 1979 a *European Charter on the Rights of the Child*[34] was enacted, containing as its first principle:

> Children must no longer be considered as parents' property, but must be recognised as individuals with their own rights and needs (p.4).

This could include litigation being initiated by children against parents, teachers or other adults. Finally, Franklin argues persuasively that 'signing international conventions is no substitute for effective government legislation intended to promote children's rights' (p.18).

Today the notion of the children's rights is no longer unusual, yet there is still some ambivalence about the legality of such claims. International and European documents relating to children's rights abound, although enforcement has been far less rigorously defined. However, support for the 'liberation' of children has been an ongoing feature of the last three decades. In 1975 Godfrey *et al* stated that:

> this is no more a 'lunatic fringe' phenomenon. Increasingly commentators and reformers are calling for the coalition of children's rights in some legal form or another' (p.3).

Furthermore, there has of late been a shift in terminology from children's 'needs' to 'rights', and change in focus away from broad educational issues to the very specific concern of 'child abuse', which at times has been associated with corporal punishment. The children's rights movement provides a plethora of issues, each group within it often defining one particular concern. For example, the Society of Teachers Opposed to Physical Punishment had one central aim of abolition which, as mentioned in chapter 3, was achieved within maintained schools by 1987.The Children's Legal Centre, Justice for Children, and the Family Rights Group focus their attention on lobbying for a variety of causes. Accordingly, no one policy emerges from the movement; rather it appears as a collection of deeply committed advocates recommending complementary proposals to enhance the welfare of the child.

The Concept of the 'Child' and 'Childhood'

What is a 'child' and who decides? What do we mean by 'childhood' and how long should it last before adulthood begins? These two related concepts affect the acquisition of rights and privileges, and the length of dependency on adult caretakers.

Definition of 'the child' concerns the acknowledgment of a young person's ability to act independently of adults. Goldstein *et al.* (1979) state that

> in the eyes of the law, to be a *child* is to be at risk, dependent and without capacity or authority to decide, free of parental control, what is 'best' for oneself (p.7).

This contrasts with the status of an *adult* who is 'presumed by law to have the capacity, authority and responsibility to determine, and to do, what is 'good' for one's children' (*ibid.*). The vulnerability of the child was described by Bentham thus: 'the feebleness of infancy demands a continual protection. Too sensitive to present impulses, too negligent of the future, such a being must be kept under an authority more immediate than that of the laws...' (p.248). That 'more immediate authority' is normally the parent or an adult caretaker. Margolin adds that 'notions of childhood as a period of helplessness and protected growth are entrenched' (p.448), and have provided justification for treating young people differently from adults. The age at which a child ceases to require adult supervision is claimed by many to be arbitrary in determination. Freeman (1983a), for example, maintains that:

> children are by definition not adults, even if the dividing line between the two is relatively arbitrary, a historical and shifting social construction. Much depends on what is understood by being an adult, for it is certainly the case that arguments used to deny children and adolescents rights, can equally well be produced to deny those of mature years those very same rights (p.1).

Likewise Wiggin states that the age of 'discretion' or majority is 'that highly uncertain period which arises very late in life with some persons and not at all with others' (p.5). However, Foster and Freed suggest that whilst the specific age of majority is 'a carry over from feudal times, and perhaps anachronistic', there is the need for an 'age line' to be delineated (p.345). 'Legislatures and courts are not unreasonable in taking an average age as regards a particular function, as long as the age set is not completely out of kilter with custom and mores' (*ibid.*). Freeman suggests, that 'age' may be used to justify 'a double standard' in the treatment of adults and children, in which the child's 'incapacity or lack of maturity' necessitates special protection for him or her (p.45). For example, 'we expect adolescents to be criminally responsible at the age of fourteen... but we are less willing to accept correlativity of responsibility and rights' (p.46).

Associated with this discussion over what constitutes a child is the concept of childhood. The notion of 'childhood' is of fairly recent vintage states Aries (1962), and the concept has different meanings at different times in history. He maintains that:

> in medieval society the idea of childhood did not exist; this is not to suggest that children were neglected, forsaken or despised. The idea of childhood is not to be confused with affection for children:

it corresponds to an awareness of the particular nature of child-hood... which distinguishes the child from the adult... In medieval society, this awareness was lacking' (p.125).

The lack of clear definition between the age of minority and majority in previous centuries concerned the changing notion of childhood. Holt (1974) describes age categorisation as 'the curve of life' which has been divided into two parts: one called childhood and the other adulthood or maturity (p.21). This sentiment is captured in Corin-thians:

When I was a child, I spoke as a child,
I understood as a child,
I thought as a child
But when I became a man, I put away childish things (1,13).

The division or 'Great Divide' of human life has caused people to think that 'the people on opposite sides of this divide, the children and adults, are very different' (Holt, p.21). This has been supported by work in psychology in which Freud and Piaget, for example, 'have emphasised the importance of childhood and its difficulties in that the child is believed not to have obtained a level of adult competence' (Thane, 1995, p.22). Moreover, child psychology provides 'further links in the long chain of justification to adult control' (*ibid.*). This is supported by rosy images of childhood, which are by no means shared by everyone.

Contrast these two views of childhood. Goodman in 'Reflections on Children's Rights' (1977) suggests that the concept of childhood is of fairly recent origin, of gradually refining civilisation rather than a device of malevolent exploitation. Accordingly, 'the key terms are not children's 'rights' or 'democracy' but their spontaneity, fantasy, animality, creativity, innocence' (pp.142-3).

Alternatively, Holt in *Escape from Childhood* (1974) regards the insti-tution of 'childhood' as being:

all those attitudes and feelings, and also customs and laws, that put a great gulf or barrier between the young and their elders, and the world of their elders; ... that lock the young into eighteen years or more of subservience and dependency, and make of them... a mixture of expensive nuisance, fragile treasure, slave and super-pet' (p.22).

This latter view challenges the notion of childhood as one of a 'Golden Age'. As Firestone (1979) suggests in 'Down with Childhood' (p.42), 'the myth of childhood flourishes so widely not because it satisfies the needs of children but because it satisfies the needs for adults', and he concludes that: 'Children are repressed at every waking minute. Childhood is hell!' (p.50).

Another way of looking at childhood is in terms of children's relationship with society. The institutional concept of childhood is described as 'a legal or quasi-legal one which in modern society is usually defined by chronological age' but may elsewhere depend on such variables as undertaking initiation ceremonies (Wringe, p.88). It is the 'institutional concepts of childhood moreover, which drastically affect, or... are actually defined by an individual's positive rights' (*ibid.*). Conversely, the 'normative' concept of childhood is employed when discussing the notion of what is right and wrong. This concept 'is connected with certain capacities, the acquisition of certain elements of knowledge and experience, ... or reasonable expectations about a person's likely behaviour at certain stages of development' (*ibid.*). Whether described as 'institutional' or 'normative', the existence of childhood is generally perceived as an interlude before adulthood. Wiggin argues that 'one of [the child's] inalienable rights, which we too often deny him, is the right to his childhood' (p.10).

Finally, some groups do not fit within the concept of childhood. For example, street children have been described as 'outside of childhood', and notions of happiness, play and innocence within the conventional family model do not exist, for they function in the context of forced independence and powerlessness which renders them particularly vulnerable (Ennew, 1995). Indeed their basic 'right to life' can be at stake! Furthermore the label 'children' belies the responsibilities they have forced upon them.

What's in a name?

In addition to the debate over the concept of childhood a host of terms are used to describe the person who has not yet reached the age of majority: 'young persons', 'babies', 'infants', 'children', 'youths', 'minors', 'adolescents', 'pupils' and 'teenagers'. Furthermore, the question 'what is a child?' is answered by adults, who 'impose their conceptions of childishness on beings whom they consider to be children' (Freeman, 1983a, p.7). Adults may not necessarily be well placed to determine clearly the definition of a child, since they may have 'less contact with children now than in medieval times [for] our society is marked by greater segregation of ages than earlier societies were' (pp.7-8). Likewise Farson (1978) argues that ideas of childhood are being 'developed and reinforced not through contact between adults and children, but through lack of it' (p.22).

Franklin (1995) notes that the term 'child' was initially used to describe someone of low status and that being a child says more about power relationships, limited access to economic resources, and exclusion from political participation. As such he sees the terms 'child' and 'childhood' as articulating society's attitudes towards children which are both ageist and negative.

Academic and statutory authorities attempt to provide an answer to the question 'what is a child?' The draft copy of the *United Nations Convention on the Rights of the Child* states that 'a child is every human being to the age of 18 years unless, under the law of his State, he has attained his age of majority earlier' (Article 1).

This view is reflected in British legislation such as the *Education (No.2) Act* (1986)[35] which states with reference to the prohibition of corporal punishment that a pupil is any person who is under eighteen (section 47(5c)). Similarly, the *Family Law Reform Act* (1969)[36] stipulated that a child becomes an adult in the eyes of the law when he/she has reached eighteen, the age of majority. Wringe states that part of the controversy surrounding the children's rights movement has not been about whether a child can have rights of freedom but whether particular individuals or groups of individuals 'are in fact still children... or whether they are, morally speaking, adults being treated as children in conformity with misapplied institutional labels' (p.107). The answer to this varies, for across different cultural groups, age limits designating childhood are socially constructed and are relative to other factors affecting the organisation of society.

Legally therefore the age of eighteen in Britain and elsewhere generally determines the point at which a person is no longer classified as a 'child'. It makes no allowance for different maturity levels, nor does it require competence tests to assume adult rights. The label 'child' can be used for both the day-old baby and the seventeen-year old. Not only is childhood perpetuated within an ideology of happiness and safety, but a situation has developed in which through the raising of the school age, and alterations in social security benefits, we now have a prolonged adolescent dependency on adults. Further, there are ambiguities in the concept of 'child', with legal responsibility being determined at a much earlier age than the commensurate autonomy in decision-making or the recognition of rights. Finally, childhood in Western societies serves as a part of the life-cycle, a social construct shifting through historical and cultural change. It does not require a rite of passage in terms of 'an initiation ceremony', but instead formal proof of an eighteenth birthday in order to assume adult rights and privileges.

Justification of Children's Rights

Are children denied rights in law which are morally theirs, or are we taking the issue of children's rights too far? If children have more rights, does this mean that adults have fewer? These are some of the questions we need to consider when justifying children's rights and the implications they have for teacher authority and family autonomy.

Theories about children's rights have tended to be polarised, protection or paternalism versus liberation or self-determination. Traditional values put forward to justify children's rights have involved the 'protectionist theory'. Hobbes described the status of children in the 17th century as 'like the imbecile, the crazed and the beasts, over... children there is no law'.

Accordingly fathers could dispose of the lives and liberties of their children as they saw fit. Locke perceived the parents' role more in the nature of protection and nurture: 'all Parents were, by the Law of Nature, under an obligation to preserve, nourish and educate the children they had begotten'.

John Stuart Mill stated that 'the only purpose for which power can be rightfully exercised over any member of civilised community, against his will, is to prevent harm to others.' This might appear a promising line of approach for justifying children's rights, but he entered a caveat that 'it is, perhaps hardly necessary to say that this doctrine is meant to apply to human beings in the maturity of their faculties. We are not speaking of children, or of young persons below the age which the law may fix as that of manhood or womanhood'.[37] Moreover, Mill stated that the power of the state over children's lives could be justified since 'the existing generation is master both of the training and the entire circumstances of the generation to come'.[38]

Of the traditional theorists Freeman notes that:

> only in Locke are there really any hints of children's rights and these are muted. Yet within Locke are the seeds of a liberal paternalism which... can be used to justify children's rights (p.54).

'Paternalism' has been used to justify intervention into a person's private life for that person's best interests. The problem inherent in the children's rights movement is the *degree of intervention* by parents, adults or state agencies. While the issue of children's rights provokes complex problems with no easy solutions, a fine balance is required, continues Freeman, 'so that the personality and autonomy of children are recognised and they are not abandoned to their rights' [p.i]. Moreover he argues that 'a child has rights whether or not he is capable of exercising any autonomy' (p.57). Protection of children is necessary, therefore, only until they become rational autonomous agents, and justification rests on this vulnerability.

> Talk of children's rights in the twentieth century has predominantly been couched in child-saving language, in terms of 'salvation'. It has usually referred to children's rights, but its essential concern has been with protecting children, rather than their rights (pp.18-19).

The need to protect children which provided the justification for much of the early child legislation of the 19th century mentioned earlier in this chapter, originally focused on conditions of the workplace and the needs of schooling. Today this theory has been extended into the home and, some would say, threatens to violate family autonomy.

Margolin notes that 'the early child-savers were concerned with special needs, but contemporary liberationists stress equality' (p.446).

Notions of equality are found in a further theory of rights conceived in terms of liberation and self-determination. The American writer Holt (1974) is a fervent advocate of this philosophy which is concerned with the proposal that young people be given 'the rights, privileges, duties and responsibilities' normally available to adults (p.15). This theory gives children 'the right to do, in general, what any adult may legally do' (p.16). Holt sees himself as belonging to the school of advocates interested in protecting children's rights rather than in protecting children *per se*. The 'liberation' approach to children's rights calls for their rights to be equal to that of adults and, as proposed by Holt, this includes voting and contractual rights. Similarly, Farson (1978) states, overriding all 'birth rights' is the right of 'self-determination' and believes that 'children, like adults, should have the right to decide the matters which affect them most directly' (p.27). He anticipates opposition to such an idea from those who are closest to the situation, parents and teachers.

So far we see a dichotomy between 'protecting' children and protecting their 'rights' but the two need not be mutually exclusive. The liberationist case proposed by Holt and Farson has received severe criticism for the degree to which it would extend children's rights. Freeman sees it as doing the cause disservice, for it is 'grist for the media's mill which, on the whole, would ridicule the whole notion of children's rights,' and due to such theories of child liberation, 'it is easy to dismiss the credibility of the whole argument for children's rights' (1983a, p.3).

A further theory of children's rights is that contained within Freeman's model of 'liberal paternalism'. He contends that:

> the general justification of children's rights lies within an overarching theory of human rights. A theory of human rights requires the treatment of persons as equals. It expresses a normative attitude of respect for individual autonomy' (p.54).

Whilst there is an element of paternalism in Freeman's theory, he argues that when children display capability of rational autonomy, they should be entitled to a more liberal type of treatment. In brief, this theory can be described as quasi-paternalistic, drawing on both paternalism and liberalism.

If we look at recent legislation we see a shift from concern with protecting children to protecting their rights. *The Children Act* (1989) was introduced as the most comprehensive and far-reaching reform of child care law in living memory.[39] Prior to this, note Lyon and Parton (1995), English law was 'too reliant on notions of welfare paternalism which viewed children as defenceless.... and in need of protection by state agents.... who knew what was in children's interest' (p.41). There was no attempt to desegregate the rights of the child as distinct from those of the parents. The 1989 Act was the first attempt to redress this balance and 'the first English Law in which children's rights are taken seriously and not simply identified within a unified notion of welfare' (*ibid.*). 'Parental responsibility' rather than 'parental rights' is a key characteristic of the legislation, a move which implies 'a re-conceptualisation of children as persons to whom duties are owed, rather than as possessions over which power is exercised' (*ibid.*).

Accommodating children's views, recognising their ability to act independently, and giving special attention to the older 'child', ie 16-17, all feature within the 1989 Act. This can be seen potentially to challenge and diminish the rights of adults. Lyon and Parton note:

> The way children's rights are framed in the legislation is not primarily concerned with improving the rights of children *per se*, but in providing a legal mechanism for opening up the private household, and parental behaviour in particular, and thereby making the family more visible to social regulation (p.40).

Following this line of argument, welfare professionals such as teachers and social workers are also more likely to come under scrutiny and be more accountable for their decisions in relation to children and their rights.

Defining the Concept of 'Rights'

Before considering some of the rights advocated for children it is useful to examine the notion of 'rights' *per se* and to set the ambiguity which surrounds the concept in a philosophical context. Further particular reference is made to the context of the school and how the child's right not to be subjected to sanctions such as corporal punishment limits the rights of the teacher.

Rodham (1973) describes children's rights as 'a slogan in search of a definition' (p.487). Six years later she observes that 'although that search is still continuing, there has been significant progress in our efforts to define and achieve children's rights.' Freeman (1983a) states that discussion of children's rights is 'essentially ambiguous' embracing 'a number of disparate notions' (p.72), (as highlighted in this chapter). Accordingly, it is important to attempt definition of the term 'rights' and separate it from other terminology before considering what rights children should be entitled to.

The term 'rights' is suffuse with connotations of moral and legal rights, liberties and freedom, positive and negative claims and entitlements. It is used by campaigners lobbying for a host of different causes within society. The application of the term 'rights' to the category of children, causes further confusion. This is because, state Gross and Gross:

> The rights of children is an abstract, general, legalistic concept. It is an idea, an ideal, at best an affirmation of principle. It does not help children until it is put into practice (p.7).

For Rodham (1979) the phrase refers to a series of relations: the family, society and juvenile-orientated institutions, against which claims can be made. Freeman adds that children's rights is 'a phrase that continues to be used imprecisely' as it tends to be 'something of a catch-all idea embracing different notions' (p.32). Furthermore, when the different rights are reviewed 'it becomes apparent they are conceptually sub-divided into categories and that they are urged against different persons and have different enforcement problems' (*ibid*.). (Some of these categories are discussed later in the chapter.) She points out that:

> when we talk of children's rights we are often not talking of legal or institutional rights at all. We are referring most often to moral... rights, usually in the sense of ideal rights, against those who make society's rules, usually that is the legislature, to convert their moral right into a positive legal one (*ibid*., p.35).

So it is arguable that the abolition of corporal punishment in schools was a moral right for pupils, converted into a legal right by virtue of the pressure to implement the *Campbell and Cosans* ruling and as manifested in the 1986 Education Act. Further, states Freeman, 'many references to children's rights turn out on inspection to be aspirations for the accomplishment of particular social or moral goals' (p.37). Again, this is applicable to the desire to abolish corporal punishment which was for many a 'social or moral goal.' Furthermore, anti-discrimination legislation has tended to express the language of aspiration, of how we expect people should be treated.

A definition of the term 'human rights', states Hunter (1979), can be broad in scope, in order 'to throw a mantle of respectability around whatever private interest is being espoused at the moment', or narrow, 'focusing on what might more accurately be called anti-discrimination legislation' (p.78). Fairweather (1979) classifies human rights as

> rights, liberties and freedoms [which] define the relationships between an individual or group and the state and between individuals and groups themselves (p.309).

There is an important distinction to be made between 'rights, liberties and freedoms'. A 'liberty' tends to be very broad in nature, and enables a person to do anything which is not specifically prohibited by law. The words 'freedom' and 'liberty' are often used interchangeably. Fundamental freedoms which are stated in a Bill of Rights, such as that proposed for the United Kingdom, normally include freedom of religion and freedom of assembly.[40] A 'right' is more narrowly defined, and is something granted to a person which requires positive action on the part of the government to ensure it – such as the 'right to education', discussed in chapters 2 and 3. Further, the word 'rights' is an umbrella which incorporates political, legal and egalitarian rights, which were noted in the previous section concerning the justification of children's rights. Finally, Wasserstrom (1964) states that human rights are not absolute, in that 'there are no conditions under which they can properly be overridden' (*ibid.*). A case in point is that under the Education Act, (1986) children's rights not to be inflicted with corporal punishment is overridden under certain circumstances, such as when averting injury to people or property.[41]

Discussion of 'rights' also brings into question the correlative with 'duties'. Feinberg (1966) delineates ten kinds of duties: including duties of respect, status and obedience (pp.137-142).[42] Of particular relevance to this book is his argument that:

> a duty, whatever else it be, is something required of one. That is to say first of all that a duty, like an obligation, is something that *obliges*. It is something we conceive of as *imposed* upon our inclinations, something we must do *whether we want to or not* (p.140).

Teachers may now be said to have a duty to refrain from corporally punishing their pupils whether they 'want to or not'. Unless that is, they are prepared to accept the consequences, or what Feinberg calls the 'liability'. Similarly, the notion of 'duty' has application for 'the right to education'. This right, as discussed in chapter 3, often implies obligations and duties on the part of the state and schools to provide education for children of a certain age and also imposes duties on the child to adhere to school regulations. Contradictory and confusing ideas have been expressed in education policy in the past decade regarding duties. The Government has espoused the notion of children's and parents' rights but has said very little as to their responsibilities. Conversely teachers have been bombarded with demands, increasing their responsibilities but there has been mostly silence as to their rights and we will return to this issue later. But there is still one way in which rights can be delineated, and that is as substantive and procedural rights. The former refers to legal claims such as the right to education as stipulated under the *European Convention on Human Rights*. The latter ensures fairness during the process of decision making. King and Trowell (1992) note that:

> the concept of procedural rights may extend to any situation where adults have power over children's lives, such as schools... and may require some complaints procedure to enable the child's grievances to be heard (p.116).

This point that the principle of 'due process' should be incorporated into disciplinary policy and codes of conduct was raised in chapter 4. Finally, there is the issue of setting aside other people's rights. Wringe contends that though... in certain circumstances it may be legitimate or even obligatory to set aside or overrule a right, the person on the receiving end of such an action remains the victim of a wrong (p.29).

Presumably, therefore, if a child was debarred from receiving education, perhaps for unruly behaviour, the right to education might be seen as having been violated and the child becomes 'the victim of a wrong', despite the cause of the debarrement. Likewise, teachers may be perceived as 'the victims of a wrong' now that education legislation effectively fetters their Common Law right to administer corporal punishment. The abolition of corporal punishment might well be seen, therefore, as the overruling of one group's rights for 'the greater good' of another. Teachers may feel that the loss of their right to administer corporal punishment is a 'wrong', or a legitimate 'right' has been unfairly overruled. Thus the issue of corporal punishment in schools serves as a useful example for exploring the concept of rights and the various ways in which the term may be applied, limited or imposed on others. For the purpose of this discussion, therefore, we can summarise that a 'right' may be defined as a claim or entitlement to an action or service which may be legally enforceable and may place obligations on others to uphold.

Specific Rights Advocated for Children

We turn now to exploring specific rights recommended for children. Advocates of the children's rights movement maintain that there are several important rights which children are entitled to claim. These range from the child's right to be treated as a person, of equal status to that of an adult, as noted earlier in the chapter; to the right to be treated differently, in some cases deferentially with certain immunities. What the movement has brought to public attention is the belief that children do possess rights. Wringe suggests further that: 'not only are children held to have rights, but certain established practices are held to infringe these rights and to justify protest' (p.1). He argues that many of the rights advocated belong clearly to a liberal tradition of long standing. The only new characteristic in the situation is their applicability to children.

Freeman (1983a) identifies four categories of rights under the general heading of children's rights: Welfare rights, Protection rights, Rights of social justice and Rights of autonomy.

Welfare Rights

Many of the rights found in international manifestos discussed earlier may be regarded as the most fundamental of children's rights, such as education. These rights 'are not easily formulated as rights against anyone: rather they are rights against everyone' (Freeman, p.41). Accordingly, 'it is a question in each case of deciding on whom the duty falls and who is failing to carry it out' (ibid.). We saw that parents have alleged that Local Education Authorities have failed to implement 'the right to education' when their children were debarred from receiving education. Unlike other kinds of rights, there is no difficulty in applying welfare rights to children.

Rights of Protection

These focus on the vulnerability of children, especially the very young and they place a caretaker role upon parents. Further, 'when rights are spoken of in this context, it is to inject more responsibility into the parental role. This approach to children's rights is the oldest and the most firmly entrenched' (ibid.). Child abuse and corporal punishment can be categorised under protection rights. Freeman maintains that children have 'a moral right not to be beaten which the law should recognise' (p.114). He feels that it is important to abolish this practice in schools and state institutions since it would 'symbolize society's rejection of violence against children' (ibid.). Not until 1987, however, has this been achieved and then not for all children. Freeman adds, moreover, that 'protection as rights is, of course, a highly paternalistic notion' and that even when children are represented by legal counsel, 'the latter will invariably see their role as deciding what is best for the child, rather than representing the child's opinion to the court' (p.44). He contends, nevertheless, that 'whatever may be the public feeling on children's rights generally, there can be no doubt as to the strength of the sentiment supporting child protection' (pp.44-5).

Social Justice Rights

The third group is 'grounded in social justice' and is 'a claim that rights which adults have should be extended to children as well' (p.40). Freeman states that this argument is clearer to determine in countries like America where a written constitution and a Bill of Rights exist, and in which adult rights are more strictly delineated. Further, despite the absence of a constitution, 'the claim is no less important in this country' (*ibid.*). In the United Kingdom it would be difficult to itemise clearly what rights children should have in order that they be 'treated like adults', when adult rights are not easily recognisable. This situation should change as constitutional reform, as highlighted in chapter 2, ensures that human rights are entrenched within a Bill of Rights.

Autonomy Rights

The final category of rights under Freeman's model requires more freedom from control for children, a greater recognition of their capacity to choose from alternatives, and greater autonomy over their lives. Cousins (1996) proposes 'empowerment and autonomy from babyhood', which requires children to talk and adults to listen. These rights are often set against parents, for they concern 'the claim that children should be free to act independently of their parents before they reach the age of maturity' (p.48). The right to make independent decisions ranges from the relatively trivial issue of a child's appearance to those concerning where they reside. Freeman's model employs both parents and the courts in recognising the importance of a child's wishes, but also 'a workable criterion for overruling them in certain cases' (*ibid.*). He bases this right's typology on the theory of 'liberal paternalism' discussed earlier.

Rights Concerning Education

Next we turn to rights specially related to children in schools. These are drawn from international treaties and children's rights advocates (see figure 6), and a discussion of some of the main ones follows, along with the implications for teachers.

'If one assertion seems particularly fundamental to the children's rights movement it is that *children should be seen as persons in their own right*' (Wringe, p.11 emphasis added). This contrasts with the traditional assumption that children are in fact the property of their parents, a theme explored earlier in the chapter. It would appear to be the most basic of rights, for the National Council for Civil Liberties (1971) has made the point that 'children are the property of someone – if not of parents then the state'. Wringe adds that:

> in spite of their lack of legal status, it is suggested, pupils in school have a moral right to the same consideration as anyone else and the same amount of respect from their teachers as the clients of any other professional body (p.11).[43]

Figure 6: Children's Rights Concerning Schools

- The right to be seen as persons in their own right.
- The right to education.
- The right to direct and manage one's own education.
- The right not to attend school.
- The right to work for money.
- The right to freedom in personal appearance.
- The right to religious freedom.
- The right to educational democracy.
- The right to participate in school governance.
- The right to appeal, representation and redress.
- The right of access to knowledge.
- The right to freedom of thought and expression.
- The right to be free of corporal punishment.
- The right to be free of degrading or humiliating treatment or punishment.
- The right to sexual freedom.
- The right to live away from home.

The Advisory Centre for Education (ACE) maintains that children are denied even basic rights as detailed in the *United Nations Declaration of Human Rights* and conclude that children's rights 'are no greater than the rights of others and no less' (p.107). This in itself is a debatable point; it could be argued that as young children are particularly vulnerable their protection rights, as discussed earlier, may need to be greater than those afforded adults. Furthermore, the right to be taken care of consequently restrains the liberty of others, such as parents and teachers.

'The right not to attend school' is an interesting claim, given that so much is argued for 'the right to education', a service which is normally provided in some form of educational institution. Wringe states that advocates of this right see compulsory schooling in terms of the infringement of personal autonomy and schooling is perceived in terms of 'imprisonment'. Jeffs (1995) provides a very robust defence of the right not to attend school.

> Until we begin to reassess the place of compulsion within school it is difficult to see how real progress can be made with respect to extending children's rights in the context of schools... the bottom line being that they, unlike adults, have no option but 'to put up and shut up' about the way in which they are treated (p.36).

He sees compulsory school attendance as causing teachers to keep children contained against their will which contradicts their primary role as educators. We noted in chapter 4, concern over the compulsory nature of schooling and that some teachers may be serving the role of social controller rather than that of educator. This leads to the imposition of rules and management styles which 'undermine the rights, freedoms and dignity of the majority of young people' (ibid.).

The educational claim suggesting that children should be able to *direct and manage their own education*, is also associated with this issue of compulsory school attendance. Holt sees this as:

> ... the right to control and direct their own learning, that is, to decide what they want to learn, and when, where, how much, how fast, and with what help they want to learn it... the right to decide if, when, how much, and by who they want to be *taught* and the right to decide whether they want to learn in school and if so which one and for how much of the time (p.183).

He argues that 'except [for] the right to life itself', no human right is more fundamental than this educational right, since it concerns freedom of thought and expression (*ibid.*). He substantiates this by arguing:

> the requirement that a child go to school, for about six hours a day, 180 days a year, for about ten years, whether or not he learns anything there, whether or not he already knows it or could learn it faster or better somewhere else, is such a gross violation of civil liberties that few adults would stand for it (p.184).

Moreover he contends that presently there is not in fact 'the right of children to go to school' but really 'the right of the State to compel them to go whether they want it or not' (p.185). This is reflected in the Education Act (1944) which places a duty on parents to ensure their children of compulsory school age receive education. Under European law 'the right to education' has been given expression, and this has been more difficult to guarantee since the Convention, as discussed in chapter 2, is not yet entrenched within our legal system. The whole de-schooling debate concerns the legitimacy of keeping children in school and the issue of compulsion. Farson concludes that:

> school has been a babysitter. School is the place where we want children to be, we don't want them anywhere else. School serves that custodial function extremely well by incarcerating children almost all day, every day (*ibid.*).

The right to 'educational democracy' concerns pupils, their views on educational matters, and their participation through such vehicles as school councils. As those under 18 are currently excluded from serving on governing bodies, there is less opportunity for their involvement in school democracy and governance (Education Act, 1986). A great deal depends upon the individual school as to the extent of the right of the pupil's voice to be heard. It clearly makes a mockery of the concept of whole-school policy, about which Jeff remarks:

> it is difficult to envisage a more dishonest term, for any notion that 'whole school' might involve young people in a debate regarding what values could or should reside at the heart of the community, is always absent (p.34).

This right to be heard does not necessarily mean that children automatically get their own way, rather it is about ensuring they have an effective mechanism within a democratic structure to ensure that their wishes are heard. Given the key issues which schools today are facing, such as bullying, this would appear to be self-evident. Furthermore, the practicalities of pupil involvement have been explored by Holt (1995), who identifies a model of various steps on a ladder determining increasing levels of genuine participation.

The rights of appeal, representation and redress have particular relevance to the school setting since 'many specific abuses of children's supposed civil rights are held to result from the authority relationship existing in schools and in particular from the power of the head teacher' (p.13).

Wringe argues that with regard even to excessive cases of corporal punishment, for example, pupils have had little form of redress against teachers. As the cases discussed earlier in this book demonstrate, children have relied on parents who themselves have found insufficient redress within the domestic courts to instigate proceedings. Presumably, therefore, if parents did not feel strongly about the physical chastisement of their child, there was little likelihood of proceeding against the teacher. Finally, on the theme of appeal and redress, ACE suggests that

> Children (shall) have freedom of access to suitably trained and appointed people to whom they can take their complaints and grievances. *They shall have freedom to make complaints about teachers, parents and others without fear of reprisal.* (p.107, emphasis added).

The Children Act (1989) does provide some scope for redress, for children to acquire legal representation, and have their views taken into consideration.

The right of 'freedom in personal appearance' also has direct relevance to schools, for the majority at secondary level stipulate requirements on school dress, hair styles, and the wearing of jewellery. School policy on this would need to incorporate rules which are equitable and based on gender, cultural and religious factors. The NCCL maintains that when parents are requested to sign an undertaking ensuring that 'their children will wear school uniform', this constitutes a 'mild form of blackmail on parents' and is possibly invalid, since pupils 'have not signed nor necessarily been consulted about signing the undertakings in question' (p.6). Interestingly a case has been taken to Strasbourg in which a mother complained that the rules governing school uniform in her children's school, violated their rights under Article 8 of the Convention. This states that 'everyone has the right to respect for his private and family life, his home and his correspondence'. Whilst *Stevens v. UK*[44] ultimately failed at the admissibility stage, the Commission did imply that school rules which prevented children from expressing an opinion or idea by means of their clothing, might be a breach of the Convention's guarantee of freedom of expression under Article 10. This was found in the American case of *Tinker v. Des Moines*, highlighted earlier, in which it was held that a student has the right to freedom of political expression through school dress.

A further right concerning education is 'the right of free access to knowledge' which has been advocated by many campaigners and is contained in various declarations. ACE states on this theme:

> Children have the right, at the appropriate age, to such knowledge as is necessary to understand the society in which they live. This shall include knowledge of sex, contraception, religion, drugs, including alcohol, and tobacco and other problems which confront every growing child (p.107).

This right may be opposed by parents who hold strong religious convictions (Parker-Jenkins 1995). Likewise, in *Gillick v, West Norfolk and Wisbech Area Health Authority* (1984),[45] the parent objected to contraceptive information being given to her 15 year old children. In cases where there is clearly a situation of rights in conflict, whose should take primacy? In *Gillick*, the courts were persuaded that provided the child has sufficient maturity, its rights should be recognised, and that in fact parents' rights dwindled according to the age and maturity of the child.

Finally, the right to be free of corporal punishment is one which has received particular attention and support. Mental humiliation is not yet unlawful, but the abolition of physical punishment has been achieved for children in the state school system, and those on the

'Assisted Places Scheme' in non-maintained schools. Advocates continued to lobby for *all* children. Jeff argues that 'disrespect for young people is nowhere more evident than in the continued use of physical punishment in some private schools'(p.25). As the European Convention is applicable to everyone within a European country's jurisdiction, it is arguable that this right should be extended to all British pupils, regardless of the nature of their school. Further, the *Education Act* (1993) declares it unlawful for any maintained school to use inhuman or degrading punishment. As of 1998 the law has changed, and the ban on physical chastisement of pupils extended to all children (*TES*, 1998).

Implications for Schools

> Children begin loving their parents.
> After a time they judge them.
> Rarely, if ever, do they forgive them (Oscar Wilde).

Do children forgive their teachers?[46] Application of many of the rights advocated for children has implications for schools and especially regarding discipline and authority of the teacher. Many issues have traditionally been dealt with by reference to school rules and as evidenced by the foregoing list of rights, many of these traditional practices may appear to violate children's rights. Indeed as the majority of children between the age of five to sixteen are at school, and as their attendance is compulsory, unless alternative arrangements have been made, discussion of children's rights in many instances is actually that of 'pupils' rights'. Wringe notes one argument that

> becoming a pupil is an act of complete subordination to one's teacher, incompatible with any notion of rights of participation in the control of the institution in which both find themselves (p.126).

There are areas in which a conflict of rights emerges in the school setting and today's administrators find themselves compelled to define the extent of pupils' rights *vis-à-vis* the teacher. Unlike the situation in other institutions the child may not actually be in school willingly. Some might contend that it is difficult to justify children's rights to be involved extensively in the running of schools and in personal choice in curriculum matters. This has been attempted, though on a very limited time scale (Croce *et al*, 1996), but these authors argue that 'the pupil has rarely done anything to 'give' him the right to say how school should be run, or how qualified teachers should conduct themselves' (p.18).

Teachers may respond by asserting their rights and responsibilities, which may require the curtailment of pupils' rights. Invoking philosophical and hypothetic rights and applying them to the reality of the school situation in which teachers are charged with the education, moral and safe welfare of large numbers of children, could render them inoperable. Furthermore, notwithstanding the logistics and dynamics of implementing rights of participation in school business or of personal appearance by pupils, there is the need to gain the acceptance of such claims by the teaching profession. As Wringe adds: 'it is often not what the pupil does which is considered offensive, but the assertion of his right to do it' (p.19).

Current talk of children's rights might appear a trivial and impertinent intrusion which challenges the authority and rights of teachers, and schools are unlikely to welcome the notion of children's rights as suggested, for example by Holt and Farson.

The discussion so far has explored the issue of the children's rights and the implications they raise for schools, but they do not need to be seen in terms of necessarily challenging, undermining or conflicting with authority. Instead school can be the place in which the rights and responsibilities of everyone in the community receive recognition. This point was raised earlier in chapter 4 within the context of formulating a 'code of conduct'. Here values and attitudes should be translated into a framework of good practice. Osler (1994) highlights the role which teachers can play because 'the formal education system is likely to be the main means by which most children will become familiar with their rights' (p.143). Further, children's rights can be a legitimate area for academic study. Starkey (1991) recommends that teachers should use international treaties as a point of reference in their lessons. Given the increasing significance of globalization, there is scope for international issues to be addressed, possibly within 'World Studies' and there are places for this within the National Curriculum. Lansdown (1995) advocates teaching children to think about rights seriously, and Griffiths and Davies (1995) argue that schools where children are treated with fairness and justice create better societies for everyone.

> Respecting children's rights is not about allowing children to become dictators. It is about creating personal and social relationships which acknowledge children as participants in their lives and social structures which include and value rather than exclude and denigrate them' (Osler, p.23).

Thus there is sufficient justification for children's rights, and these can be explored within the school setting, using both the formal and informal curriculum. But as with any social programme there are resource implications, as Freeman (1992, p.61) points out. Likewise Franklin (1995) argues that 'rights do not come on the cheap', rather that

> the issue of children's rights is fundamentally an issue about resources and their distribution. Securing rights for children will require government to reallocate resources in their favour (p.18).

Talk of children's rights may stop at the level of aspiration if there is inadequate resourcing to implement them.

Conclusion

Even the youngest of children have rights; indeed much has been made of the need to provide them with special protection due to their vulnerability. There is support for the children's rights movement lobbying from a variety of disparate groups.

Whilst ensuring the safety and well-being of children, there is, nevertheless, a danger that we prolong adolescent dependence and keep children in a vacuum marked 'childhood', ignoring their decision-making abilities. Nowhere is this more evident than by the fact that even in the children's rights movement, we scarcely hear the voice of the child! Instead, theorists and international treaties proclaim children's rights but the rhetoric is not necessarily translated into reality. Little attention is given to the resource implications of children's rights and the need for government to recognise financial obligations to support the rhetoric. We have seen that children's rights and children's needs are not necessarily the same thing, and greater emphasis should be placed upon seeing children as people in their own right. This point was explored with reference to schools and the ways in which educational institutions may infringe pupils' rights, but that is not to see the issue of children's rights within schools as a negative pursuit juxtaposed against teachers' rights. Schools can be the very place where human rights are recognised and supported for the greater good of the community. Furthermore, talk of children's rights not only raises the importance of teachers' rights in schools, but also leads us to consider how in the broader political context there has been increased central control of education and a diminution of everyone's rights in the system.

Notes

1. See *Childright* – No. 34, February 1987, pp 17-19 and *EPOCH* (1996).
2. As cited in Freeman, 1965, p.127.
3. See Rodham (1973), for more on the theme of entitlement'.
4. As cited in Zeldin, 1973, p.336.
5. *Times Educational Supplement*, 30 January, 1970, p.5.
6. *Times Educational Supplement*, 11 December, 1970, p.9.
7. *Times Educational Supplement*, 19 May, 1972, p.6.
8. Wringe (1981) describes this as the most substantial of the magazines on this theme at the time.
9. See A.S. Neill 'Freedom Works', in *Children's Rights* P. Adams, et al (Eds.)(1971), London: Elek Books, ch.4.
10. *Times Educational Supplement*, 2 October, 1970 p.6.
11. National Council for Civil Liberties (NCCL) '*Children in School*', Discussion Paper No.1 in the series *Children Have Rights* (1970-71).
12. *Times Educational Supplement*, 5 May, 1972, pp.9 and 14.
13. As cited in Wringe, p.p.8-9.
14. *Ibid*.
15. *The Protection of Minors Bill* Hansard Parliamentary Debates, House of Lords, 5th Series, vol No 347, 10 December 1973.
16. Freeman, (1983a) provides interesting discussion of this point drawing on American case law.
17. For more on the theme see Hyman I.A. and Wise J.H. (1979) (Eds.) *Corporal Punishment in American Education*, Philadephia: Temple.
18. *In the Matter of the Application of Paul L Gault and Marjorie Gault, Father and Mother of Gerald Francis Gault a Minor. (1967)* US Supreme Court Reports (annotated) vol.387 (U.S. 387).
19. *John F. Tinker and Mary Beth Tinker (Minors) et al., Petitioners v Des Moines Independent Community School District et al (1969)* US Supreme Court Reports (annotated) vol. 21 (US 393).
20. *In the matter of Samuel Winship (1970)* US Supreme Court Reports, vol. 25, (US 397).
21. *James Ingraham and by his mother and the next friend, Eloise Ingraham et al Petitioners v Willie J. Wright I. et al (1997)* US Supreme Coaurt reports (annotated) vol. 51 (US 430).

22. As cited in Chanlett and Morier (1968) p.5.
23. United Nations Declaration of Human Rights cited in I. Brownlie (1981) (Ed) *Basic Documents on Human rights* (2nd Edition) Oxford; Clarendon Press.
24. *United Nations Declaration of the Rights of the Child* US General Assembly Resolution 1387 (XIV) 20 Nov, 1959.
25 Advisory Centre for Education 'Draft Charter of children's Rights' (1971), *Where* vol. 56, p.105.
26. As cited in Freeman MDA (1993a) *The Rights and Wrongs of Children*, London: Frances Pinter, p.20.
27. Children's Legal Centre (1986) 'Briefing of the UN Rights of the Child, London: CLC; and Childright (1985() No.18, June p.7.
28. *Campbell and Cosans v UK* (1982) European Court of Human Rights, Series A, Nos.48 and 60, 25 Feb and 22 March.
29. *Tyrer v UK* (1978) European Court of Human Rights Series A, No.26, 25 April.
30. Children's Legal Centre (1986) 'Briefing on the Drafting the UN Rights of the Child', London; CLC.
31. *Council of Europe; Collected Texts* (1972) 8th ed. Strasbourg.
32. *Childright* (1987) No.39 July/Aug p.11.
33. The cases discussed in chapter 3, illustrate this point. A notable exception, however is *Neilson v Denmark* (1986) (App No.1092/84 European Commission of Human Rights, Decision as to Admissibility, 10 March.
34. As cited by Children's Legal Centre (1986) Children's Charters. London; CLC.
35. The Education No.2 Act (1986) London, HMSO, C61.
36. The Family Law Reform Act (1969) c.46, section 1.
37. As cited in Hafen B.C. (1976) 'Children's Literature and the New Egalitarianism', *Brigham, Young Law Review* p.612.
38. As cited in Freeman (1983a) p.54.
39. *The Children Act (1989)* London: HMSO, preamble.
40. See *The Guardian* (1997a) 'Judges Win Power in Historic Bill', October 25, p.1.
41. *Education No.2 Act in (1986)* London HMSO, section 47(3).
42. For a further discussion of this theme see Brandt, A. (1959) *Ethical Theory* Englewood Cliffs, New Jewsey.
43. See also Worsfolds (1974) 'A Philosophical Justification for Children's Rights' *Harvard Educational Review* vol.44, No.1 pp.142-157; and Sachs C. (1973) 'Children's Rights' in Bridge J.W. et al, *Fundamental Rights* London; Sweet and Maxwell.
44. *Stevens v UK* (1986) Application No.11674/85, European Commission of Human rights, March 3.
45. *Gillick v West Norfolk and Wisbech Area Health Authority* and another (1984) ALL ER 365; ALL 533.
46. This point was raised by one of my former Masters' students, Kate Gray, as part of a course she took with me on Children's Rights.

Conclusion
Reflection and Reality

> Our democracy is based on the premise that groups of people will stand up for their own interests and rights, but children are not in a position to do this (Rosenbaum and Newell, 1991, p.3).

Throughout this book, we have been looking at the issue of school discipline from a legal perspective, while drawing on international development. European initiatives demonstrated that Britain was behind the rest of the Continent in its thinking on corporal punishment, and that it still is out of step with countries which have challenged parental chastisement. However we have not been alone in hanging on to traditional methods of disciplining children, as elsewhere there is a reluctance to adopt alternative santions. Here we bring together the major themes and the ramifications for educators, school governing bodies and local education authorities. We reflect on the impact of Strasbourg; the removal of the cane from schools and how this causes us to question the adequacy of the *in loco parentis* doctrine today. Implications for teachers are explored in the light of their legal and contractual obligations and the broader socio-political climate. We examine the position of children today and some of the debates concerning protection for and protection from children, and consider the way forward and how children's rights should be implemented if the theory is to become reality.

The Impact of Strasbourg

As we saw in chapter 1, corporal punishment was an intrinsic and traditional feature of our schools, supported with entreaties not to 'spare the rod and spoil the child'. Such was the widespread application of physical chastisement in our public schools in the last century that it became known as 'the English vice'.[1] Not until the 20th Century was the practice seriously challenged and only then through a European forum. It is unlikely that the framers of the Convention in the 1940s conceived of it applying to corporal punishment in schools, but the treaty has a dynamic character which permits it to be tailored to contemporary values. In the 1980s the European Court was prepared to consider instances of physical chastisement in British schools as akin to 'degrading treatment', so that in certain circumstances the sanction could amount to a violation of human rights. We saw that even the threat of corporal punishment could be tantamount to violating the philosophical convictions of parents opposed to its use. Over thirty cases were lodged at Strasbourg during the 1980s, and the Government suffered a humiliating loss of face in trying to defend physical chastisement. Yet we now hear of calls for the reintroduction of the practice on grounds of youth indiscipline in schools and society.[2]

Realistically, a return to corporal punishment in schools would be highly problematical. The Government has entered into a convention and is bound by the decision of the European Court that if we fail to respect parents' philosophical convictions on physical chastisement, we are in breach of their human rights. That means that no domestic law can be in conflict with principles contained in the European Convention.

How then can we avoid alienating Strasbourg? The Government could attempt to introduce a bill whereby parents could opt in or out of corporal punishment: in other words, sign your child up to be whacked! This might appeal to those who believe that 'it never did me any harm'. But how could schools implement such a system? Should children in classroom wear different colour badges to assist teachers in deciding whether to cane or not to cane? Or could schools be divided into cane and cane-free zones?

When this two-tier scheme was mooted in 1985 by Sir Keith Joseph, Secretary of State for Education, it united all factions on the issue of corporal punishment to declare it ludicrous, unworkable and educationally indefensible. Common sense prevailed and only complete abolition of the practice was deemed acceptable. The same would be true today. Even if parents were inclined to sign up their children for caning, teachers would be left in the absurd position of having to arbitrate different punishments for the same misdemeanour. And since corporal punishment was traditionally used more frequently for boys than for girls, schools could also fall foul of the *Sex Discrimination Act* which quite rightly conceives of gender as a two-way street.

Legally it is a non-starter and socially there are also difficulties. Abolition of corporal punishment has caused us to reconsider how we perceive children, not only in schools but in society in general, and the concerns surrounding children's rights. Is a return to corporal punishment the only way in which discipline and respect for others can be enforced in a violent society? Unruly and disruptive behaviour in the young, so clearly evidenced in recent cases at Manton[3] and The Ridings[4] schools, has been attributed to a number of factors including inadequate parenting and a general lack of deference to authority, and some may be persuaded that a move towards legitimising force is the only viable option left to teachers who have to instil discipline in the classroom. Corporal punishment as retribution could be seen as a deterrent to others, a clear signal that the school has not 'gone soft' on pupil disobedience. Yet analysis of school punishment books prior to abolition reveals that the same pupils' names appeared repeatedly, suggesting that the sanction was ineffective. Research by the Society of Teachers Opposed to Physical Punishment in the 1980s provides evidence that some schools used the cane not as a last resort but regularly and abusively. Meanwhile, other European countries have moved on to challenging parents' authority in the home, as part of an increasing condemnation of violence in society. For all these reasons the return of the cane to British classrooms is ill-conceived, legally problematic and socially retrogressive.

The Court, as intended by the Convention's framers has acted as 'the public conscience of Europe', to encourage international co-operation through the Council of Europe. We discussed, in chapter 2, how human rights problems could not be left to the internal jurisdiction of any one country and how 'the voice of Strasbourg' has been continually heard across the continent. There has been a move towards a policy of harmonisation through educational changes, and interest in each others' educational arrangements, particularly about pupil behaviour and social justice. Furthermore, the Convention has served, observe Bailey *et al*, as 'a useful educational and promotional role by providing convenient, positive statements of civil liberties that can be used as a point of reference as authority in argument' (p.12). This is well-evidenced by Ritchie and Ritchie (1981) who describe the efforts of a New Zealand pressure group to achieve abolition of school-based corporal punishment by citing as persuasive argument the judgements of the Court in British cases. Likewise South African courts have made reference to the Strasbourg decisions during their own move towards abolishing physical chastisement.

In the past the United Kingdom has been pilloried, some would say unfairly, for its record of violations of the Convention. Britain's 'frequent appearance in the dock'[5] has resulted in losing 19 out of 26 cases, as of November 1987, and being called to respond to three out of every five complaints lodged with the Commission.[6] Many writers ask how it is that 'the cradle of democracy' could have such a poor record in human rights violations. It was predicted in 1985 by Bailey *et al* that:

> the number of applications to Strasbourg would clearly decrease if, in the exhaustion of local remedies, one had first to go to a British court which would... apply the Convention (pp.583-4).

As we are now moving towards having an entrenched Bill of Rights with incorporation of the European Convention, it will be interesting to see the extent to which this will happen.

In the meantime, what is most evident is the impact which the Convention has made on British parents who have been willing to seek redress in Strasbourg over educational disputes. Through its alliance with the Council of Europe, Britain has been thrust into a new phase in the development of human rights. By adopting a broad interpretation of the notion of parents' 'philosophical convictions', 'the right to education' and 'degrading punishment', the Strasbourg organs found that Britain has breached the Convention which she has agreed to uphold. In these cases the Court and Commission appeared to move faster than the British government in the condemnation of corporal punishment.[7]

The potential effect of the Convention's provisions on education policy-making and teaching practice in general is far-reaching. Pressure groups such as End Physical Punishment of Children World-wide, may advocate educational objectives through Convention-based litigation and, as in the spate of corporal punishment cases lodged during the past decade, these may provide a catalyst for reform in the absence of initiative by government. The provisions of the Convention are capable of being applied in new directions, such as the rights of children with learning difficulties.[7] New areas presently under investigation may prove fertile in Strasbourg, such as special educational needs, school accountability, exclusions and curriculum content. Further, rights may be broadened by extending the notion of 'philosophical convictions' to include such concerns as choice of schooling based on cultural mix.[8] New cases emerging from litigant parents could provide judicial clarification from Strasbourg on several contentious issues and there is still room for a number of test cases on the extent of 'the right to education'.

With the changing emphasis away from protecting children to protecting their rights, as detailed in chapter 7, young people may be encouraged to litigate on their own behalf (see *Neilson v Denmark* (1984).[9]

Removing the Cane

Ten years on, the implications of the removal of corporal punishment in Britain have to some extent been digested. While the practice of corporal punishment has been effectively abolished for pupils in maintained schools and a percentage in the non-maintained sector, schools have been developing alternative forms of punishment. The legal consequence for teachers of continued use of corporal punishment in defiance of the *Education (No 2) Act (1986)* has been removal of the defence under Common Law to be acting *in loco parentis* when using physical chastisement, and the majority now risk prosecution by parents, or disciplinary proceedings by local authorities. If corporal punishment is being used illegally, there has been little or no reporting of the fact.[10] The implications for local education authorities, head teachers and governing bodies have also been significant. What may be classified as the symbol of authoritarianism has been replaced by a greater emphasis on care and guidance nurtured within a non-violent context. Furthermore, the Assistant Masters and Mistresses Association (AMMA) stated in 1985 that:

> whatever their attitude towards disciplining their own children, perhaps fewer parents are as unquestioningly willing to delegate the right to others to chastise their own children as has been the case in the past (p.9).

This was also found in Australian studies highlighted in chapter 5. AMMA notes that 'the real significance of the ...European Court and Commission judgements' may well be 'that British schools abide by parental wishes whatever they may be' (*ibid*., p.12). Certainly, schools are increasingly obliged to listen to parents over issues concerning school management.

The context of the debate today is no longer about pro- and anti-caning lobbies but about what should replace corporal punishment. Before 1986 some local authorities abolished corporal punishment in the absence of statutory enactment and so have attempted to deal with this question.[11] Despite the fact that the whole country has been instructed to eliminate corporal punishment from maintained schools, shortcomings of the 1986 Act mean that pre-schoolers, for example, are not afforded protection under the legislation. For the majority of children, however, there have been significant changes in the way discipline has been handled in schools. More recently, all schools, maintained and non-maintained, have become 'caneless' by virtue of the School Standards and Framework Bill (TES, 1998a).

It was recommended at the time of general abolition in 1986 that:

> Schools must be given clear discipline policies, supportive arrangements and other resources ... if the policy and practice are to be more than pious hope or paper exercise, (AMMA, p.15)

To what extent has this happened? It is difficult to assess the level of support made available. The legislation which removed corporal punishment said nothing about what should replace it. Unlike some Australian states, it provided no guidelines, no in-service training or networking information. Instead a great deal has been left to individual education authorities and schools, some of which had already abolished the practice to develop alternatives according to their particular circumstances. The Education Reform Act (1988) which followed the abolition of corporal punishment introduced not only a National Curriculum but new policy on assessment, league tables, Local Management of Schools and the demise of support services traditionally provided by local authorities. Accordingly, funding for the development of alternative sanctions to corporal punishment has had to compete with other demands. As political agendas have been formed in response to legislation, we have witnessed a steady and alarming increase in exclusion rates.[12] It is simplistic to equate this increase with the removal of the cane alone, but the cane was cheap and its replacement is not. Some schools may have taken the view that a disruptive pupil may be too costly to keep in terms of providing adequate pastoral care support, and exclusion may have appeared the most feasible option. What we do know is that the customary role of teachers in Britain has been modified in light of legal change and the development of alternative disciplinary sanctions.

The Inadequacy of the *In Loco Parentis* Doctrine

It still remains unclear who is *in loco parentis* now that teachers have been forced to vacate the position with regard to corporal punishment. Does the concept still apply and, if so, in what circumstances? The teacher's role in Britain was given a much broader interpretation than on the Continent. Indeed it was said during a Hansard debate in 1976 that:

> In many of our more difficult areas the teacher is increasingly *in loco parentis*. The teacher has the job of seeking to instil civilised values and a proper sense of order into very often extremely rebellious children.[13]

However, the traditional definition of *in loco parentis* has been inadequate since long before abolition of corporal punishment. The idea was that teachers stood in the place of the parent and that parents' rights were delegated – but as education became compulsory there could be no automatic assumption of these delegated rights.

What needs to happen now is that the traditional doctrine of *in loco parentis* and the ways in which it can be applied is re-appraised. Since the policy shift away from physical chastisement teachers are *in loco parentis* in a more limited sense. There is still a duty of care which teachers must carry out, but how do we define when, and in what circumstances, in *loco parentis* applies? I would argue that the doctrine needs re-defining within a broader, more democratic notion of the school. We need to ask what fundamental principles should be incorporated into school discipline guidelines. The policy should send a positive signal about the working environment, rather than focus on a list of punitive sanctions. This could include a 'Code of Conduct' based on social justice, the result of a consultative process with teachers, pupils, parents, governors and any other concerned parties, so as to foster ownership, representation and equity. It is the principles, not a list of sanctions or roles of authority, which matter for ensuring that everyone's welfare in the school community is recognised. The doctrine of *in loco parentis* would thus be not only updated in the light of new social and legal norms, more realistically defining the status of the teacher, but also seen as a part of the process of protecting children's rights rather than undermining them.

If some teachers are no longer to assume the role of *in loco parentis* as formerly understood, where would they stand as regards negligence? Furthermore, do teachers still have pastoral duties if and when the pedagogic duty ceases? In light of concern with teachers' duties and responsibilities, it would be appropriate to consider these issues particularly when the 1,265 hours of a teacher's working year are exhausted. Presumably, the school management would not always be available to deal with the pastoral and disciplinary needs of pupils. Without definite guidelines, serious problems concerning safety within the school could emerge, and responsibility rests clearly with the headteacher. This was highlighted by the tragic death in 1986 of a thirteen year old boy at the hands of a fellow pupil in a Manchester comprehensive school. The perpetrator was known to staff as a disruptive and violent pupil who had previously been suspended from school. An investigation of the school revealed that there had been complaints about assaults by pupils on teachers and other children, which went unpunished and, significantly, that the teachers had 'low morale because they felt their efforts to maintain order were not supported following the abolition of corporal punishment'.[14]

Although this was an isolated case, problems in the 1990s still necessitate regular debate on the fundamental issue of the teacher-pupil relationship and school disciplinary sanctions. Current legislation requires that the headteacher outline the school's discipline system in its prospectus, and that governors develop regulations concerning exclusions. School managers need to be mindful of the potential for parental challenge when formulating policy on discipline, not just in the light of the Strasbourg findings, but also given the encouragement of active consumerism in education. Ideally the self-motivation of the pupil will contribute to the learning process, but teachers will have to have discipline, whether imposed by themselves or others. It is becoming increasingly difficult to recruit and retain teachers in some subject areas. How much more difficult this will be if effective discipline is not firmly established in schools.

Along with a new definition of 'a teacher' with the attendant duties and responsibilities, the position of the teacher *vis-a-vis* disruptive and violent pupils still requires thought. Teachers' contractual obligations have been to carry out reasonable requests of the headteacher. The presence in a classroom of a particularly violent or disruptive pupil may cause problems if a teacher is no longer to be in *loco parentis* as previously understood. *The Health and Safety at Work Act* (1974) places an obligation on the employer to take all reasonable steps to ensure that teachers operate in a safe environment. The *Local Government (Miscellaneous) Provision* (1982) section 40, 'creates a criminal offence of causing a nuisance or disturbance on educational premises'. In cases where a pupil is highly disruptive or violent, the Local Education Authority may have to resort to excluding the pupil pursuant to Articles 23 to 27 of the 1986 Act, in order to ensure the safety of employees in the school. There is also the question of Local Authority liability for pupils' safety as well as that of teachers – a pupil's 'right to education' may need to be qualified by the teacher's right to operate in a safe environment. The reprimanding and discipline of disruptive pupils will need to be well-conceived if teachers assume a more limited role *in loco parentis* or none whatsoever.

Perhaps local authorities may need to assume the *in loco parentis* mantle and clearly designate those who assume the position in the school. Teaching associations, ever more disturbed by their members' complaints of personal attacks by pupils, will try to ensure that along with delineated duties, teachers' rights are given serious considera-tion, particularly as they relate to safety at work.

The responsibilities of parents in ensuring their children's good behaviour requires attention and, in particular, the development of policy regarding recalcitrant parents. During the House of Lords debate on the *Abolition of Corporal Punishment Bill* (1973), Lord Ferrer remarked that:

> one must remember that one of the teachers' troubles is that at the end of the scale there are too many parents who utterly fail to instil any sort of discipline in their children when they send them to school (p.928).[15]

Teaching associations echo the concern that parents must be involved and accountable, as teachers alone cannot solve the problem of dis-ruptive children. In practical terms this means discussion, surveys, open-days and other means to gain advice and support from parents on discipline issues.

Greater emphasis on parental involvement would bring Britain into line with European countries who expect far more from parents. In West Germany, for example, parents who do not support the school's policy and who fail to attend school conferences concerning their chil-dren, can find themselves deprived of Child Benefit. Parents may now be expected to assume greater responsibility for their children's behaviour, since teachers are no longer able to assume the position of parent substitutes. Perhaps greater accountability could be achieved with punishment directed at parents in the form of financial penalty, as in the German model, rather than simply excluding the child. If parents cannot guarantee the good behaviour of their children, schools may require greater powers to *compel* parental responsibility, conceivably with statutory underpinning.

If the problems of indiscipline are to be solved, time and resources need to be allocated to provide an effective pastoral care system. Schools have worked to develop other sanctions but the number of pupils excluded from school has increased. Writing in 1983(a) Free-man warned that:

rights can easily backfire. Reform movements intended to enhance children's rights and the concomitant development of professional structures to implement such reforms often generate their own set of problems and ultimately have deleterious effects on children's rights...The reforms of one era are apt to become the problems of the next. (p.34)

The pupil's right not to receive corporal punishment has 'backfired' when alternative sanctions are draconian. As the notion of *in loco parentis*, changes, unwarranted or unreasonable school regulations will also have to go.

Implications for Teachers

As noted in chapter 6, some teachers have feared that the elimination of corporal punishment would undermine school discipline and limit their authority in exercising care and control over pupils. Some would argue that teachers cannot teach unless they have control and that this can only come about through their own authority. Can this authority be backed by non-physical sanctions, and will teachers be given the right conditions in which to work and adequate support for their task? The lack of deference to authority has meant that some people feel the pendulum should swing towards giving greater authority to adults.

Teachers are finding that they undertake more and more responsibilities, experience a fall in salary comparable to other occupational groups, have their disciplinary rights limited and still operate within the confines of 'professionalism'. Writing in 1986 at the time of abolition George Walden, former Conservative Education Minister, maintained that:

It would be disastrous for everyone to allow our teachers to be demoralised, or to demoralise themselves further... they must be decently paid. Teachers' pay has drifted down over the years, in relative terms, together with society's esteem.[16]

This still holds true. The educational reforms of the 1980s mean that teachers have had to adjust to major changes to the profession. Whether from Strasbourge or Westminster, changes have been imposed rather than negotiated and have significantly affected the status of teachers in the UK. The European Court and Commission produced findings in corporal punishment cases demonstrating its unwillingness to endorse the practice, and instead it supported parents' and children's rights. Strasbourg waved the stick which brought British teachers into line with their European counterparts.

Simon (1988) observed that sympathy for children's rights was not always forthcoming as there has been a progressive weakening of teachers' rights in relation to teaching unions. Today general resistance amongst teachers, parents and students at grass roots level often seems to be the only constraint upon the will of the government (Meigham, 1992). This is directly related to pupils, for 'increasing control of teachers has implications for the rights of children' (Jeffs, 1995, p.29). Ironically, while a liberal/monetarist policy pertains, allowing organisations to operate freely in the marketplace with a minimum of interference, education has been subject to a number of centrally-imposed reforms and the New Labour Government does not suggest a major departure.

As the Court has so effectively been used by parents and pupils to secure their rights, teachers might well be persuaded that Strasbourg could be a useful forum for their own grievances.[17] The Convention does not cover economic and political rights of the workplace but reliance might be placed on 'the right to education' as inclusive of specific matters in the curriculum. Likewise, teachers might invoke Article 8 when a school's employment or disciplinary policy appears to breach 'the right to a private life.' To date however, teachers have felt that Strasbourg rulings have not enhanced their rights but fettered them. With the greater valuing of children must come the valuing of teachers – they also have rights in the educational process and should be supported by an effective and fair system. There are no quick-fix solutions to the present problems in school. To call for the return of the cane is to underestimate the problem and over-simplify the answer!

To rectify continuing concerns over discipline, a broader view is needed of what is happening in schools. This begins with relaxing further the National Curriculum straitjacket and supporting curriculum offerings which engage pupils' interests and strengths. In the present climate of uniformity, the less academic children struggle to keep pace in a system characterized by assessment, budgetary restraints and league tables.

Increasing selection will undoubtedly exacerbate the situation, for who will select the child who is unable to contribute highly to a school's academic performance? Within the contemporary ethos of competition, pupils may feel alienated from what is happening in schools. Furthermore, long-term fears of economic decline and unemployment makes the value of education to the young more questionable.

Children in Society Today

Abolition of corporal punishment has caused us to reconsider how we perceive children generally, and creates the concerns surrounding children's rights. At the same time, unruly and disruptive behaviour in the young is persuasive grounds for the 'flog 'em' lobby that legitimising force is the only option left to teachers who have to instil discipline in the classroom. Typically, the school is expected to respond to the needs of society as an enforcer of discipline, yet it cannot perform what the law does not allow.

Throughout this book we have noted the need to see children as people in their own right. Yet institutions are remarkably resistant to change. Traditionally children have been cast in the role of powerless subjects, reliant on the ideologies of paternalism or libertarianism to modify or improve their position. Many writers claim that no institution impinges more on their daily lives than the school. Moreover, support exists worldwide to extending rights to children. Archard (1993) argues that giving rights to children 'is a public and palpable acknowledgement of their status and worth' (p.169).

There are conflicting views over young people and there are calls for protection both for and from children. The 1980s especially was a period of public outcry for increased protection rights, following the deaths of Maria Colwell,[18] Jasmine Beckford,[19] Tyra Henry[20] and Kimberly Carlisle.[21] Significantly, 'much abuse of children is the result of corporal punishment which has gone wrong' (Freeman, 1983a, p.113). These cases also shattered the myth that children's best interests lay within the family, and pointed to domestic violence being a legitimate matter of state concern.

Protection from children has been forcefully called for too, particularly since James Bulger was killed.[22] Here children's wrongs rather than their rights attracted media attention and created panic over juvenile

crime. The case helped to undermine the notion of children as inno-
cents, and to demonise children with calls for stricter control and
punishment. Franklin (1995) observes:

> society constructs the children it needs. Instead of policies to pro-
> tect children in the community, the government and media have
> preferred to promote policies to protect the community from chil-
> dren. (p.5)

The talk about some children being inherently evil echoes the Victorian
views with which we began, and the maxim that children should be
seen and not heard may be given fresh interpretation. The New Labour
Government is contemplating proposals aimed at creating children's
prisons, fast-track sentencing and night curfews.[23] This departure
from children's rights – what Franklin calls ' a policy retreat' challenges the ideology of childhood as a time of innocence and instead
seeks to stress children's responsibilities to society and take scant
account of their rights.

Protection *from* children can also be seen in forthcoming legislation
concerning schools. A proposed clause for the *Education Act (1997)*
is concerned with 'physical restraint' of children on school premises
or beyond, such as during a school trip. Under section 550A, a member of staff will be able to use such force as is reasonable to prevent a
child committing an offence, injury or damage to people or property,
or engaging in any behaviour prejudicial to the maintenance of good
order and discipline. Importantly 'the clause was introduced as a
result of pressure from the teacher unions, all of whom supported it!'[24]

The problem here is the relationship between physical restraint and
corporal punishment – which can be defined as any attack on the
physical body. At what point does one sanction end and another
begin? Guidance will need to be crystal clear about what constitutes
physical restraint and in what circumstances. Otherwise, children may
feel they are being given corporal punishment, and teachers may be
legally vulnerable, especially if any injuries are sustained. As we saw,
litiagation over personal injury and negligence has been filed by
aggrieved parents in the past. How much more likely will this be when
with one hand we remove corporal punishment and with the other we
extend the idea of 'physical restraint'? Is the new proposal retrogressive? Certainly it is problematic. The proposal moves away from the

more positive supports which schools have been developing in the absence of corporal punishment and as alternatives to violence.

Ambiguities and contraditions can thus be seen in the way we view children's rights in society. This book has shown how the welfare of the child has been paramount and has been fostered through legislation in Britain and elsewhere. Advocacy of children's rights is an international phenomenon, with heighted media attention, but there is a danger that, once espoused, rights are somehow thought to have become a reality. We will need to translate the theory into practice. What we have been more properly describing is the language of aspiration and entitlement. Until there is sufficient political will, talk of children's rights remains pious but empty rhetoric. This raises a number of significant questions for schools and society:

- Will the recognition of 'children's rights' actually make a difference to their lives?

- Are the necessary resources available?

- What are the staffing implications?

- Do teachers have the requisite knowledge and skills?

- Is there popular support for a policy of promoting children's rights?

A range of ideas has been put forward, such as a Ministry of Children, Youth Councils and the creation of a Children's Rights Commissioner. The appointment of Children's Right Officers in local authorities has demonstrated a commitment to children's rights (Franklin, p.13). Comparative perspectives point to the use of ombudswork in New Zealand, Norway, Israel and Costa Rica (ibid., p.3). If we restructure the debates around implementing rights and the sorts of initiatives needed to provide voice, representation, participation and empowerment, we move beyond children's rights as a concept or ideology towards one of reality. At school level, too, there are a number of possibilities such as Student Pupil Councils, and analytical models for children's participation, as suggested by Hart (1995), which provide for levels of genuine involvement and consultation. To achieve this move towards children empowerment, Franklin maintains that adults 'must assume an enabling role that necessarily carries the germs of its own destruction' (pp.18-19).

It is in the interest of *adults* that children be educated and trained to assume rights and responsibilities. Rather than viewing the giving of rights to children as possibly denying rights to adults, we need to recognise that everyone in the community has rights and consider how these can realistically be balanced, and how situations where rights conflict can be reconciled.

Finally, it has been argued that implementing children's rights is difficult because as minors they lack political power. Accordingly,

> giving more young people the right to vote would not resolve the many difficulties which they confront, but it would place the responsibility for protecting children's rights where it properly belongs. Not in the hands of well meaning but potentially paternalistic adults, but with those who have the greatest interest in ensuring that those rights are not infringed: children themselves (p.20).

Lowering the age of majority to 16 years would go some way to giving voice to adolescents, many of whom are young adults being treated as children. But who would speak for those under 16 years? Adult involvement and support will still be needed for the vast number of children in society. This can clearly be justified on a number of grounds and the future depends on how we treat children today. The rights rhetoric masks enormous areas of life with which legislation cannot adequately deal and which remain dependent on the commitment and goodwill of adults in fostering a better society. We are in an ideal position to reflect on how we percieve children in our society and to determine what needs to be done on a number of fronts, not only to continue the momentum, but to give value and meaning to the lives of those people who will ultimately be responsible for us all in the future.

Notes

1. See Gibson, T. (1978) *The English Voice: Beating, Sex and Shame in Victorian England and After*. London: Duckworth.
2. See Parker-Jenkins, M. (1996) 'A Simple Answer that never Worked', *Times Educational Supplement*, Nov. 15 p.26.
3. Nottinghamshire Education Committee, *Manton Junior School: Management Inspection* (1996), Nottinghamshire Notts County Council. See also 'Manton Re-opens As Transfer is Agreed', *Times Educational Supplement* (1996a), November 15, p.7.
4. The Ridings School (1996b) 'Shephard Orders Ridings Inquiry', *Times Educational Supplement* October 25, p.11.

5. See for example Grosz, S., *The Times*, 25 June 1985, p.2.

6. *Forum* (The Council of Europe Quarterly), No.1, 1985, p.2.

7. *The Guardian*, March 17, 1987.

8. See *Education*, vol 170 No.17, 23 October 1987.

9. *Neilson v Denmark* (1984) (Application No.1092/84). *European Commission of Human Rights*, Decision as to Admissibility, 10 March 1980.

10. Reported cases on the illegal use of corporal punishment are rare and normally the teacher has received disciplinary action. See for example "Smack Row Teacher Suicidal" *The Guardian*, April 17, 1998, News 3.

11. See *Childright*. No 30, September, 1986, pp.13-14.

12. See for example, 'Exclusion Rise Linked to Paperwork', *Times Educational Supplement* (l997b) November 7, p.15.

13. Patrick Cormack, in *Hansard Parliamentary Debates*. *House of Commons*, vol.903, 20 January 1976, p.1158.

14. *The Sunday Times*, 8 February, 1987, p.3.

15. *Hansard Reports, House of Commons*, 1973.

16. As cited in *The Daily Telegraph* (1987), 5 February, p.4.

17. See for example the case of the Surrey Headteacher in dispute over the 'traditional' style of education, *The Times*, 2 September, 1986.

18. *Report of the Inquiry into the Care and Supervision Provided in Relation to Maria Colwell* (1974) Field-Fisher Report, London, HMSO.

19. *A Child in Trust: The Report of the Panel of Inquiry into the Circumstances Surrounding the Death of Jasmine Beckford*, London, Brent Council, 1985.

20. See *Whose Child?: The Report of the Panel Appointed to Inquire into the Death of Tyra Henry* (1978), London: London Borough of Lambeth.

21. See *Inquiry into Death of Kimberly Carlisle* (1987), London: London Borough of Greenwich and Greenwich Health Authority.

22. See the case of *James Bulger, Times Educational Supplement* (1993) leading article, November 25, p. 19a. See also 'Bulger Tragedy Still Haunts Mothers', (1994) *Leicester Mercury*, 16 June, p.14.

23. Labour party proposals regarding measures to respond to juvenile crime.

24. 'Physical Restraint of Children: A New Sanction for Schools *Childright* (1997) July/Aug, No. 138 pp.14-16. See also 'DfEE Draft Guidance for Section 550A of the Education Act 1996: The Use of Reasonable Force to Control or Restrain Pupils', *Childright* (1998) March, No 144, pp. 11-14; and 'May the Force be With You', *Times Educational Supplement* (1998b) April 3, p.35.

Bibliography

A Child in trust: The Report of the Panel of Inquiry into the Circumstances Surrounding the Death of Jasmine Beckford (1985), London: Brent Council.

Adams, N. (1984) *Law and Teachers Today*. 2nd Ed. London: Hutchinson.

Adams, P., Berg, L., Berger, N., Duane, M., Neill, A.S. and Ollendorf, R. (1971) *Children's Rights: Towards the liberation of the Child*. London: Elek Books.

Advisory Centre for Education (1971) 'Draft Charter of Children's Rights', *Where*, Vol. 56, pp. 105-108.

Alexander, K. and Alexander, M.D. (1985) *American Public School Law* (2nd Ed), St. Paul, Minnesota: West Publishing Co.

Alston,, P., Parker, S., Seymour, J. (1992) *Children's Rights and the Law*, Oxford: Clarendon Press.

Andrews, J. (1983) 'Just Satisfaction Under the Convention'. *European Law Review*, Vol. 18, pp. 286-290.

Archard, D. (1993) *Children: Rights and Childhood*, London: Routledge.

Aries, P. (1962) *Centuries of Childhood*. New York: Vintage.

Assistant Masters and Mistresses Association, (1985) *After Strasbourg: A Policy for Discipline in Schools*. London: AMMA.

Ayres, P. (1962) *Centuries of Childhood*, London: Routledge.

Bailey, S.H., Harris, D.J. and Jones, B.L. (1985) *Civil Liberties: Cases and Material*. London: Butterworth.

Bantock, G.H. (1970) *Freedom and Authority in Education: A Criticism of Modern Cultural and Educational Assumptions*. London: Faber and Faber.

Barnard, H.C. (1971) *A History of English Education from 1760*. London: University Press.

Barrell, G. B. (1985) *Teachers and the Law*. 6th Ed. London: Methuen.

Barrell, G (1978) *Teachers and the Law*, 5th Ed, London: Methuen.

Bauer, G.B., Dubanoski, R., Yamauchi, L.A., and Honbo, K.M. (1990) 'Corporal Punishment and the Schools', *Education and Urban Society*, Vol. 22, No. 3, May, pp. 285-299.

Bean, P. (1981) *Punishment: A Philosophical and Criminological Inquiry*. Oxford: Martin Roberts.

Beazley, K.E. (1984) *Education in Western Australia: Report of a Ministerial Inquiry into Education (Beazley Report)*, Perth: Education Department of Western Australia.

Beddard, R. (1993) *Human Rights and Europe*, Cambridge: Grotius Publications.

Beddard, R. (1973 and 1980) *Human Rights and Europe: A Study of the Machinery of Human Rights of Europe*. 1st and 2nd Eds, London: Sweet and Maxwell.

Bel Geddes, J. (1977) 'The Rights of Children in World Perspective'. *The Children's Rights Movement: Overcoming the Oppression of Young People*. Gross, B. and Gross, R. (Eds), New York: Anchor Press.

Benn, S.I. and Peters, R.S. (1959) *Social Principles and the Democratic State*, London: George Allen and Unwin.

Bentham, J. (1840) *Theory of Legislation*. Vol 1, Boston: Weeks Jordan..

Bentham, J. (1970) *Principles of Morals and Legislation*, J.H. Burns and H.L.A. Hart, (Eds) London: Athlone Press

Berger, V. (1995) *Case Law of the European Court of Human Rights*. Dublin: The Round Hall Press.

Bernstein, B. And Brannen, J. (1996) (Eds) *Children, Research and Policy*, London: Taylor and Francis.

Birch, I.K.F. (1976) *The School and the Law*. Melbourne: Melbourne University Press.

Bishop, H.L. and Miles, A.S. (1998) *Due Process Handbook for Alabama Public School Principals: A Guide to Preventative Law*, Montgomery Alabama: Alabama State Department of Education.

Bloom, S. (1995) 'Spare the Rod, Spoil the Child? A Legal Framework for Recent Corporal Punishment Proposals', *Golden Gate University Review*, Vol. 25, No.1, Spring, pp. 361-389.

Blyth, E., Milner, J. (Eds) (1996) *Exclusion from School: Interprofessional Issues for Policy and Practice*. London: Routledge.

Bonner, P., Delius, P. and Posel, D. (Eds) (1993) *Apartheid's Genesis 1935-1962*, Braamfontein: Wits University Press.

Booth, T. and Coulby, D. (1987) (Eds) *Producing and Reducing Disaffection: Curricula for All*. Milton Keynes: Open University Press.

Borstelmann, L.J. (1983) 'Children Before Psychology: Ideas About Children from Antiquity to the 1800s', in W. Keesen (Ed.) *Handbook of Child Psychology*, Vol. 1, New York: Wiley.

Bradley, F.H. (1927) *Ethical Studies*, Oxford: Clarendon Press.

Brandon, S., Duncanson I. and Samuel G (1979) *English Legal System*, London: Sweet and Maxwell.

Brandon, S. (1979) *Criminal Law*, London: Sweet and Maxwell.

Brandt, R. (1959) *Ethical Theory*, New Jersey: Prentice-Hall.

Bratton, W., Pollard, C., Orr, J., Mallun, R., Dennis, R. (Eds) (1997) *Zero Tolerance: Policing a Free Society*, London: Institute of Economic Affairs.

British Psychological Society (1980) *Report of the Working Party on Corporal Punishment in Schools*. Leicester: BPS.

Brodie, I., Berridge, D. (1996) *School Exclusion: Research Themes and Issues*. Luton: The University of Luton Press.

Brownlie, I. (1981) *Basic Documents in International Law* 2nd Ed., Oxford: Clarendon Press.

Burns, J.H. and Hart, H.L.A. (1970) (Eds) *Principles of Morals and Legislation*, London: Athlone Press.

Butler, S. (1921) *The Notebooks of Samuel Butler*, edited by H. Fe, London: Cape.

Bybee, R.W. and Gee, E.G. (1982) *Violence, Values and Justice in the Schools*, Boston, Massachusetts: Allyn and Bacon.

Canter, L. And Canter, M. (1976) *Assertive Discipline*, Santa Monica: Lee Canter Associates.

Chanlett, E. and Morier, G.M. (1968) 'Declaration of the Rights of the Child', *International Child Welfare*, Vol. 22, pp.4-8.

Charles, C. (1996) *Building Classroom Discipline*, New York: Longman

Children's Legal Centre (1986) *Children's Charters*, London: CLC.

Children's Legal Centre (1986) *Briefing on the Drafting of a New United Nations Convention: The Rights of the Child*, London: CLC.

Childright (1998) *DfEE Draft Guidance for Section 550A of the Education Act 1996: The Use of Reasonable Force to Control or Restrain Pupils*, No 144, March, pp. 11-14.

Childright (1997) *Physical Restraint of Children: A New Sanction for Schools*, No 138, July/ Aug, pp. 14-16

Childright (1987) No 34, February.

Childright (1985) No. 15, March, p.9 and p.14.

Childright (1987) No 39, July/August.

Childright (1997) 'Physical Restraint of Children: A New Sanction for Schools' No. 138, pp. 14-16.

Childright (1997) 'Government Plans for Youth Justice', Nov. No. 141, p.4.

Childright (1997) 'Pupil Exclusion', No. 142, December, p.22.

Childright (1985) No 18, June, p.7.

Childright (1986) No 30, September 30, pp.13-14.

Colmar, S. (1991). The New Positive Teaching Package: An Initial Evaluation: *Positive Teaching*. Vol. 2 No. 2, pp. 65-78

Commonwealth Department of Human Services and Health, (1995) *Legal and Social Aspects of the Physical Punishment of Children*. Canberra: Commonwealth Department of Human Services and Health.

Connell, R., Ashden, D., Kessler, S. and Dowsett, G. (1982) *Making the Difference*, Sydney: George Allen and Unwin.

Conway, R.W.F., Tierney, J. and Schofield, N. (1991) *The Fair Discipline Code Project: A Review of the Application of the Fair Discipline Code in New South Wales Secondary Schools*. Newcastle: University of Newcastle, School of Education.

Cook, T.G. (1974) *The History of Education in Europe*. London: Methuen

Coulby, D. (1987) 'It's nothing personal: Class Opposition to the Curriculum', in T. Booth and D. Coulby (Eds) *Producing and Reducing Disaffection: Curricula for All*. Milton Keynes: Open University Press.

Council of Europe, Press Release (1997) *Registry of European Court of Human Rights*, April, F- 67075, Strasbourg, Council of Europe.

Council of Europe (1994) *The Evolution of the Role of Children in Family Life*, Strasbourg: Council of Europe.

Council of Europe (1987) *Press Release*, B(87)7, 5 February.

Council of Europe (1987) *Press Release*, B(87) 27, 21 August.

Council of Europe. (1987) *Press Release*, 1(87) 32, 26th June.

Council of Europe, *Press Release* (1985) B (85) 1, February 11.

Council of Europe (1985) *Forum: The Council of Europe Quarterly*, No 1, p.2.

Council of Europe. (1972) *Collected Texts*, 8th Ed., Strasbourg: Council of Europe.

Cousins, J. (1996) 'Empowerment and Autonomy from Babyhood: The Perspective of Early Years Research', in M. John (Ed) *Children in Charge*. London: Jessica Kingsley.

Crittenden, B. (1991), 'Thre Aproaches to Classroom Discipline: Philosophical Perspectives', in M.N. Lovegrove and R.Lewis (Eds), *Classroom Discipline*, Melbourne: Longman Cheshire.

Croce, O., Hill, B. And Williams, M. (1996) 'Running Our School' in *The Child's Right to a Fair Hearing*, London: Jessica Kingsley.

Cryan, J.R. (1995) 'The Banning of Corporal Punishment' *Dimensions of Early Childhood*, Spring, pp.36-37.

Curtis, S.J. and Boultwood M.E. (1966) *An Introductory History of Education Since 1800*, 4th Ed, London: University Tutorial Press.

The Daily Telegraph (1987) (Re teacher morale) February 5, p.4.

De Mause, L. (1974) *The History of Childhood*. London: Souvenir Press (Educational and Academic).

De Smith, S.A. (1977) *Constitutional and Administrative Law*. Harmondsworth: Penguin.

Department of Education and Science (1983) *Consultative Document on Corporal Punishment*, London: DES

Derbyshire HMSO County Council (1997) The Exclusion of Pupils from School, *Report of the Chief Education Officer*, Matlock: Derbyshire County Council.

Derbyshire County Council (1993) *Good Behaviour, Discipline and Managing Violence*, Matlock: DCC.

Dettman, H.W. (1972) Discipline in Schools in Western Australia: *Report of the Government Secondary School Discipline Committee (Dettman Report)*. Perth: Education Department of Western Australia.

Dewey, J. (1916) *Democracy and Education*. New York: The Free Press

Dickinson, G.M. and Wayne MacKay, A. (1989) *Rights, Freedoms and the Education System in Canada: Cases and materials*. Toronto: Emond Montgomery.

Docking, J. (1990) *Managing Behaviour in the Primary School*, London: David Fulton.

Docking, J.W. (1990) *Primary Schools and Parents: Rights, Responsibilities and Relationships*. Sevenoaks: Hodder and Stoughton.

Docking, J.W. (1980) *Control and Discipline in Schools: Perspectives and Approaches*. London: Harper and Row.

Donnellan, C. (1996) (Eds) *What are Children's Rights*? Cambridge: Cambridge Independent.

Dubanoski, R.A., Inaba, M.; and Gerkewicz, K.(1983) 'Corporal Punishment in Schools: Myths, Problems and Alternatives'. *Child Abuse and Neglect*. Vol.7, pp.271-278.

Eaglesham, F (1956) *From School Board to Local Authority*, London: Routledge and Kegan Paul.

Edmund, S.M. (1996) *The Puritan Family*. New York: Harper and Row

Edulaw, (1995a) Corporal Punishment: A Human Rights Issue, pp.4-5, Vol.1, No.2.

Edulaw (1995b) 'Corporal Punishment: Legal Update', Vol 1, No 3.

Elton Report (1989) *Discipline in Schools: Report of the Committee of Inquiry*, London: HMSO.

Elvin, L. (1981) *The Educational Systems in the European Community: A Guide*. Windsor, Berks: NFER-Nelson.

End Physical Punishment of Children (EPOCH) (1996) *Hitting People is Wrong – and Children are People Too*. London: Approach.

Ennew, J. (1995) 'Outside Childhood: Street Children's Rights', in B. Franklin (Eds) (*op.cit.*)

Entwistle, H. (1970) *Child Centred Education*. London: Methuen.

Ewing, A.C. (1929) *The Morality of Punishment With Some Suggestions for a General Theory of Ethics*. London: Kegan Paul, Trench and Trubner.

Faber, A. and Mazlish E. (1980) *How to Talk So Kids Will Listen and Listen So Kids Will Talk*. New York: Avon Books.

Fair Discipline Code: Guidelines for Discussion by Government School Communities. (1989) New South Wales: NSW Department of Education.

Fairweather, R.G.L. (1979) 'The Canadian Human Rights Commission' in *The Practise of Freedom*, McDonald, R.S.J. and Humphrey, J.P. (Eds) Toronto: Butterworth.

Farran, S. (1996) *The UK Before the European Court of Human Rights: Case Law and Commentary*. London: Blackstone Press.

Farson, R. (1978) *Birthrights*, Harmondsworth, Penguin.

Feinberg, J. (1966) 'Duties, Rights and Claims', *American Philosophical Quarterly*, Vol. 3, No. 2, pp. 137-144.

Finnish Child Welfare Act (1983) Available from: Central Union for Child Welfare in Finland, Armfeltintie, 1,00150, Helsinki 15, Finland.

Fischer, L., Schimmel, D. and Kelly, C. (1995) *Teachers and the Law* 4th Edition, White Plains, New York, Longmans.

Firestone, S. (1970) *The Dialectic of Sex*, London: Jonathan Cape.

Firestone, S. (1979) 'Down with Childhood', in M. Hoyles (Ed) *Changing Childhood*. London: Writers' and Readers' Publishing Cooperative.

Ford, P.L. (1962), *The New England Primer*, New York: Teachers' College Press.

Foster, H.H. and Freed, D.J. (1972) 'A Bill of Rights for Children', *Family Law Quarterly*, Vol. 6, pp. 343-375.

Foucault, M. (1979) *Discipline and Punish: The Birth of the Prison*, Harmondsworth: Penguin.

Franklin, B. (1996) (Ed) *The Rights of Children*. Oxford: Basil Blackwell.

Franklin, B. (1995) (Ed) *The Handbook of Children's Rights: Comparative Policy and Practice*, London: Routledge.

Freeman, C.B. (1965) 'The Children's Petition of 1669 and its Sequel'. *British Journal of Educational Studies*, Vol. 14, pp. 216-223.

Freeman, M.D.A. (1983a) *The Rights and Wrongs of Children*, London: Frances Pinter.

Freeman, M.D.A. (1983b) 'Children's Rights – the Literature', *Childright*, No.2, November, pp. 19-21.

Freeman, M.D.A. (1992) 'Taking Childrens Rights More Seriously' in P. Alston *et al*. *Children's Rights and the Law*. Oxford: Clarendon Press.

Fryers, H. (1996) *Perspectives on Behaviour*. London: David Fulton.

Gathorne-Hardy, J. (1977) *The Public School Phenomenon*, Harmonsdsworth: Penguin.

Gathorne-Hardy, J. (1975) *The Fall of the British Nanny*. Harmondsworth: Penguin.

Gibson, I. (1978) *The English Vice: Beating, Sex and Shame in Victorian England and After*. London: Duckworth.

Gilkey, L. (1965) *Maker of Heaven and Earth: The Christian in the Light of Modern Knowledge*, New York: Anchor Books.

Godfrey, G. (1975) *Parental Rights and Duties and Custody Suits*, London: Stevens.

Goldstein, J., Freud, A. and Solnit, A. (1973) *Beyond the Best Interests of the Child*, New York: Free Press.

Goldstein, J., Freud, A. and Solnit, A. (1979) *Before the Best Interests of the Child*, New York: Free Press.

Gomien, D. (1995) *Judgements of the European Court of Human Rights: Reference Charts*. Strasbourg: Council of Europe.

Goodman, P. (1977) 'Reflections on Children's Rights', in *The Children's Rights Movement: Overcoming the Oppression of Young People*, Gross, B. and Gross, R. (Eds) New York: Anchor Press.

Gould, R. (1954) 'The Status of Teachers: Five Objectives for Professional Advancement', *Schoolmaster and Woman Teacher's Chronicle*, Vol CLXV, pp. 647-654.

Government White Paper (1997) *Rights Brought Home*. London: HMSO CM3782, November

Griffiths, M. and Davies, C. (1995) *In Fairness to Children*. London: David Fulton.

Gross, B. and Gross, R. (1977) (Eds) *The Children's Rights Movement: Overcoming the Oppression of Young People*. New York: Anchor Press.

Grosz, S. (1985) 'Keeping Britain out of Work', *The Times*, June 25.

The Guardian (1998) 'Smack Row Teacher Suicidal', April 17, News p.3

The Guardian (1997a), 'Judges Win Power in Historic Bills', October 25, p.1.

The Guardian (1997b) 'Why the Jury Is Still Out On Zero Tolerance' , December 9, p.2.

The Guardian (1987) (Re special needs) March 17, p.1.

Hafen, B.C. (1976) 'Children's Liberation and the New Egalitarianism'. *Brigham Young Law Review*, No. 6, pp. 605-658.

Halls, W.D. (1965) *Society, Schools and Progress in France*, Oxford: Pergamon Press.

Hansard Parliamentary Debates, House of Commons (1986), Vol 102, no 154, July 22.

Hansard Parliamentary Debates, House of Lords (1973) 5th Series, Vol 347, December 10.

Hansard Parliamentary Debates, House of Commons (1976), Vol 903, January 20, p. 1158.

Harris, D. (1984) *The European Social Charter*, Charlottesville: University Press of Virginia.

Harris, D.J. (1973) *Cases and Materials on International Law.* London: Sweet and Maxwell.

Harris, D.J., O'Boyle, M. and Warbrick, C. (1995) *Law of the European Convention on Human Rights*. London: Butterworths.

Hart, A. (1992) as cited in Franklin, B. (1995) (Ed) *The Handbook of Children's Rights: Comparative Policy*, London: Routledge.

Highfield, M.E. and Pinsent, A (1952) *A Survey of Rewards and Punishments in Schools*, (A Report by the National Foundation for Educational Research in England and Wales), London: Newnes.

Hill, G.B.N. (1897) *Johnsoniam Miscellanies*. Vol. 2. Oxford: Clarendon Press.

Hirst, P.H. and Peters, R.S. (1970) *The Logic of Education*, London: Routledge, Kegan and Paul.

Holt, J. (1974) *Escape from Childhood*, Harmondsworth: Penguin.

Hughes, T. (1890) *Tom Brown's School Days*. London: Macmillan.

Humphrey, J. (1970) 'Human Rights and Authority', *University of Toronto Law Journal.* Vol.20, pp.412-421.

Hunter, I. (1979) 'The Origin, Development and Interpretation of Human Rights Legislation', in R.St.J. Macdonald and J.P. Humprhey (Eds), *Practice of Freedom*, Toronto: Butterworths and Co. (Canada), pp. 77-109.

Hyams-Parish, A.C. (1996) *Banished to the Exclusion Zone: School Exclusions and the Law from the Point of View of the Child*, Colchester: Children's Legal Centre.

Hyman, I.A. (1988a) *Corporal Punishment in American Schools*. Philadelphia: Temple University Press.

Hyman, I.A. (1988b) 'Eliminating Corporal Punishment in Schools: Moving from Advocacy Research to Policy Implementation' paper presented at the 96th Annual Convention of the American Psychological Association, Atlanta, American Psychology Association.

Hyman, I.A. (1990) *Reading, Writing, and the Hickory Stick: The Appalling Story of Physical and Psychological Abuse in American Schools*, Lexington: Lexington Books.

Hyman, I.A. and D'Allessandro, J. (1984) 'Good, oldñfashioned discipline: The Politics of Punitiveness' *Phi Delta Kappa* 66(1) 39-45,

Hyman, I.A. and McDowell, E. (1979) 'Corporal Punishment An Overview, in I.A. Hyman and J.H. Wise (Eds) *Corporal Punishment in American Education*, Philadelphia: Temple University, pp. 3-21.

Hyman, I.A., McDowell, E. and Raines, B. (1978) 'Corporal Punishment and Alternative in the Schools: An Overview of Theoretical and Practical Issues', *Inequality in Education*, 23, pp 5-20.

Hyman, I.A. and Wise, J.H. (1979) *Corporal Punishment in American Education: Readings in History, Practice and Alternatives*. Philadelphia: Temple University Press.

Imber, M. and Van Greel, T. (1993) *Education Law*, New York: McGraw-Hill.

The Independent (1997) 'Tony Blair Promises the Right to Smack', November 8th, p.1.

The Independent (1997) 'Girl of 12 Thrown into Jail on the Isle of Man', June 7, p.3.

Inner London Education Authority (1970) *Discipline in Schools*, London: ILEA.

Irving, B.A. and Parker-Jenkins, M. (1995), 'Tackling Disaffected School Pupils and Positive Support Strategies'. *Cambridge Journal of Education*, Vol. 25. No. 2, pp. 225-235.

Jackson, P. (1973) *Natural Justice*, London: Sweet and Maxwell.

Jacobs, F.G. (1975) *The European Convention on Human Rights*, Oxford: Clarendon Press

Jacobs, F.G. and White R.C.A. (1996) *The European Convention on Human Rights*. Oxford: Clarendon Press.

Jeff, T. (1995) 'Children's Right's in a New Era?', in B. Franklin (1995) *The Handbook of Children's Rights*, London: Routledge.

John, M. (1995) (Ed) *The Way of Children's Rights*, London: Routledge.

Kaestle, C.F. (1983) *Pillars of the Republic: Common Schools and American Societies 1780-1860*, New York: Hill and Wang.

Kay-Shuttleworth, J. (1841) *On the Punishment of Pauper Children in Workhouses*, London: London College of St. Mark and St. John (Occasional papers No. 1).

Keaney, M.K. (1995) 'Substantive Due Process and Parental Corporal Punishment: Democracy and the Excluded Child'. *San Diego Law Review*, Vol. 32, No. 1, pp. 1-51.

Kelly, J.C. (1987) Improving Writing Production in 12-13 Year Olds of Positive Reinforcement. *Behavioural Approaches with Children* Vol. 11, No. 2, 87.

Kelly, P.C. (1985) 'A Survey of Parental Opinions on Corporal Punishment in Schools', *Developmental Pediatrics*, 6, pp. 143-145.

Kempee, P. (1996) *A Systematic Guide to the Case Law of the European Court of Human Rights 1960-1994*, The Hague: Martinus Nijhoff.

Kessen, W. (1983) (Ed), *Handbook of Child Psychology*, Vol. 1, New York: Wiley.

Khan, A. and Williams, S. (1993), The Liability of Negligence of Teachers and Schools in Australia', *Education and the Law*, Vol 4, p 155-163.

Kimberley Carlisle Inquiry: Death of Kimberley Carlisle (1987), London: London Borough of Greenwich and Greenwich Health Authority.

King, E.J. (1969) *Education and Development in Western Europe*. London: Addison-Wesley.

King, M. (1981) (Ed) *Childhood, Welfare and Justice: A Critical Examination of Children in the Legal and Childcare Systems*. London: Batsford Academic and Educational.

King, M. and Trowell, J. (1992) *Children's Welfare and the Law: The Limits of Legal Intervention*, London: Sage.

Kozol, J. (1968) *Death at an Early Age: The Destruction of the Hearts and Minds of Negro Children in the Boston Public Schools*, Harmondsworth: Penguin.

Landsdown, M. (1995) 'Taking Children's Rights Seriously', in John, M (1995) (Ed) *The Way of Children's Rights*, London: Routledge.

Lawson, F.H. (1952) *Roman Law and Common Law: A Comparison in Outline*, Cambridge: Cambridge University Press.

Leach, P. (1990) *Baby and Child: From Birth to Age Five*. Harmondsworth: Penguin.

Leach, P. (1990) *Children First*. London: Michael Joseph.

Leach, P. (1993) 'Should Parents Hit their Children?', *The Psychologist*, Vol. 6, No. 5, May, pp. 216-220.

Leach, P. (1994) *Children First – What our Society must do – and is not doing,* Harmondsworth: Penguin.

Leicestershire Education Department (1996) Exclusion of Pupils from School, *Report of The Director of Education*. Leicester: Leicestershire County Council.

Leicester Mercury (1994) 'Bulger Tragedy Still Haunts Mothers', June 16, p. 14.

Leinster-Mackay, D.P. (1977) 'Regina v. Hopley: Some Historical Reflections on Corporal Punishment', *Journal of Educational Administration and Law*, Vol.9 (1), pp.1-6.

Lemmer, E.M. and Badenhurst, D.C. (1997) *Introduction to Education for South African Teachers*, Cape Town: Juta and Co.

Lewis, R., Lovegrove, M.N. and Burman, E. (1991) 'Teachers' Perceptions of Ideal Classroom Disciplinary Practices', in M.N. Lovegrove and R.Lewis (Eds) *Classroom Discipline*, Melbourne: Longman Cheshire.

Lloyd, D. (1964) *The Idea of Law*, Harmondsworth: Penguin

Lloyd, D. (1972) *Introduction to Jurisprudence*, 3rd Ed., London: Stevens

Locke, J. (1960) *Two Treatises of Government*, Laslett, P. (Ed), London: Cambridge University Press.

London County Council (1952) *Punishment in Schools*, London: LCC.

Longford, 7th Earl of (F.A. Packenham), (1961) *The Idea of Punishment*, London: Chapman.

Louden, L.W. (1985) *Disruptive Behaviour in Schools: Report of the Ministerial Working Party on Disruptive Behaviour in Schools*, Perth: Education Department of Western Australia

Lovey, J. (1992) *Teaching Troubled and Troublesome Adolescents*, London: David Fulton.

Lovey, J., Docking, J., Evans, R. (1993) *Exclusion from School: Provision for Disaffection at Key Stage 4*, London: David Fulton.

Lyon, C. and Parton, N. (1995) 'Children's Rights and the Children's Act 1989' in Franklin, B. (1995) (Ed) *The Handbook of Childrens Rights: Comparative Policy and Practice*, London: Routledge, pp. 40-56.

Maclaine, A.G. and Selby Smith, R. (1971) *Fundamental Issues in Australian Education: A Book of Essays and Readings*, Sydney: Ian Novak.

McManus, M. (1995) *Troublesome Behaviour in the Classroom*, London: Routledge.

McPhillimy, B. (1996) *Controlling Your Class: A Teachers Guide to Managing Classroom Behaviour*. Chichester: John Wiley.

Maddocks Report (1983) as cited in Slee, R. (1995) *Changing Theories and Practices of Discipline*. London: Falmer Press.

Mallinson, V. (1980) *The Western European Idea of Education*. Oxford: Pergammon Press.

Margolin, C.A. (1978) 'Salvation versus Liberation: The Movement for Children's Rights in a Historical Context', *Social Problems*, Vol. 25, No. 4-5, PP. 441-452.

Marshall, J.D. (1984) 'John Wilson on the Necessity of Punishment', *Journal of Philosophy of Education*, Vol.18, No.1, pp.92-104.

Martin, S. (1994) 'A Preliminary Evaluation of the Adoption of Assertive Discipline of Robinton High School', *School Organisation*, Vol. 14, No. 3, pp. 321-330.

Mason, J.D. (1989) 'Positive Teaching on Teaching Practice', *Behavioural Approaches with Children*, Vol. 13, No. 3, pp. 170-171.

Maurer, A. (1984) *1001 Alternatives to Corporal Punishment*, Vol.1, Berkeley, Ca: Generation Books

Meacham, M.L. and Wiesen, A.E. (1989) *Changing Classroom Behaviour: A Manual for Precision*. Scranton, Pennsylvania: International Textbook Company.

Meigham, R. (1992) *Anatomy of Choice in Education*, Ticknall, Derby: Education Now.

Miles, A.S. (1997) *College Law*. (Second Edition) Northport, Alabama: Sergo Press.

Mill, J.S. (1910) *On Liberty*. London: Dent.

Mitchell, B. (1975) *Teachers, Education, and Politics: A History of Organisations of Public School Teachers in New South Wales*, Brisbane: University of Queensland Press

Moghadam, H. And Fagan, J. (1994) *Attention-Deficit Disorder*, Calgary, Detsely.

Mongon, D. (1987) 'Going Against the Grain: Alternatives to Exclusion' in T. Booth and D. Coulby *Producing and Reducing Disaffection: Curriculum for All*. Milton Keynes: Open University Press.

Moore, T.W. (1982) *Philosophy of Education: An Introduction*. London: Routledge and Kegan Paul.

More, M. (1799) as cited in Rodham, H. (1973), 'Children Under Law', *Harvard Educational Review*, Vol 43, No 4, pp 487-514.

Morgan, E. (1966) *The Puritan Family*, New York: Harper and Row.

Morrish, I. (1970) *Education Since 1800*, London: Allen and Unwin.

Mowbray, A. (1994a) 'A New European Court of Human Rights', *Journal of Public Order*, Legal Notes and Commentaries Winter, pp. 540-552.

Mowbray, A. (1994b) 'Corporal Punishment in Private Schools', *Journal of Forensic Psychiatry*, Vol 4, No3, pp. 546-550.

National Association of School Masters (1963) *Education in Europe*. London: NAS

National Council for Civil Liberties (1971) *Children in Schools*, (Children Have Rights, 1), London: NCCL.

National Council for Civil Liberties (1972) *Bill of Rights for Children*, London: NCCL.

National Union of Teachers (1983) *Corporal Punishment: The Alternatives*, London: NUT.

National Union of Teachers (1992) *Education for the Disaffected (1990-1992)*. London: NUT.

National Union of Teachers (1993) *Pupil Behaviour in Schools*. London: NUT.

National Union of Teachers (1998) *Perceptions of the Teaching Profession*, London: NUT.

Neill, A.S. (1971) 'Freedom Works' in *Children's Rights*, Adams, P. (Ed), London: Elek Books.

Newell, P. (1987) 'A Proper Regard For Authority: Regulating Schools by Rights', in T. Booth and D. Coulby (Eds) *Producing and Reducing Disaffection: Curricula for All*. Milton Keynes: Open University Press.

Newell, P. (1972) *A Last Resort? Corporal Punishment in Schools*, Harmondsworth, Penguin.

Newell, P. (1995) 'Respecting Children's Rights to Physical Integrity', in Franklin, B. (Ed) *The Handbook of Children's Rights: Comparative Policy and Practice*, London: Routledge.

Newson, J. and Newson, E. (1986) *The Extent of Parental Chastisement in the UK*, London: Approach.

New South Wales (1989) *Fair Discipline Code*, NSW: Department of Education

New South Wales (1995) *Legal and Social Aspects of the Physical Punishment of Children*. Sydney: Commonwealth Dept. of Human Services and Health.

Nottinghamshire Education Authority (1982) *Report of the Working Party on Pastoral Care and Counselling in Schools,* Nottingham: Nottinghamshire County Council.

Nottinghamshire County Council (1990) *Education and Attitudes*. Nottingham: Nottinghamshire County Council.

Nottinghamshire County Council (1994) *Children's Behaviour in Schools*, Nottingham: NCC.

Nottinghamshire Education Committee (1996) *Manton School: Management Inspection* HM: NCC.

OFSTED (1996) *Exclusion from Secondary Schools 1995/6: A Report from the Office of Her Majesty's Chief Inspector of Schools*, London: HMSO

Olmesdahl, M.C.J. (1984) 'Corporal Punishment in Schools', *The African Law Journal*, Vol. 101, No. 3, pp. 527-544

Oppenheim, L. (1953) *International Law: A Treatise*, Oxford: Clarendon Press.

Osler, A. (1994) 'The UN Convention on the Rights of the Child: Some Implications for Teacher Education', *Educational Review*, Vol. 46, No. 2, pp 141-150.

Parker-Jenkins, M. (1996) 'A Simple Solution that Never Worked', *Times Educational Supplement*, November 15th, p. 26.

Parker-Jenkins, M. (1995) The European Court: Signalling a New Trend in School Discipline, *Journal of Social Policy and Family Law*, Vol. 17, No2, pp. 248-255.

Parker-Jenkins, M. and Irving, B.A. (1995) 'Tackling Truancy: An Examination of Persistent Non-Attendance Amongst Disaffected School Pupils and Positive Support Strategies', *Cambridge Journal of Education*, Vol. 25, No. 2, pp. 225-235.

Partington, A. (1984) *Law and the New Teacher*, London: Holt, Rinehart and Winston.

Peters, R.S. (1966) *Ethics and Education*, 2nd Ed. London; George Allen Unwin.

Piele, P.K. (1979) 'Ingraham v. Wright' in *Corporal Punishment in American Schools*, by I.A. Hyman and J.H. Wise (Eds) Philadelphia: Temple University Press.

The Plowden Report: Children and Their Primary Schools (1967). London: Department of Education and Science.

Pugh, G. (1996) (Ed) *Contemporary Issues in the Early Years*. London: National Children's Bureau.

Report of the Inquiry into the Care and Supervision Provided in Relation to Maria Colwell (1994) Field-Fisher Report, London: HMSO.

Rich, R.W. (1933) *The Training of Teachers in England and Wales during the Nineteenth Century*, London: Cambridge University Press.

Ritchie, J. and Ritchie, J. (1981) *Spare the Rod*. Sydney: George Allen and Unwin.

Ritchie, J. and Ritchie, J. (1993) *Violence in New Zealand,* Lincoln, New Zealand: Lincoln University Press.

Robertson, A.H. (1982) *Human Rights in the World: An Introduction to the Study of the International Protection of Human Rights*, 2nd Ed., Manchester: Manchester University Press

Robertson, A.H. (1966) *European Institutions: Co-operation, Integration, Unification*, 2nd ed., London: Stevens

Robertson, A.H. (1961) *The Law of International Institutions in Europe*, Manchester: Manchester University Press

Robertson, A.H. (1963) *Human Rights in Europe*, 1st Ed., Manchester: Manchester University Press.

Robertson, A.H. (1993) *Human Rights in Europe: A study of the European Convention on Human Rights*, 3rd ed., Manchester: Manchester University Press.

Rodham, H. (1979) 'Children's Rights: A Legal Perspective' in P.A. Vardin and I.N. Brody (1979), *Children's Rights*, New York: Teachers' College Press.

Rodham, H. (1973) 'Children Under the Law', *Harvard Educational Review*, Vol 43, No 4, pp. 487-514.

Rodley, N.S. (1984) *Offence to Human Dignity: The Treatment of Prisoners under International Law,* Unpublished report written for the Council of Europe. Strasbourg: Council of Europe.

Rosen, M. (1994) *The Penguin Book of Childhood*, Harmondsworth: Penguin Books.

Rosenbaum, M. And Newell, P. (1991) *Taking Children Seriously: A Proposal for a Children's Rights Commissioner.* London: Calouste Gulbenkian Foundation.

Royce, R.J. (1984) 'School-based Punishment', *Journal of Philosophy of Education*, Vol.18, No.1, pp.85-95.

Rumbold, E. (1992) 'Time Off for Good Behaviour' *Special Children* No. 54, pp. 21-27.

Rutter, M., Maughan, B., Mortimore, P. and Ouston, J. (1979) *Fifteen Thousand Hours: Secondary Schools and Their Effects on Children.* London: Open Books.

Ryan, F.J. (1994) 'From Rod to Reason: Historical Perspectives in the Public School, 1642-1994', *Educational Horizons*, Winter, pp.71-77.

Sachs, C.J.B. (1973) 'Children's Rights' in *Fundamental Rights*, Bridge, J.W. (Ed) , London: Sweet and Maxwell.

Schofield, H. (1972) *The Philosophy of Education: An Introduction*. London: Allen and Unwin.

Scholland, K. (1996) *Shogun's Ghost: The Dark Side of Japanese Education*. London: Bergin and Garvey.

Schostak, J.F. (1983) *Maladjusted Schooling: Deviance, Social Control and Individuality in Secondary Schooling*. Lewes: Falmer Press.

Scott G.R. (1938) *The History of Corporal Punishment: a Survey of Flagelation in its Historical, Anthropological and Sociological Aspects*, London: T.Werner Laurie.

Scott R. (1992) 'Encouraging Better Behaviour', *Education Views*, Brisbane: Queensland Department of Education, June 5, p. 2.

Shenstone, W (1742) 'The Schoolmistress', as cited in Barnard (1971), *A History of English Education from 1760,* London: London University Press.

Short, P.M., Short, R.J. and Blanton, C. (1994) *Rethinking Student Discipline: Alternatives that Work*. London: Corwin Press.

Simon, S. (1988) as cited in Franklin, B. (1995) *The Handbook of Children's Rights*, London: Routledge.

Siogfolk, P. (1852) 'The Rights of Children' *The Knickerbocker.* 396, pp. 487-491.

Skinner, B.F. (1968) *The Technology of Teaching*. New York: Appleton-Century-Crofts.

Slee, R. (1995) *Changing Theories and Practices of Discipline*. London: Falmer Press.

Smith, A. (1985) *Freedom and Discipline*, London: George Allen and Unwin.

Society of Teachers Opposed to Physical Punishment. (1982) *Britain's Violent Teachers: A Dossier of Beatings*, London: STOPP.

Society of Teachers Opposed to Physical Punishment. (1982) *The Case Against Judicial Beating: A Briefing Paper*, London, STOPP.

Society of Teachers Opposed to Physical Punishment. *STOPP News,* June/July (1983), June/July 1984. London: STOPP.

Society of Teachers Opposed to Physical Punishment, *STOPP News,* June/July (1994) London: STOPP.

Society of Teachers Opposed to Physical Punishment. *STOPP News*, June/July (1985). London: STOPP.

South African Department of Education (1997) *Understanding the South African Schools Act*, Pretoria: Dept of Education

Squelch, J. (1997) 'Education and the Law', in *Introduction to Education for South African Teachers: An Orientation to Teaching Practice*, E.M. Lemmer and D.C. Badenhorst, (Eds), Cape Town: Juta.

Staatskoerant, Government Gazette (1990) 'Law Schedule of Regulations Governing Corporal Punishment', Pretoria: Ministry of Education, No 12381.

Starkey, H. (1991) (Ed) *The Challenge of Human Rights Education*, London: Cassell.

Stenhouse, L. (1967) *Discipline in Schools*. London: Pergamon Press.

Steyn, T. (1997) 'Schools in Transition' in *Introduction to Education for Teachers: An Orientation to Teaching Practice*, E.M. Lemmer and D.C. Badenhorst (Eds), Cape Town: Juta.

Straus, M.A. (1994) *Beating the Devil Out of Them: Corporal Punishment in American Families*. Oxford: Maxwell Macmillan.

Straus, M.A. (1990) *Discipline and Deviance: Physical Punishment of Children and Violence and Other Crime in Adulthood*, University of New Hampshire: Family Violence Research Programme.

Straus, M.A. and Kantor, G.K. (1994) 'Corporal Punishment of Adolescents by Parents: A Risk Factor in the Epidemiology of Depression, Suicide, Alcohol Abuse, Child Abuse and Wife Beating', *Adolescence*, Fall, Vol. 29, No. 115, p 543-562.

The Sunday Times (1987) (Re teachers' low morale) February 8, p.3.

The Sunday Times (1996) 'Anarchy Rules Okay' (re: the Ridings School) November 13, p. 14.

The Sunday Times (South African) (1997) 'Pupils Cell Trauma Sparks Legal Battle', September 21, pp. 1 and 7.

The Sydney Morning Herald (1997a) 'Legal Threat Over School Beating Ban', Jan 13, p.3.

The Sydney Morning Herald (1997b) 'Christian Schools Look for Loopholes to Keep Caning', April 6, p.6.

The Sydney Morning Herald (1997c) 'Hard Lessons', August 11, p.10.

The Sydney Morning Herald (1989a) 'Schools Reject Re-Introduction of Cane, June 20, p.3.

The Sydney Morning Herald (1989b) 'Cane Returns to Class', April 9, p.9.

The Sydney Morning Herald (1988) 'Corporal Punishment Makes a Comeback', November 18, p. 4.

Tattum, D.P. (1989) 'Alternative Approaches to Disruptive Behaviour' in *School Management and Pupil Behaviour*, Jones, N. (Ed) Lewes: Falmer Press.

The Times (1986) (Corporal Punishment In Religious Schools) August 10, p.5.

The Times (1985) (UK in the 'dock') June 25, p.2.

The Times (1973) Re right of Appeal at Strasbourg) November 14, p.3.

Thompson, D. and Sharp, S. (1994) *Improving Schools: Establishing and Integrating Whole School Behaviour Policies*. London: David Fulton.

Times Educational Supplement (1970) (Re school strike) January 30, p.5.

Times Educational Supplement (1970) (Re corporal punishment cases) October 2, p.6.

Times Educational Supplement (1970) (Re pupil input into curriculum) October 2, p.6.

Times Educational Supplement (1972) (Re rights for school children) May 5, pp 9 and 4.

Times Educational Supplement (1972) (Re school demonstration) May 19, p.6.

Times Educational Supplement (1987) (Re Settlement of Corporal Punishment Cases) October 2.

Times Educational Supplement (1993) 'James Bulger Trajedy', November 25, p.19.

Times Educational Supplement (1996a) 'Manton Re-opens as Transfer is Agreed', November. 15, p.7.

Times Educational Supplement (1996b) 'Shepherd Orders Ridings Inquiry', October 25, p.11.

Times Educational Supplement (1997a) 'Taking Children's Views Seriously', December 5, p20.

Times Educational Supplement (1997b) 'Exclusion Rise Linked to Paperwork', November 7, p.15.

Times Educational Supplement (1997c) 'Pressure and Prozac', November 7, p.22.

Times Educational Supplement (1998a), 'Caneless into the Dawn of a New Era', March 27, p.7.

Times Educational Supplement (1998b) 'May the Force Be With You', April 3, p. 35.

Tropp, A. (1957) *The School Teachers: The Growth of the Teaching Profession in England and Wales from 1800 to the present day*, London: Heinemann.

Tulleys, M. (1995) 'Student Teachers and Classroom Discipline' *Journal of Educational Research* Vol. 88, (3), pp. 164-171.

Turner, B. (1973)(ed) *Discipline in Schools*. London: Ward Lock Educational.

Tyra Henry Inquiry: *Whose Child? The Report of the Panel Appointed to Inquire into the Death of Tyra Henry* (1978), London: London Borough of Lambeth.

Valente, W.D. (1994) *Law in the Schools* (Third Edition), New York: Macmillan.

Van Zyl, A. (1997) 'A Historical Overview of South African Education', in *Introduction to Education for Teachers: An Orientation to Teaching Practice*, E.M. Lemmer and D.C. Badenhorst (Eds), Cape Town: Juta.

Vardin, A.A. and Brody, I.N. (1979) (Eds) *Children's Rights: Contemporary Perspectives*, New York: London: Teachers' College Press.

Vissir, J. and Upton, G. (1993) *Special Education in Britain After Warnock*. London: David Fulton.

Wardle, D (1976) *English Popular Education 1780-1975*, 2nd Ed, London: Cambridge University Press.

Wheldall, K. and Merrett, F. (1989) *Positive Teaching in the Secondary School*, London: Paul Chapman.

Wiggin, K.D. (1892) *Children's Rights: A Book of Nursery Logic*, New York: Houghton Mifflin.

Wilson, P.S. (1971) *Interest and Discipline in Education*. London: Routledge and Kegan Paul.

Wilson, P.S. (1974) 'Perspectives on Punishment', *Proceedings of the Philosophy of Education Society of Great Britain*, Vol 8, No 2, pp. 103-134.

Wolfgang, C.H. (1980) *Solving Discipline Problems*. London: Allyn and Bacon.

Worsfield, V.L. (1974) 'A Philosophical Justification for Children's Rights'. *Harvard Educational Review*, Vol. 44, No 1, pp. 142-157.

Wragg, T. (1997) 'Too Hot to Trot in the Discipline Dance', *Times Educational Supplement* Sept. 19th, p.44

Wringe, C.A. (1981) *Children's Rights: A Philosophical Study*. London: Routledge and Kegan Paul.

Zeldin, T. (1973) *France 1848-1945*, Vol 1, Oxford: Clarendon Press.

Table of Cases

A v. UK (1994) *Childright*, Nov. No. 141, p.21

A and B v. UK (1994) Application No. 25599/94; *Childright* (1997) No. 138, 16

Beaumont v. Surrey County Council (1968) 66 LCR 580; 112 Sol.Jo 704

Becky Walker v. Derbyshire County Council (1964)

Blom v. Sweden (1982) Application No. 8811/79; Report of the European Commission of Human Rights, Decision as to Admissibility 13th May 1982

Cambell and Cosans v. UK, European Court of Human Rights, Series A, No. 48 and 60, 25th Feb 1982 and 22nd March 1983

Campbell and Fell v. UK, EHRR 165 (1984)

Clearly v. Booth (1893) 1 QB465; 9 TLR 260; 17 COX CC 611

Cook v. Attock (1955) Evening Standard 13 January

Connor v. MacDonald (1912) 6 QJP 119

Costello-Roberts v. UK (1993) The European Court of Human Rights, 89/1991/341/414

Craig v. Frost (1936) 30 QJP 140 18

De Wilde, Ooms and Versyp v. Belgium, European Court of Human Rights, Series A, No.12, 28 May 1970; YBECHR 788

Fitzerald v. Northcote and another (1865), 4 F&F 656

Gillick v. West Norfolk and Wisbech Area Health Authority and another, High Court (1984) ALL ER 365; ALL 533; The Times 18th October 1985

Goss v. Lopez (1975) 419 US

Re. Gault (1967) US 387

Handyside v. UK (1976) Series A, ECHR 24

Hudson v. The Governors of Rotherham Grammar School and Selby Johnson (1937) Yorkshire Post 248, 25 March 1937; G.Barrell, Legal Cases for Teachers, 303

Hutt and another v. The Governors of Haileybury College and others (1888) 4 TLR 623

Ingraham v. Wright (1977) US Supreme Court Reports 430, (annotated 51)

Ireland v. UK, European Court of Human Rights, Series A, No.25, 29 April 1978; 2 EHRR 25 (1978)

King v. Nichols (1939) QJP 171

Lyes v Middlesex County Council (1962)

Mansell v. Griffin (1908) I KB 947; 24 TLR 431; 52 Sol.Jo.376

Mrs X v. UK (Application No. 7907/77) The European Commission of Human Rights, Decisions and Reports Vol. 14, June 1979, Decision as to Admissibility, 12 July 1978; 140th Session Minutes DH (79) 6, 31 October 1979, p.11

Mrs X and Ms X v. UK (1981) Application No.9471/81 European Commission of Human Rights, Decision as to Admissibility 13th March 1984; 166th Session Minutes 5-16 March 1984 DH (84) 4; Childright (1987) No. 42, Nov-Dec, 5

Myton v. Wood and others (1980), *The Times*, 11 July 1980, 11

Neilson v. Denmark (1984) (Application No. 1092/84) European Commission of Human Rights. Decision as to Admissibility, 10 March 1980

R. v. Jeffs (1955) *The Times*, 11 January

R. v. Hopley (1860) 2F&F 202

R. v. Newport (Salop) Justices, ex parte Wright (1929) 2 KB 416; 151 LT 563, 28CC 658

S. v. Meewis (1970) 4 SA 532 (T) (South Africa)

S. v. W. and others (1994) (2) BCLR 135 (C) (South Africa)

S. v. Williams and Others (1995) (3) South African Law Reports, pp. 632-658

Smyth v. O'Byrne (1894) Ex parte O'Bryne, 5 QLJ 125

Stevens v. UK (1986) Application No. 11674/85, European Commission of Human Rights, 3 March

Swedish Engine Drivers' case, (1976) The European Court of Human Rights, Series A, No.20, 6 February

Tinker v Des Moines (1969) US 393

Townend v. UK (App. No.9119/80), European Commission of Human Rights. Decision as to Admissibility, 6 March 1985; Council of Europe, Press Release B (87) 7, 5 February 1987

Tyrer v. UK, (1978) European Court of Human Rights, Series A, No.26, 25 April 1978

Re *Winship* (1970) US 397

Williams v. Eady (1893) 10 TLR 41

Index